MODERN RUSSIAN COMPOSERS

Da Capo Press Music Reprint Series

MODERN RUSSIAN COMPOSERS

by
Leonid Sabaneyeff

Translated from the Russian by
JUDAH A. JOFFE

DA CAPO PRESS • NEW YORK • 1975

Library of Congress Cataloging in Publication Data

Sabaneev, Leonid Leonidovich, 1881-
  Modern Russian composers.

(Da Capo Press music reprint series)
  Reprint of the ed. published by International
Publishers, New York.
  1. Composers, Russian—Biography.
I. Title.
  [ML390.S123M6 1975]   780'.92'2 [B]   75-14232
  ISBN 0-306-70673-3

This Da Capo Press edition of *Modern Russian Composers* is an unabridged
republication of the first edition published in New York in 1927.

Published by Da Capo Press, Inc.
A Subsidiary of Plenum Publishing Corporation
227 West 17th Street, New York, N.Y. 10011

MODERN
RUSSIAN
COMPOSERS

LEONID SABANEYEFF

MODERN RUSSIAN COMPOSERS

TRANSLATED
FROM THE RUSSIAN BY
JUDAH A. JOFFE.

NEW YORK

INTERNATIONAL PUBLISHERS

CONTENTS

LEONID SABANEYEFF

THE author of the present book is a Russian musical critic and composer. Born in 1881 he was graduated from the Moscow University, where he specialised in mathematics and the natural sciences. He later studied at the Moscow Conservatory under Professors S. I. Tañeyeff and P. Shlotser. In the field of composition and musical criticism he became a zealous partisan of modernism and bold innovation in art. He was one of the first to greet the appearance of Skryabin, of whom he has written a great deal, contributing much to the disclosure of the musical essence and understanding of that composer. He was musical critic and correspondent of numerous Russian and foreign periodicals and was contributor to the magazine *Appollon* (St. Petersburg), *Melos* (Berlin), *Der Blaue Ritter* (Dresden). He has written the following books: *Skryabin,* so far the only exhaustive monograph on the composer in the Russian language; *The Music of Speech; A History of Russian Music; A General History of Music; Reminiscences of Skryabin.* In addition to these, a number of works of a theoretical and scientific nature: *Chopin's Etudes; The Phenomenalogy of the Musical Creative Process; Foundations of Positive Musical Esthetics.* While residing in Russia (until 1926), he devoted much time to musical social work, was an active member of the Russian Academy of Fine Arts and the Chairman of its musical section and the President of the Association of Contemporary Music in Moscow, around which the composers of the left wing were grouped.

7

The author has been active as a composer since 1901. He has written a number of pieces for the piano, among them an Etude-Nocturne, two grand sonatas and many preludes and poems, two piano trios and a Violin Sonata, and a Chaconne for a symphonic orchestra and organ. At present he is at work on a composition on a text of *The Revelations of St. John,* and this composition of the type of oratorio with acting has been planned on a grandiose scale.

MODERN
RUSSIAN
COMPOSERS

INTRODUCTION

THE present book is intended for the foreign reader. This has forced certain characteristics upon its structure, style and exposition. The author could not treat certain phenomena with as much detail as might be possible in a book for Russian readers who are thoroughly familiar with all the peculiarities of the Russian musical world and Russian life in general which differ so markedly from the Western European world.

On the other hand, the author deemed himself obliged to explain a series of phenomena and facts more minutely than would be necessary in the interests of a Russian reader. Many events of Russian musical life are bound up with other events of Russian life, and are either by themselves unknown to the foreigner or bound up with facts unknown to him.

Russian musical history is generally a *terra incognita* to the Western reader, frequently he possesses wrong notions about it, and the chain of influences under which Russian creative music has been developing often appears to the foreign reader in an improper, perverse or distorted light. Special attention had to be paid to all this, in order that the picture of the unusual life of contemporary Russia and the style of contemporary Russian composers might be made clear, explained and justified.

Russian music of the present day is inter-bound with the Russian music of past epochs. It is also connected with a series of phenomena of the music of the world. These connections are profoundly interesting and important in order to grasp the cultural significance of the Russian branch of the world's music, the branch which somehow has grown away from it the further, owing, perhaps, to the very fact of its later origin.

In the present book the author felt compelled constantly to mention the past of Russia's music life, and, not being sufficiently certain that the reader knows this past, he has found it necessary, in passing, to give an idea of the most important stages of Russian musical history. In this way, the book, conceived as portraits of contemporary Russian composers, was obliged to take in a series of data also about composers who had become part and parcel of Russian musical history.

The author assumes a reader, utterly unprepared, devoid of special *musical* knowledge. The book aims to give "cultural characterisations" of events and not to be of assistance to the musician. Technical terms, delving into musical details, all sorts of detail, interesting and comprehensible only to the musician, have been completely banished from the exposition. The Russian composer of the present day is taken not at all in the narrow "musician" aspect, but as a cultural value which is part of the world's cultural values.

A great number of the sketches in this work are, as it were, musical portraits or esthetic characterisations of individual, most prominent composers. Moreover, certain less important facts have been brought together into groups, if the composers do not appear clear-cut and striking phenomena individually, but are of interest in the groups.

Besides these portraits of individual composers and their groups, the book contains a special article on the interesting "revolutionary music" in Bolshevik Russia. From this article the foreign reader can obtain, to a certain degree, a clear idea of the background against which contemporary creative art is developing in that country.

Russian composers are now divided into groups. These groupings are caused not only by the difference in tendencies, but by purely political and geographic conditions as well. After "the great dispersion" caused by the Revolution, a number of Russian composers found themselves abroad in Europe and even in America, and exactly among these are the most famous and prominent representatives of the present-day, such as Stravinski and Prokofyeff. The others stayed to work within Russia. The isolation which Russia had undergone after the War, the period of civil strife and blockade, could not help affecting the psychology of those Russian composers who had previously formed, as it were, one school and one "musical faction" with those who remained abroad. Consequently, at present, a fatal line has already been laid between them. Their paths have diverged in spite of their own wishes.

Nevertheless, the Russian musical family is essentially still something integral, in the opinion of both the Russian composers themselves (abroad or within Russia) and the foreigners who know the composers now living in Russia either slightly or not at all, yet do not essentially distinguish them from the Russian living abroad. The former and the latter are *Russians* and their music is naturally and normally considered Russian and not general European. Hence we have not thought it necessary to distinguish these composers from those who have remained in Russia, and the present series of characterisations has taken in the former and the latter on an equal footing as members of one family of Russian musicians.

The present book has been written for the sake of information, not of propaganda,—in particular, not for purposes of propaganda for any special musical *school*. Being a composer who does not belong to any of the groupings, the author has not felt justified here to express any thoughts save with the utmost objectivity.

The modern Russian composers have been taken here not with the specific notion of "advanced" authors, innovators seeking and finding new paths, but in the ordinary temporal sense of the word, as composers living and labouring in a definite space of time. Hence alongside composers, modern in the full sense of the word, contemporary both in birth and style, our sketch also admits composers who essentially have not contributed a single new word to the tonal art. They have repeated the old more or less successfully, yet we did not think it right to exclude them, the more so as their ranks include composers who have gained popularity on a large scale, and also because at this moment it appears difficult to form an absolutely exact criterion of the merits of this or that school.

All that seems glittering, striking and new, sometimes merely because it has glittered for the first time in the world, does not prove capable of passing the test of time, that testing by time so dreaded by the composer. In this test many things wither that appeared new and dazzling at the time of their birth, and, on the other hand, there is resurrected much that appeared obsolete and uninteresting during the life of its authors. The last decade alone has proven to us the insecurity and vanity of many prognostications that were put forth as unshakeable and categoric. As to what the decades of the future hold in store for us, it is difficult even to surmise.

One thing is indubitable in any event,—that in our times of rapid change of fashions and tendencies, in our times of precipitous destruction of the tradition of old art, such forecasts are particularly difficult. With a view to objectivity and the widest possible and most exact information for people who are interested in Russian music, but have a vague idea of it or none at all, the above considerations have made us take in composers of various creeds and schools indiscriminately, conservative and reactionary as well as the most advanced, withal striving in the characterisation of the creative art of each to give not so much an appraisal as a series of objectively observed traits, perfectly neutral for deductions, yet helpful for an orientation in these complicated phenomena. Only in a few cases, where an estimate is already possible, where it is perfectly clear that the composer in question is of interest only as a rank and file representative of the composer's art in Russia, and perhaps does not himself lay claim to a prominent place, have we made exceptions in the sense of more categorical résumés of the impressions left by his music.

This very Rubicon, the temporal or historical trait that may be recognised as the beginning of "modernism" in music, is of course, an extremely indefinite conception. Here one has to rely upon a sort of "inner sense." The author has not included in his book the composers who, admittedly belonging to the past, have completely expressed themselves and have been appraised. At present these are few, really Glazunoff alone, the patriarch of Russian composers, who may be deemed to belong to that class. On the other hand, the author thought it his duty to include in this book the composers who, though the seniors of that very Glazunoff, have not as yet been appraised even by Russia, let alone on a world-scale. These are more numerous. Names such as Tañeyeff, Ryebikoff, Gryechaninoff, undoubtedly have world-fame still ahead of them, and yet the importance of some of these for Russian music is vitally essential.

Nearly all the living and labouring composers (except Glazunoff, for he has uttered himself) have found a place in the book in our gallery of portraits, as well as those who are dead, but whose creative work manifestly belongs to the new formative period. Naturally the author of these lines has been left out of the sketch of composers as such self-criticism would be out of place.

Biographical data play the least important rôle in this book—the centre of gravity lies in the characterisations—and the biographical details are given only in the cases where these determined, in a definite manner, the creative work in this or another direction of it.

Lately Russian music has achieved world-recognition. Its popularity is ever on the increase. In the persons of the world's most prominent composers of to-day, Russian music has well-nigh reached the position of world-leadership. The interest it calls forth is still rising. But simultaneously with this interest and its growth, there is observable not only in the wide circles of the foreign public, but even among foreign composers, an extremely low amount of information on particular phenomena of Russian music, regarding the relative positions of individual composers, their artistic genealogy, the connection of Russian art with the Western, and *vice versa*.

Not alone the group of contemporaries, selected by us, the most vivid at present and, as a matter of fact, the most interesting to the world, but even the Russian classical composers beginning with Glinka and ending with the famous Russian National School (Borodin, Balakireff, Rimski-Korsakoff, Cui and Musorgski), are utterly unknown to the Western world in the sense of being clearly seen in their connection with the rest of music and with each other. In passing opinions about them, even the prominent European musicians admit and manifest unpardonable ignorance, a dilettantism of judgment and non-comprehension of the inter-connection of individual phenomena.

Yet, in order to get a clear view of modern Russian music, it is imperatively necessary to know and understand these connections. The present work, while discussing the moderns, aims partly also to give a clear idea of the connection between the Russian past and present, and thereby to aid in the fullest understanding of the present itself.

In the characterisations proper, the author has sought as far as possible, to preserve the tone of complete objectivity, striving to search out positive traits even in the facts for which personally, as far as his tastes go, he feels an antipathy. This objectivity is absolutely necessary in a book which aims, as I have already pointed out, first and foremost at information and not agitation, and must, accordingly, avoid by all means bringing in the elements of personal tastes and individual sympathies.

LEONID SABANEYEFF.

PARIS, *August, 1927.*

SERGEY TAÑEYEFF

(1856–1915)

TANEYEFF was not only a great Russian composer, whose
true worth has begun to loom clear only since his death,
but for the Russian musical world he was something infinitely greater, the teacher of several musical generations,
and the living and shining ideal of the musician as a priest
of pure art. He was an idealistic personality as a man, and
all those who in any way came in contact with him, carried
away memories not only of a serious, profound and original
composer, "a Russian Brahms," but also in a higher degree
of a pure, honest and ideal human being, so typically Russian that he could not have been duplicated in other surroundings or in another nation.

Tañeyeff was not recognised in his lifetime, and yet,
somehow, he was. The special conditions of the Moscow
musical world gave birth to this odd anomaly. In general,
in order to understand Tañeyeff, his importance, his influence, his meaning, we must transfer ourselves temporarily
into the atmosphere of "Old Moscow" of the eighties and
nineties of the century when Tañeyeff's life and creative
art were being shaped. That atmosphere even many Russians no longer remember at present, to say nothing of
persons belonging to other cultures.

During those years the Moscow Conservatory had been
founded and won its cultural importance, barely five or six
years after the founding of the St. Petersburg Conservatory. The brothers Rubinstein, the pianist-genius Anton
and the less famous but perhaps no less gifted Nikolay, as it

were, divided between them their importance as founders of the musical nursery-gardens of education in Russia. Anton Rubinstein founded the St. Petersburg Conservatory; Nikolay Rubinstein, that of Moscow.

These conservatories immediately became the nurseries not only of musical education, but also of musical tradition. Russian musicians, who until then had all been more or less amateurs, who had hardly undergone any connected course of training in the art, flung themselves with the zeal of neophytes at musical science, the traditional science that was already beginning to wane in the West at the time. But to Russian culture it was still very new. This newness explains the queer phenomenon which the generation of musician-innovators, those active geniuses of the Russian National School including Rimski-Korsakoff, Borodin, Musorgski, Balakireff, and Cui (*see* Appendix), exhibited in contrast to the generation of "conservatory musicians," who won this appellation because they had been graduated from a conservatory, and because of the literal meaning of the word "conservator" as well.

Musical tradition was something new for Russia and her still amateurish musical world. It was a peculiar "novelty," and many seized upon this novelty with great ardour. To the dilettantism of the former-day Russian composers, the new generation of "conservatories," with a pride that was not devoid of vanity, opposed its musical culture and its succession from the West with which the "musical nationalists" would have nothing to do. As opposed to the amateur "subversion of foundations" and their scorn of "scholastic grind," this new generation bowed to the Western European musical culture and, perhaps, even too uncritically accepted the musical lore that was beginning to wither in the West itself.

For the enlightenment of the reader who is not initiated into the interrelations and currents then existing in the musical world of Russia, it is not devoid of interest to observe that between the two capitals of Russia, the old capital, Moscow, of landowners and merchants, where dwelt chiefly the famous and characteristic "Russian spirit," and St. Petersburg, the new bureaucratic capital, where were concentrated the Court, the aristocracy and the officialdom, and the European "spirit," there existed a suppressed rivalry and struggle in the musical as well as in other matters. Each of these wished to have "the best forces" in all fields. And each thought its own forces the better.

The Moscow musical world treated the St. Petersburg composers with a certain amount of scepticism and pushed to the fore their own, principally Chaykovski, as the most prominent product of the Moscow Conservatory. In turn, St. Petersburg hesitated long about the recognition of Chaykovski and tried, in general, to disregard the musical doings of Moscow.

This antagonism and rivalry explains why in Moscow the real recognition of the composers of the Russian National School came comparatively late (in the twentieth century). Until then, relying on the authority of Rubinstein and Chaykovski, the Moscovites had had no liking for Borodin or Rimski-Korsakoff or, particularly, for Musorgski, who was considered a "half-witted," half-tutored, and crazy being.

For the same reason, in Moscow, which had neither Musorgski nor Balakireff, nor any of the revolutionary-innovating or nationalist "Slavophile" spirit of the Russian National School, the conservatory Western traditions had taken root more easily and firmly. In St. Petersburg, Anton Rubinstein alone fought against dilettantism at the Conservatory, but the contest was uneven, as the side of the adversaries had the force of men endowed with genius.

And thus it came to pass that Moscow became the guardian of conservatory Western traditions, while St. Petersburg guarded the innovator tendencies and Russian nationalism. In this respect life queerly mocked the habitual sympathies of Moscow for Russia and St. Petersburg for the West. Moscow became the city of musical conservatism and remained so until the second decade of this century, when the new geniuses springing up there, changed the relationship about.

In this conservative midst, devoted to the newly revealed musical traditions and to the old composers, and the classic art of Europe, in accordance with the taste dictated by the authority of Chaykovski and N. Rubinstein who were not at all inclined to innovations,—in this atmosphere S. Tañeyeff was educated, inevitably predestined to become the real conservator of tradition.

Sprung from an ancient noble family of modest and retiring nature, with a keen and searching mind, and inclined to the solution of complicated problems,—the typical mind of a chess player or lawyer,—Tañeyeff was, as a man, the most typical representative of the Russian noblemen's traditions of the latter half of the last century. He possessed in the highest degree that typical irony of an always sceptical and watchful mind, which at all times worked behind the screen of an immobile and apparently lazy body. He possessed the moral irreligiousness, if one may express it so, peculiar to this class of Russians, the scientific positivism of thought, a complete aversion towards all mysticism with miracles and tricks, an esthetic conception of religion as something nationally, historically, "scientifically" valuable, and necessary for study. He bowed before Western culture, before the classic world of beauty, before the great art of Europe. He had the mind of a chess player or a mathematician who everywhere seeks problems to be solved, a peculiar love of brain gymnastics. He was a man of broad, liberal enlightened political convictions, but convictions only, and not deeds, for this kindly man devoted to his world of art, could never sail out upon the poisoned ocean of political passions. An original in life, about whom many anecdotes were current, locked up in himself and hating society, he had consecrated himself to music at an early age, as in the middle ages people would consecrate themselves to a monastery, and throughout his life he unswervingly fulfilled the dictates of his order with a punctuality and accuracy that were religious.

After graduation from the conservatory, a brilliant career was in store for him. Barely a youth, he was appointed director of the Conservatory to succeed Nikolay Rubinstein. A splendid pianist (a pupil of N. Rubinstein) he could have won world renown in concerts. But the fame of the market place and the wandering life of a "world artist" ran counter to this original and consistent nature. He could not think of such an existence but with aversion. And so we find that Tañeyeff resigned from the post of director which he had held for five years, gave up the career of a virtuoso, locked himself up in his inner world, and retired into quiet and "wilderness." Almost an anchorite, a rigid ascetic, he lived a life in which there never flashed the light of any romance, or any infatuation save that one single ideal one of "man for music," of which he was the living embodiment.

There was a strange and most complete harmony with this image of his, in that life in the Moscow "wilderness" in which Tañeyeff prayed to his god—Art. Fleeced by his relatives after the death of his parents, who had left him considerable means, he raised no objection and treated with stoic equanimity this manifestation of human insignificance. For his residence he picked, with stubborn persistence, lone little houses of which there were at that time many in the quiet outskirts of the "big village," without improvements, without running water, without electricity, which last he viewed (as he did the telegraph) with hatred, as base attempts to "mechanise life."

Thus he lived quietly with his aged nurse who had stayed with him since the time of serfdom. The new electrical age went past him, just as contemporary music did. For Tañeyeff, time had stopped. In his dreams he was with Palestrina and Bach, or in a world of classical antiquity which he passionately loved, surrounding himself with books of ancient wisdom and art. Only a feeble reflection of the contemporary era penetrated into his sequestered world, and nearly all of it was greeted with disapproval by the hermit.

Of course he was a hermit only in the conventional sense of the word. The spirit of any mystic asceticism whatever was unconditionally foreign to Tañeyeff. On the contrary, there was in him a mass of earthly clarity and devotion to this world, this earth. To the earth, but not to its perversions through false culture, "civilisation," enslavement by the machine, annihilation of personality in the collective mass. A great individualist, valuing the freedom of personality above everything else, Tañeyeff hated the cultural civilising wiles as contributing to the enslavement of the spirit. In many respects, he shared the theories and ideas of Lyof Tolstoy, the friend with whose family he was so closely and intimately acquainted, although he never was a "Tolstoyan" in the accepted sense of this word.

Tañeyeff's whole framework was especially fitted to cultivate and conserve the past. In the world-views of this man, there was something "museumlike." His passionate devotion to the valuable things of culture was a fear of hurting or losing them. He was the embodiment of the Moscow musical view of the world of that time. His musical deities were Palestrina, Bach, the old Netherlanders, whose musical-mathematical conception possessed so much in common with Tañeyeff's own; and, more modern, the radiant and antiquely joyous Mozart, Mendelssohn and "partly" Beethoven, for whom he felt great respect, but did not possess that

devoted exaltation that he felt, for instance, for Palestrina
or Mozart.
  With far greater equanimity he passed by the romantic
musical world—Chopin, Schumann. Liszt, Wagner and
Berlioz, he did not understand, knew imperfectly, and what
he knew, he hated almost to his very death in the year
1915. Of course time did its work, and once I recall that
having noticed a score of *Parsifal* on his desk in 1910, and
expressing surprise, I received this answer from the in-
veterate hater of Wagner: "Do you know, it turns out to
be magnificent music. . . ."
  Profoundly honest, incredibly truthful, incapable of lying
even to himself, Tañeyeff penetrated beauties with difficulty
and effort, and he required much time to grasp what was
new to him. But having once grasped, he became a devoted
admirer forever.
  Of the Russian composers, he loved only Glinka and Chaykovski, retaining only bitter feelings for Musorgski and
the *Koochka* (the "great five"). He made an exception
during the latter years for Rimski-Korsakoff who fascinated
him with the geometric harmoniousness of his musical structures, and for the then youthful Glazunoff, Aryenski, and
Rakhmaninoff.
  It goes without saying that all the later ones, Skryabin,
Debussy, Ravel, Strauss, either left him cold, peculiarly
"grieved" him, exasperated him, or roused him to indig-
nation.
  "Murky waves are running in music," he said bitterly.
  The infinite honesty of an ancient master emanates from
this Tañeyeff. Having worked stubbornly, effortfully all
his life and only for himself, far from any thought of some
"recognition," "success," "fame," Tañeyeff despised dilettantism and scorned the appreciation of the masses. Even
towards the external and generally accepted expressions of
homage and success he showed derisive irony and scepticism

behind which was felt the enormous pride of the artist as such, side by side with "personal" humility. Tañeyeff was not characterised by arrogance even in the slightest degree. But his absolute uprightness and honesty made a great appeal and he was respected and feared like unto the voice of conscience.

Tañeyeff had set himself to be a master-composer. There were mixed traits in his make-up. On the one hand the urge of an honest artist thoroughly imbued with the conception of the importance and meaning of art. On the other hand, the bent of a research scholar who wished to pierce with his "analytic" eye the spiritual laboratory of creative art, and divine "the secrets of beauty." This duality runs through his whole life. Perhaps in the depths of his soul, this spirit, honest and somehow oddly devoid of intuition, was persuaded of the possibility of a rational construction of beauty. This theory harmonised with his personality. By stubborn labour and study, he wished to seize the secrets of creative art, believing that this was possible and that the different paths, intuitive inspiration (for which he felt a profound respect), and a searching mind and toil, lead to the same object, the creation of the beautiful.

In this respect for the gifts of intuition, with which nature had not endowed him in due measure, Tañeyeff proved himself no "crumb-picker," no dull musical savant destitute of the true sense of art; not one of those tonal druggists who do not even know where beauty is. Tañeyeff understood beauty, loved it, felt it, but he believed in another, a rational way of achieving it by the side of the ordinary path of intuition.

All his life Tañeyeff spent under these stimuli of creative art: scientific thought and seeking of intuition. Apparently he knew there was "something" which had not been given him. In his correspondence with his teacher and friend, Chaykovski (who, by the way, frequently treated his opinions not as if he were Tañeyeff's teacher, but rather as a pupil, so high was even then the authority of Tañeyeff), Tañeyeff speaks at length of his ideas of a rationally constructed musical beauty, in which he saw something mathematical, something akin to geometrical beauty. His lack of a philosophic training, despite his enormous endowments therefor, prevented Tañeyeff from exactly formulating his ideas, but their essence was apparently his opinion that only that beauty was eternal which possessed mathematical attributes and premises, simple mathematical results of certain rigid laws which must be sought and found.

And he sought these laws lovingly and obstinately. He endeavoured to find their roots in the works of the old contrapuntists of the XIII-XVI centuries. He studied Josquin-de-Pre, Orlando Di Lasso, Palestrina. He devoted a great mass of time to the study of "severe style" counterpoint, of which he became professor at the Conservatory after he had resigned from the post of director. He believed that therein were to be found the keys to musical beauty. There have remained as a monument of his researches, two great works of scientific music, unparalleled in wealth of contents even on a European scale, let alone in Russia, where at the time, they were absolutely unique. These are *Counterpoint of Rigid Writing*, published by Byelyayeff in 1907 and the *Canon*, still unpublished.

I do not know any composer that would with such preciseness represent the idea of devotion to music. This is verily pure devotion, and verily to music and nothing else. His image of musical beauty and artistic beauty in general puts into shade all images of other beauties. Other composers knew infatuations and passions, for many of them the very music and creative art were somehow "means" of expressing the earthly passion that had seized them. Tañeyeff knew neither earthly passion nor religious mysticism. He knew only the beauty of Art, the beauty of rhythm, and the mystery of orderliness, the secret of which lured him on always. Is not his creative art perhaps so strange for this reason? Does it not appear occasionally dry for the reason that in an art which is devoid of the emotional premises of love and reverence, there fatally remain only the mathematical characteristics of orderliness, the mathematical laws of beauty? These only were felt by the great Russian composer, great in his odd blindness, great in his sterile morality which knew neither a moral lapse nor a moment of repentance. Perhaps an artist dare not be too pure, too sinless; perhaps the true artistic sanctity even needs a preliminary passing through some sort of abyss of sin.

He was a pure musician and from his idea of music was excluded both the idea of passion and the notion of anything that was unmusical. But one must not think that music came to him easily. No, Tañeyeff in general was in this respect, as it were, a "hard" composer. It came to him painfully and with difficulty, only by means of work and stubborn toil which he loved in itself. His life was adapted to the "painstakingness" of his creative art.

Alone of all Russian composers, Tañeyeff was celibate and teetotaler, so that it became a matter of course, and all his intimate friends no longer paid any attention to it. And his music, too, was just as sober and chaste: he did not even divine the states of intoxication, infatuation, or passion.

A certain kind of mathematic quality played a great part in his musical ideas. He loved bizarre tonal half-ornaments, half-problems. He loved the wise and ingenius concatenations of the separate voices. He was fond of overcoming tonal matter with human wisdom, setting for the latter a series of conditions with the proviso of preserving beauty and clarity. Many years he devoted to the unriddling of old contrapuntal "secrets" of the ancient masters, all those secrets of "mirror canons," "riddle canons" and all the other tricks and magic miracles with which those queer semi-mathematicians, semi-chess players and semi-musicians had delighted themselves and others. He believed that there was some rational "path" in all this. And he proved to be right. In his *magnum opus* on counterpoint of which we have already spoken, all those secrets have been solved, revealed, reduced to simple calculations, and, in passing, a great mass of new and still more ingenious possibilities have been discovered. The pure infatuation of the chess player used to seize Tañeyeff whenever he entered this world of musical tricks. To him music connoted a combination of orderliness, mind, and withal some feeling, even though devoid of earthly passion and "blood," yet, in its own way, very, very intense.

Before setting out to compose, he would prepare a special copy book and jot down in it the various themes that came to his mind. Then he wrote various exercises in contrapuntal style on these themes and only after having "mastered the material," as he put it, would he set to work. Persistent and accurate, he discarded a mass of sketches until he found what he needed. After his death there was found among his papers a mass of perfectly finished compositions which he, at the time, had not wanted to publish. Three completed symphonies, six quartettes, a mass of minor compositions—all this had not satisfied him and he had never even mentioned them.

His first compositions go back to the years of his graduation from the conservatory. He made his début brilliantly, with the Cantata *Johannes Damascenus* to a text by the poet Aleksey Tolstoy. In certain respects this is his composition of profoundest warmth and soulfulness. Behind the influences of Chaykovki and even Rubinstein, there is felt an original spirit and genuine greatness of thought clad in contrapuntal forms unusual for a Russian composer. For already in these early compositions, the future admirer of Bach reveals an enormous technique in the mastery of polyphonic interweaving of voices.

In this cantata the listener has not to look for attempts at innovations. Tañeyeff was too determined a foe of novelty. On the contrary, here all efforts converged on the old, on the restoration of the great and monumental style of the old-time religious music. Tañeyeff declares war on the fidgety and too mobile style of modernism and harks back to the majestic tones, slow and solemn, as are all great thoughts.

Then he turns his glances towards opera. But here, too, he remains faithful to himself. No traditional operatic subject with a love intrigue and a lyric centre of gravity appeals to him who has remained through his life devoid of love and has turned away in disgust from the fidgety and rushing "civilised" world. His glance turns far away. He drew his libretto from the monumental creations of the antique world. The tragic world of Æschylus is his style and his sphere. Having adapted for operatic purposes the trilogy of the Hellenic author of *Oresteia*, he employed it as the groundwork of his opera *Oresteia* on which, with the painstaking sluggishness peculiar to him, he worked for ten years without hope of even having it published, let alone of having it produced on the stage.

In the musical spirit and the conception of this opera, completed in 1893, Tañeyeff again approaches Chaykovski, but this time in a lesser degree than in his Cantata *Johannes Damascenus*. Here there are clearly more influences of Rubinstein and particularly of his sacred and oratorio operas (*The Macabbees, The Tower of Babel*). It is hard to say positively that the antique spirit had been embodied in this opera. The terrible and ominous theme of Æschylus, this gloomy and oppressive chain of crimes on the part of men and gods and the bloody waves of Fate in some way harmonised too little with the quiet, meek and wise character of Tañeyeff, for if he were to draw upon the antique world, it would have been more fitting for him to set to music

Hellenic philosophy rather than the bloody dramas of Æschylus. However strange it may appear in *Oresteia*, there turned out to be too much of the "operatic" pomp and circumstance, too much mixing of styles, and only the last act, as it were, begins to seize the antique atmosphere and spirit. This stupendous work was dedicated to the very same Rubinstein whose style was reflected in the music of the opera and who had died shortly before the piano-score of the opera had seen the light of day, so that the dedication reads, "To the memory of Anton Rubinstein."

Oresteia was produced several years later at the Mariinski Theatre in St. Petersburg. The opera had no success, due partly to its excessive length, the stubborn composer allowing no single cut, but chiefly owing to the unfamiliarity of the public with the antique world. Many years later, the opera was revived at the private theatre of Zimin in Moscow and then enjoyed considerable success.

Tañeyeff now began to devote a considerable part of his creative work to the perfection of his chamber style. This style, which had reached its culmination in the quartette compositions of Beethoven, was especially akin to Tañeyeff, as it embodied the idea of "serious music" without any concessions to the changing tastes, fashions and the wide "public opinion." The world of four instruments, each of which is independent and all together form a unity, particularly attracted our composer, for he could make complete application of his polyphonic mastery here. And Tañeyeff began to work in this department. He completed as many as six quartettes by way of "experiments," and finally decided to publish only the seventh.

Modest and hesitating, helpless in the extreme in practical affairs, he did not know for a long time how musical compositions were published. It required the interference of friendly disposed musicians to convince the new Bach that the times are past when it was possible for a composer to write music, to engrave it himself, and to pile it up on the shelves in the hope that some two hundred years later another Mendelssohn would unearth these treasures. Tañeyeff was very much surprised when the publisher Byelyayeff proposed to publish his opera and his quartettes and even paid money for them. Tañeyeff argued a long time with him, maintaining that it was not really worth the money, but this odd bargaining, utterly contrary to nature, ended after all with the victory on Byelyayeff's side. The opera and the quartettes were published.

Thereafter Tañeyeff assiduously wrote chamber music. Of all Russian composers he devoted himself with the greatest love and strictest adherence to principles of this intimate and serious and isolated chamber world. He wrote a long series of quartettes for strings, then a quintette, and later passed to ensembles with piano, trio, quartette and quintette. Here he found the true field for applying his masterly technique painstakingly built up in long years of solitude. Tañeyeff's style, formerly similar to Chaykovski's and Rubinstein's, lacking individual characteristics when taken as a whole, here became specific and original, yet not even for a moment becoming in any way inclined to innovation or modernism.

Great events in the musical world were taking place around Tañeyeff. His own pupils brought him news about them. New talents were blooming. Richard Strauss was breaking down the old laws of euphony and introducing decorative principles into music; Debussy was creating a new world of harmonies constructed on entirely different principles; Skryabin was striving to combine music with eschatological mysticism and simultaneously creating also a specific world of harmonies; all around him at his very elbows were working the more conservative young composers—Rakhmaninoff, Gryechaninoff; Rimski-Korsakoff himself was beginning to be carried away by musical innovations. But Tañeyeff, as though living in a different world, was doing his work and taking no account of it all. He accepted and approved but little of all these new things. Most of them he met with decisive enmity. Straightforward in the extreme, he always spoke bluntly, without fear of making enemies, and, strange to say, he never made them thanks precisely to this. On the contrary, the musical world, independent of his leanings, was filled with reverence for the "teacher" who never darkened his life with one word of flattery or hypocrisy, who told composers to their faces the truth however unpleasant, but told it blushing and growing confused himself, as though performing an unpleasant duty.

In respect to quartette style, Tañeyeff stands out as a master of the highest rank. It is hardly possible to mention another composer after Beethoven, save perhaps Brahms, who can stand comparison to him in respect to maturity of style in the sense of making the most of the instruments and creating a tonal web that commands interest. But at the same time there are apparent also the characteristic faults of all his creative work: dryness of the melodic line, abstractness of the melody, lack of inner emotional temperament, an occasional odd blindness to artistic differences of style, a blindness that permits Tañeyeff in one and the same composition to combine imitative traces of Mozart and Chaykovski.

It is interesting that one so closely kindred to Brahms in temperament, in his convinced conservatism, in his striving towards something serious, monumental, even in his sympathies for the oratorial, symphonic and chamber styles, that Tañeyeff nevertheless hated and even did not understand this very Brahms, doubtless following the traditional unfavorable recommendation that Chaykovski had once given Brahms, and which, thanks to Chaykovski's authority, had thereafter shut the door of the musical world of Moscow and Russia in general in the face of Brahms. Yet, there is no doubt that if Tañeyeff's significance for Russian music can be characterised very briefly, this characterisation will be exactly: "The Russian Brahms." Just as profound and holy a musician, pedantically and disinterestedly devoted to art, a man without compromises, an admirer of the old traditions, and just as austerely dryish in his creative work. But here, however, justice requires it to say that with Tañeyeff all these traits, both positive and negative, are more sharply expressed so that the result of the sum total is not perhaps to the advantage of his music.

At the same time Tañeyeff conceived an enthusiasm for the *lied* and created in this field a series of works that exhibited great merit and underscored more profoundly his kinship with Brahms. It is the very same austere music, self-restrained, without too frank lyricism; having only a trace of sentimentality it is music in which all emotions are somewhat stifled by chaste austerity. In the field of song, Tañeyeff has rather numerous productions and this department of his compositions of late has been enjoying considerable vogue among artists. Tañeyeff who knows his instruments perfectly in chamber ensemble, proves just as great a master of the voice and its nuances.

He composed also in the symphonic style, but his first symphonies he himself rejected as unsatisfactory. His Fourth Symphony (published as the "First") in C-minor, is written throughout in monumental almost Beethovenish tones. A similarity with Brahms is noticeable here too, particularly in the Adagio, which is full of contemplative majesty. This music, utterly devoid of any intention to make an impression by external means, and in particular by the "newness of harmonies" then so fashionable and which had caught almost all composers, could not but appear somewhat old-fashioned, purposely reactionary. More and more Tañeyeff was gaining the odd position of a "teacher revered by all" but with whose opinions almost nobody agreed. He was loved with tender love, loved even by his opponents of different schools, as, for instance, by Skryabin. They loved him and did not agree with him, and he, too, kindly disposed to everybody as much as possible, disagreed with them. Between Tañeyeff and the musical world an abyss was growing bridged only by respect for his extraordinary musical erudition and his upright and noble personality. This abyss was natural and it opened quite normally. The world was moving forward and Tañeyeff remained in an isolated state on some sort of a fantastic island in the midst of the sea, an island on which not only in the musical sense, but in the most literal as well, there was neither running water nor electricity, where life did not flow in a contemporary nervous and hot tempo, but with a tempo of the century before the last which contemporaries could not but look upon as deadening. People came into this world of his to rest from the tumult of the new times and to rejoice in the philosophic calmness of a man who could stop the march of time for himself, but to abide long in this quietude was hard. And the unbending and irreconcilable Tañeyeff, unwilling to accept the new, made no surrender even in a single trifle.

Apparently the atmosphere of isolation was beginning to grow somewhat burdensome even for Tañeyeff. He felt his isolation not only from the present but, most important, even from the future. New generations of musicians enthusiastically gave themselves up to new revelations in music, but the influences of the old master-teacher left no impression on them. With his rational mind, Tañeyeff felt and understood that surely there must be some sort of truth even in this new music, since there was such great mass enthusiasm for it. And so, already in his declining years, he resolved to study the contemporary with the same painstaking and persistence characteristic of him as in former times he had studied the old Flemings and Bach.

He began with Richard Wagner whom he considered the transition composer separating the new from the old. The fair and objective Tañeyeff, who always strove to find the good everywhere, found rather soon what he had sought in Wagner. He found mastery, which reconciled him with Wagner, found also "splendid music," as he expressed it himself. But Wagner was not sufficient, all contemporary music continued to be a "book under seven seals" for Tañeyeff.

He felt this world was getting away from him and apparently it was to him the source of a great inner tragedy. Whether he dreaded that what he had all his lifetime considered an indisputable verity, a truth in art in which he believed as some believe in a religious truth, seemed to be tottering and that the whole work of his lifetime was brought under a question mark, or whether he simply began to feel the isolation which he had not noticed earlier because it was not so noticeable while the musical world of Moscow itself had been conservative, are questions hard to answer. But one felt hurt for this pure, devoted man of convictions who had dedicated all his life to the service of a single idea. One felt hurt that this creative art of his, so pure, so devoted, this service of his to art, so ideal, historical destiny doomed to oblivion and perhaps even to ridicule.

The final years of his work were passing unnoticed. Other events, more striking, had crowded him out and completely occupied the attention of musicians and the public. His last work, a grandiose Cantata *After Reading the Psalm,* with monumental aims, with its Bachlike majesty in form, with an enormous sweep of mastery, and although it was performed, still left behind it only opinions of "esteem." Recognised as the moral and scientific musical authority, recognised as a theoretician, as a teacher, and above all as an "ethical personality," Tañeyeff at the same time had the queer fate of witnessing the gradual annihilation of his authority as a composer and his recognition in this field.

He died a lone death, a man out of fashion, against a background of unfolding new events, in the era of the victorious march of militant modernism that swept away all traditions.

But the time that has elapsed since his death (1915) has shown that many were wrong. A great deal of what in the days of the onward march of Modernism had seemed to them irrefutable, extremely interesting, epoch-making, dazzling, proved to be no such thing. A great deal of it has now turned out to be but flashy fireworks, a dazzling display that leaves fading memories behind. A great deal proved the whim of the ever-changing fashion that forever thirsts for the new. All the new harmonies were now devised and even the innovations of Debussy and Skryabin paled before the audacities of the succeeding composers. And when all these new things had been achieved and thereby became old, what stood behind these new things grew clear.

The artistic verity, that the new is valuable only in so far as it finds new words for expressing new and interesting significant experiences, proved correct. As soon as the flash of once new words had grown dim, as soon as the means of expression had lost the attraction of unusualness, it turned out that the simple language of Tañeyeff could be compared with the modernist language of the new authors, for both he and they ceased to be new each in his own time. And then there emerged to the foreground a comparison of the contents. It was a joy to many to whom the figure of Tañeyeff was dear, that his compositions that had seemed obsolete and old-fashioned were suddenly gaining new life, that they were proving interesting and more alive than a great many things that had crowded them and put them in the shadow with their false and ephemeral flashiness. It turned out that in his compositions were hidden purely musical inner potentialities which surpassed by far the flash of the artificial gems of rank and file modernism.

At present Tañeyeff is rising from the ashes, rising slowly but steadily and convincingly. Mastery is the most enduring thing in art. Tastes and fashions change, also the demands for one sort of contents or another, but mastery ever remains necessary and desirable, it makes the works of the classics and antiquity live. And Tañeyeff always possessed mastery in the highest degree, in minute things as well as in large things. He was a conscientious and exacting artist who took pains with his art to the minutest detail and found no rest until everything reached his ideal. But mastery was not the only thing. Also the inner side, the content, of Tañeyeff's creative art possessed such solid merits that it stands the "test of time" so dreaded by every artist.

Twelve years have passed since his death and his creative art is gradually and persistently gaining recognition, making a path for itself, as the creative work of the great Russian classic. Serious programmes are no longer made up in Russia without Tañeyeff's compositions, his quartettes are becoming an indispensable part of the quartette repertory, his songs invariably figure on the programmes. Soon there will come the time for the rehabilitation of his symphonic and oratorio works as well, perhaps the most valuable things he left. The recognition of Tañeyeff moves slowly, just as his creative work moved, but it moves steadily.

At present his fame is spread only throughout Russia which formerly also turned its countenance away from the excessive chastity and austerity of this music, but there is not the slightest doubt that it will spread to Europe and America as well, for always and everywhere that which has in it seeds of eternity will gain a path for itself. And just as the Russian romantic Musorgski has conquered the world, even though half a century behind time, exactly so the Russian classic, Tañeyeff, will in time gain recognition, thereby proving that he was right, that the pure and holy service to the ideal of musical beauty proves truer and more

enduring than the restless seeking of new expressions and
new irritations, that the greatness which music has been called
to express may be expressed not only in the language of
new forms, but also in the majestic language of ancient
music and that this latter expression is perhaps the most
suitable for the ideas and images which appeal to human
thought loftily attuned.

Tañeyeff was an idealist. His thoughts revolved in a
select circle. He had no need of jerky phrases for giving utterance to his inner world. His world was better and more
adequately expressed in old sounds and he felt it instinctively.
And then the miracle happened which has reoccurred many
times in the field of art and has astonished every time,—
the old has proven more viable than the new. The majesty
of his thought and the purity of his spiritual vision is now
visible through the simple forms of his expression, whereas
many of those who in their time had obscured him, now
reveal behind the glittering newness of externals a poverty
and shallowness of inner content.

We are fully justified in saying that Tañeyeff is the rising
star of Russian music, still unrecognised, but destined to be
recognised with recognition similar to that of almost all the
truly great, not in his lifetime but after death. It is only
then that there emerge the true values, and the falseness
of perspective, natural in the estimation of even the most
farsighted, is rectified.

ALYEKSANDR SKRYABIN

(1871–1915)

SKRYABIN combined contradictions. A fantastic with a mystical twist, a megalomaniac who now spoke with complete conviction of his own divineness and then, on the other hand, a rationalist seeking in music a *scheme,* geometry, harmoniousness that was mathematical. Finally, a "piano" composer who only with difficulty, and not always successfully, stepped from his intimate piano world into the world of symphonic forms. Skryabin swept over the Russian musical world as some meteor or comet, foreign in its essence yet somehow logically determined by the whole course of preceding history. Like a meteor, he left behind a trail less significant than one would have expected at the time of the efflorescence of his activity, a trail growing so dim that the fatal question of the "true significance" of Skryabin has been asked with the implication that he has been overestimated.

Skryabin was born and musically educated at a time when Russian musical thoughts were still in a slumbering state. The Russian musician was almost ignorant of the contemporary achievements of Western music. The very concept of "newness" and "innovation" in music was extremely relative and timid. At any rate, in Skryabin's earliest attempts at composition, it is now difficult to divine the future great composer. In spite of a certain acridity, and super-refinement of his harmonic thought, his compositions of that period still appear somewhat clumsy, excessively epigonic with regard to Chopin whom he plainly imitated at the time. Cui, an old "bird" of a musician dropped the winged expression: "A trunkful of stolen manuscripts of Chopin." And indeed, at that time, it was difficult to discern anything else in the trunk.

But it is interesting that Skryabin's faith in himself and in his exceptional position in the history of music was chronic and early. When still a boy he had entered a world of haughty dreams. There was in him an erotic quality that found relief in the banal "cavaliership" of fashionable salon life. This maniacal, conceited demonism of self-adoration found it necessary to express itself in a form so peculiar to the salon. Russia had known the types of literary salon "demons" who possessed both posing and sincerity side by side. But in Skryabin it possessed the first example of the musical salon devil. It was Skryabin's fortune that he succeeded in evolving from this form into something higher, and if he was not fated to reach a complete enlightenment, at least he was on the right path.

Skryabin's creative work in music is very difficult to separate from his life as a whole, and the even monstrous reveries that inspired him. To him music meant utterance, and life was the soil and occasion for the birth of these utterances. He was incapable of regarding music as the art of a form, "pure" music, music for itself. To Skryabin this seemed absurd. Music was required as a means to utter and express something. Music was language, an esoteric language, comprehensible perhaps only to the one completely initiated, but grasped by all peripherically in some way. And not music alone, but every art as well. And with Skyrabin the borders separating one art from the other grew faint at an early age. His mental make-up inclined him towards schematisation and craving to know and explain everything to the end, and therefore was forced to make up schemes which seemed to him explanatory, and at an early stage made all the arts identical. He was the artist to whom the secret of combining all the arts was bound to be revealed. This ancient romantic fantasy perhaps came to him through Wagner and his dreams of a *Gesammt-kunstwerk*. But Wagner had never been so schematically rectilinear in his constructions nor forgot anywhere to such a degree the actual correlation of divine forces.

One might say that Skryabin's gifts were essentially the gifts of a salon composer, a true "twentieth century Chopin," refined and pointed, with a sort of poisoned *Weltanschauung*, more superficial and externally dynamic. But Skryabin's spirit never felt satisfied and never could have been satisfied by what, in his opinion, was the "modest perspective" of being on a par with Chopin. To be merely a musician was to Skryabin the acme of misfortune. However, fate has bitterly laughed at his megalomania, for his philosophical constructions have not, after all, been deemed worthy of anything beyond the attention of a biographer, and the rank of his genius with all its merits can hardly be compared to Chopin's.

The haughty dream of his uniqueness was characteristic of Skryabin since his earliest years. The boy began to ponder over world-problems possibly as early as the age of fourteen. His intellectual life was running perhaps a more intensive course than with his musical ancestor, Chopin, but unfortunately, neither the peculiar traits of his nature, nor the milieu in which he was born, that of an ancient Russian family of military nobility, predisposed him towards a *study* of the field that absorbed him. By nature Skryabin was not a true thinker, only something of a "scientific dreamer." Characteristic of his psychic make-up was an eternal striving to "fortify himself with science" which if I am not mistaken, has not been observed so far in any other composer in the world.

The author of the preludes of refinement and finesse, in which Chopin's world was, as it were, reborn with a new refinement and a new tragicalness, was eagerly curious to penetrate the riddles of life and art and their mystic correlations. Wherefore life? Wherefore art? What is their meaning in that orderly system which is the world and which Skryabin always conceived somewhat schematically like a geometric figure? In Skryabin's earliest records, his diary, lately published in Russia, we find curious passages bearing testimony to the tense mental urge of the youth who was eager to grasp his position in the universe. The idea of his exceptional endowments, of his being a genius already permeates all his sensations, and everything seems to be built around him as the central god.

Wherefore life, full of agitations and tragedies? Wherefore death, the inevitable end of existence? These are the questions fateful and naïve in their pristine primitiveness, which the youthful amateur philosopher poses, and which Skryabin boldly undertakes to answer. He feels within him "the forces of genius for solving the century-old riddles." He is bringing liberation and knowledge to humanity. He is the messiah, sent for the purpose of proclaiming the truth.

The tragedy of the world struggle, the tortures of man locked up in the vise of existence, all this was reflected in his music of that period. But it would be idle to suppose that this reflection is adequate for the ideas themselves. It is adequate only for Skryabin's conception of these ideas. A live and fantastic mind, inclined to the broadest and most rapid generalisations, inconsistent and at the same time schematic, Skryabin as a spiritual personality was neither Titan nor hero, but rather the average man. And in his music we discern a dream of Titanism, the dream of greatness and tragedy, but not greatness itself, not Titanism itself, examples of which have been given us by geniuses like Beethoven or Wagner. Skryabin's music shines by reflected planetary light. These ideas when reflected in Skryabin's psychic make-up, which is not deep, become more appropriate to the drawing-room; the reflection does not embody the ideas themselves.

Of course this does not diminish the enormous musical beauties of this music. Skryabin, nevertheless, remains a great, perhaps the most gifted Russian composer of genius, if considered in the strict sense of his "musical work," which should be done. ˙ But he, himself, did not wish that. He took a tremendous burden upon his shoulders. Feeble, and far from Titanic by nature, he made promises which he could not fulfil, and thereby proved his spiritual weakness.

Philosophy remained the guiding motive of his life and his creative work. It is interesting to consider this enthusiasm of the musician for philosophic problems in conjunction with the enthusiasm for abstract thought then general in Russia and particularly in Russian literature. It was especially centred upon the field of the mysterious, the unknown.

At that time the literature of the symbolists had blossomed forth gorgeously, and in their works we find notes in common with Skryabin: enthusiasm for the philosophic, enthusiasm for the unusual. The artists conceived a desire to be unusual, they were no longer satisfied with the title of talented, and in that sense "unusual," human beings. They wanted great unusualness. All of them became devotees of black magic, wizards, magicians, conjurors of spirits. There is not the slightest doubt that Skryabin is a reflection of the literary Russian symbolism in music, that he has a "mood-key" common with the symbolists who were at that time also called decadents (see Appendix). Hence his striving to prop up art with philosophy. Hence his striving after "prophetism" after occult sciences, "consecration," everything in general that has been dictated to him by the proud dream of his real or potential greatness and uniqueness.

But that which in the case of the decadents was a theme for creative work, sometimes merely a beautiful form, occasionally merely a pose, in Skryabin's case morbidly came to be a living part of his very self. He really began to believe in his uniqueness, in his prophetic mission, his messianism. The desire to be not only a mysterious "salon devil," but a real demon as well, some sort of a theurgus, competing with God in the art of creating the world, crops up in Skryabin very early. Naïve and inexperienced in philosophy, he falls early into the seductive captivity of solipsism and begins to profess the opinion that there is nothing except himself, that he is the only one, that everything is in his "conception," and that therefore he creates; consequently he is—God. . . . This naïve theory of self-deification was soon shattered against the flaws and weak points of the world created by himself. But for a long time, Skryabin would not surrender and would seriously discuss the question: Why the world created by him was not such as he had wished to have it.

An optimist by nature, and for that reason perhaps not so inclined to a profound treatment of problems, Skryabin soon found consolation in the faults of the universe. In his conception art was the principle which transformed life and made it happiness. When recreated in art, both sorrows and sufferings and tragedies turn into beauty. In this transmuting influence lies the meaning of art. Life must be transmuted by means of art. Having identified itself with life, and having penetrated it, art will eo ipso transform life into the "Kingdom of God on earth." Some great artist will be able to combine all arts and thereby become the great teacher of mankind. Of course it is hardly necessary to add that in Skryabin's mind this great artist who could combine all arts was Skryabin himself. And thus his messianic idea combined itself with his artistic idea. He became a prophet through art and an artist through his ordination.

In the first place, Skryabin's exalted opinion of himself and his desire to be the first and even . . . God, may appear, and of course will appear, abnormal to many. In his philosophic dilettantism many, and not without reason, will descry symptoms of some serious psychic ailment. Many have started on a career of insanity in exactly this way. Skryabin would disarm opponents of this kind by declaring in advance that insanity did not mean a tragedy or a disadvantage to him, but rather an advantage. He calls people to partake of insanity, maintaining that moments of utter happiness or bliss always possess the characteristics of insanity. And he is perhaps right in his dialectics, wherein he argues very ingeniously, proving the thesis necessary to him.

Of course symptoms of the well-known "dementive moment," in plain words, insanity, are present not only in Skryabin's conceptions but in his whole make-up, supererotic and woven of contradictions. In his megalomania this insanity manifests itself only the more concretely. Of course all this is nothing from the "musical" point of view, for elements of insanity have been inherent in many creators of music. Skryabin was but the first "consistent paranoiac" to reduce musical insanity to a peculiar sort of scheme and even to a theory.

At any rate, with all the insanity of these conceptions, it is impossible not to admit the fascination and even the beauties of the dreams of transforming the world by means of art. This idea is one of those that grip, that are democratic in the profoundest manner and are strong thereby. But Skryabin does not stop here; his idea develops, passes through an evolution and transforms itself before it succeeds in transforming the world, transforms itself into becoming unrecognisable.

In the sphere of music, his idea of "art the transformer" was reflected in his First Symphony with its closing chorus *Hymn to Art*. Here Skryabin makes his début, unsuccessfully it is true, as a poet, as a preliminary to his mission for the combination of arts. However, his First Symphony cannot escape the reproach of too great a discrepancy between his grandiose attempts and a miniature attainment. The transparent and childishly naïve soul of Skryabin was far better expressed in this composition than was his "second ego," that messianism and haughty notion of a superman making the gift of liberation to the world. The Symphony is written in Chopin-like and somewhat salon-like forms, despite the presence of a certain amount of Wagnerism.

The godhead idea, the indissoluble companion of Skryabin's life, continues to develop. From the artist-transformer of the world, Skryabin becomes God who creates this world, having a "notion" as he does, that this is so, that he is the author both of all his tragedies and all his joys, that he literally creates his life and consequently the whole world as well. For Skryabin has no faith in the real existence of other individualities, save his own all-embracing personality which is God. The imperfection of this God does not frighten him, just as the gloomy perspective of an "isolated personality" does not frighten him for some time. This queer and now really psychopathic replacement or substitution of a scheme instead of reality, of a sort of cheap scenery instead of the infinity of the universe, is very characteristic of Skryabin. He does not feel frightened or bewildered at the contemplation of a world in which he is the only living and real being and for a time he does not notice the extraordinary scantiness of this world that lacks life and divinity and is comfortably held in his own tiny individuality, that is schematically endowed with the attributes of omniscience.

In music this stage is reflected in his Third Symphony or *The Divine Poem*, musically perhaps the acme of his creative art. This epoch was in general the culminating point of his life; he felt an extraordinary wave of creative art and the compositions written by him at this time bore the genuine impress of the musical previsions of genius (Etudes, op. 42, the Fourth and the Fifth Sonatas, the *Poème d'Extase*,

a series of minor compositions). At the same time his thinking gradually became more mature as though straining off
the elements of psychopathism that had "stuck" to it. From
this time on along with the efflorescence of his creative
powers, there began in Skryabin also a great change in ideas
that guided him in life and in composing.

His famous idea of a "Mystery" was born. This Mystery
which was not destined and could not become reality, was
nothing but the culmination of his ideas about the meaning
of the world, ideas that in their time had brought him now
to solipsism, then to Nietzscheanism and again to self-deification. Skryabin succumbed to the influence of the ideas
of theosophy, which he recreated in his mind in a peculiarly
original manner in order to create the idea of a Mystery
which was to become the guiding principle of his life. It
is difficult to relate this idea in a few words, the more so
since apparently it was not sufficiently clear to the author
himself. But in brief, the matter reduces itself to this, that
the whole universe in Skryabin's imagination (partly borrowed from theosophists) is reduced to an "alternation of
rhythms" or as the Hindu occultists express it, to the
"breaths of Brahma." "The creative spirit" of the universe
first of all creates the world by its desire, the creative will, it
creates matter by the creative force of resistance, and when
this world has been created and everything is being material-
ised, everything being differentiated in the process of "in-
volution," there then appears in that spirit a contrary striving towards fusion (the process of evolution) of Spirit and
World. Then the two polarities are combined in the erotic
act of love, the result of which is a return to the primordial
state of chaos, after which follow new "breaths of Brahma."

This Mystery was to mark that act of love which con-
cludes the universe in Skryabin's conception. This is the
mystic love of Spirit for World, and it is easy to divine that
in Skryabin's conception spirit is he, himself, that Skryabin

conceived himself to be an "embodiment of the world spirit" on earth. In this way the transformation of the world by art of which the youthful Skryabin had dreamed, was going through an evolution, and transformed itself into an "apocalyptic idea" of the end of the world that, it is true, was not called forth without the participation of the "combined arts" as they appeared in the image of the Mystery, of which Skryabin desired to be the author.

At first this Mystery outlined itself to Skryabin as an act close at hand, that was ready to take place any day. He conceived it as a huge artistic work that combined in itself all arts. The combined influence of these arts would produce the ecstasy, the transformation, which would shatter the frail walls of this world and man would fuse with Eternity. Dazzled by the splendor of his dream, the composer could not see its tremendous remoteness from realisation, did not notice either that he himself was by no means equipped for the "combination of the arts," or that mankind was in any way disposed to close accounts with the universe. But the fact was that henceforth with Skryabin all life was reduced to the projecting and planning of the Mystery, to preparing materials for it which truly speaking were all the compositions of this period; all of them came into existence, as though they were "sketches" for the Mystery, and received a separate existence only incidentally.

The insane element in this idea comes into most striking relief. Having created for himself a world that did not resemble the real one, Skryabin did not notice that the real world went on living as usual and took no account at all of his plans. And in his music there occurred a break. It becomes still more frenetic and super-refined. Chopin's influences vanish; in their stead emerges the mighty and striking physiognomy of Skryabin himself, at times recalling somewhat the musical lineaments of Liszt, just as exquisite, just as frenetic and "orgiastic" in inspiration. Simultaneously there occurs Skryabin's obsession with a certain musical "harmony," an acid chord which fills his compositions and is so characteristic that it even cannot stand imitation, for it immediately evokes the idea of "Skryabin's style." This harmony or chord in variation fills almost the entire contents of Skryabin's last compositions, giving them the character of a sort of enclosed, narrow, isolated and sequestered musical sphere, something like a tonal hothouse wherein grow only orchids of a single species and where no other plant can survive.

Among the musical influences that affected Skryabin during this period an important rôle was no doubt played by the influences of the French impressionists, especially Debussy. Of course it is possible that in the general musical air of Europe at that time, there were floating ideas of these complex harmonic combinations. But it is indubitable that Skryabin shared the general fate of his contemporaries, which consisted in the fact that they were all carried away by the search for new chords, new "harmonies," that they were carried away by the hunt of the exquisite, the refined, and forgot the puissant, the mighty and the majestic, forgot the field of rhythm and melody which was overwhelmed and swallowed by the prodigiously grown realm of spicy and exquisite harmony.

Skryabin's innovations, which had given him a place in musical history as one of the boldest musical pioneers, consisted mainly in creating new chords. This enthusiasm of his was a sort of sport with him. Skryabin wished to outdistance all this contemporaries in creating chords "with the greatest number of notes." In this queer sport there was a little of the same naïveté which had been the earmark both of Skryabin's philosophy and his mystic "apocalyptics." As often happens, "musical nature" conquered and smoothed out much of what theoretically appeared absolutely inacceptable. During this last period to which belong

the Symphonic Poem *Prometheus* and Skryabin's last
sonatas, his style reached an extraordinary exquisiteness and
refinement, his harmony a rare complexity along with a
saturation of psychologic content. Side by side with this,
we observe a dissolution of rhythm and a reduction of
melody to the minimum, a severance of the musical web and
line which turns into a series of spasmodic exclamations and
destroys the impression of unity and wholeness.

It is peculiar that being an innovator on principle, and
consciously desiring to discover new paths in music, Skryabin
simultaneously appears here as some sort of rationalist. A
great deal in his creative work seems to be not the result
of intuition, of inspiration that had suddenly illumined
him, but the result of stubborn "research" work, that possessed, if you will, a mathematical character to some extent.
The traits of the ecstatic visionary in Skryabin lived side
by side with traits of the rational research scholar, and the
schematism which is so clear in his philosophic concepts of
the universe manifests itself no less strikingly also in his
music, in the structure of his compositions which are so
harmonious, so "rationalised" in their harmony that occasionally their form appears to be some logical conclusion
rather than the creative work of their author.

And the composer himself did not deny it, nay more, he
thought it necessary. In his opinion, the paths of intuition
and reason were different ways towards one and the same
thing and hence it is immaterial whichever one makes use
of. One can but wonder at the ease of genius with which
Skryabin would overcome his natural schematism, how, in
spite of this rationalism of his creative art, he reached striking results and produced compositions in which only the
very experienced eye of the musician may discern those
"seams" which his "rational construction" followed in erect-
ing them.

Skryabin died without having succeeded in writing either

the Mystery that was to lead to the end of the world, or even the essay at the *Preliminary Action,* a sort of huge cantata on the same theme, but still in "artistic plans." His fate was truly tragic, for having devoted his whole life to dreaming only a single dream, and having sacrificed everything for its sake, he never succeeded in carrying out that one thing. Bitter fate mocked the composer. He, the messiah in his own imagination, who had dreamed of leading mankind towards "the last festival," who had imagined himself God, and everything including himself, his own creation, who had dreamed by the force of his tones to overthrow the universe, died of a trifling pimple. He, who would speak with scorn of "musicians pure and simple" and imagined himself "the prophet musician," nay, even the synthetic artist who had mastered the mysteries of all arts, died leaving behind him a memory chiefly not of a philosopher and still more not of a prophet, but of a "piano composer," for his symphonic compositions seem, after all, to have been born from the piano and sound as if "instrumentated from the piano." His nature was alien to pure symphonism just as it was alien also to the element of might and dynamics in his creative work. The best that he has created is of course his exquisite and refined piano world in which he really builds something new, but even this new finds no continuation in the later destinies of Russian music. This new appears to be something torn apart and sterile. Either the sociological conditions had changed after the War, or the politics of people became different, but at the present time one must note a definite turn away from Skryabin, who very soon after his death had been "placed in the ranks of musical saints," and canonised in Russia, while in the West he has not gained the proper recognition even yet. With all that exquisite, perfumed and hothouse world of sonorities of his, Skryabin is foreign to the present-day consciousness, perhaps somewhat more crude, but still feeling more keenly Skryabin's lack of that for which there is a striving in Russia—grandeur and might.

Skryabin's philosophy died before it had had time to be properly born. But this is no reason why he may be considered as a pure musician only. Perhaps his music is alien to modernity for the very reason that when severed from his philosophy, it is incomprehensible and incomplete, while his philosophy suffers from too manifest faults. Skryabin very rashly bound his huge ship of musical creativeness organically by ties that were too firm, to the frail and ephemeral skiff of his philosophical views of the world. And perhaps here lies the cause of his decline and the probability of his future extinction as a composer. A genius incomplete in music, owing to these bonds, a genius incomplete in the field of thought, Skryabin threw out of his own hands the instrument with which he might have been able to communicate his gifts of genius to the world. This is becoming clear already, in spite of the fact that too brief is the time which still separates us from him, and while the tradition of his compositions and ideas is still alive. The West, which is not conversant with Skryabin's philosophy, appreciates him differently from Russia and more cautiously and timidly.

Considered from the point of view of musical-historical perspective, Skryabin at first appears "by himself" among Russian composers. His roots are not in Russian music, not in the Russian folk melody as are nearly all other Russians. He is a Westerner, whose peculiar talent could hardly have flourished anywhere else save on Russian soil. In addition to Chopin, Liszt, Wagner and Debussy which we have named among his musical ancestors, there may be mentioned also, perhaps, Ryebikoff, and Grieg, and even Chaykovski, whom Skryabin himself hated. Time was when Skryabin was the standard-bearer of new Russian music, when around him was grouped everything young and fresh. He was a convinced innovator, and with his innovations he illumined the path

of Russian art. Times have changed now. Rakhmaninoff
and Skryabin who had been antipodes are now representatives of one school, if they are compared with the music
of the present day which rests upon foundations completely
different. And Skryabin himself would no doubt admit that
he is nearer to old music than the new. After the shatter-
ing essays of the new art, the innovations of Skryabin from
the formal point of view appear more than modest, so much
so, that many no longer even claim Skryabin's right to this
title of honor.

In him have been fused in a bizarre way the features of
academism with those of the most unbridled and turbulent
romanticism; the urge towards the mysterious, the mysticism
of his thoughts, all his eroticism. Academism gave rise
to his "rationalism," his formal finish, his clinging to tradition, which oddly enough managed to live side by side with
the spirit of innovation. Certain laws Skryabin did not
want to break, while he was exceedingly desirous of breaking others. And now, when all laws have been broken long
ago, and called into question, his position has become conservative at one bound and even more academic than romantic. Among the composers of the whole world, Skryabin,
perhaps with Debussy alone as a companion, appears the
most exquisite and refined, the most transparent in the musical fabric he weaves. But he is not always such. Even
in his earliest compositions we find lapses into coarseness,
into unexpected banality, into some sort of cliché of thought
and even of feeling, and occasionally there is apparent an
inartistic desire to impress by mere external means; an increase in the number of instruments played, or in the number
of notes in a chord, or even by an athletic pursuit of loudness. Here comes to mind his make-up as a thinker and as
a man: this man had all the time desired "the superlative
degree" of everything. He wanted to be first everywhere:
in the complexity of harmony, in the number of notes in

a chord, in the exquisiteness of music, in the loudness of sonority. His megalomania in this way invaded the world of art, making him forget the old axiom of artistic practice, that in art, quantity plays no part whatever. And precisely that quantitative content in Skryabin has been growing obsolete faster than his other qualities.

In spite of its "megalomaniacal number of movements"— six instead of the usual four—his First Symphony appears childish, naïve, and sonatina-like. In spite of the forty-two lines in its score, his orchestration of *Prometheus* never constituted an era in music in general and it is even difficult to say how good an effect is produced by the grandiose, deliberately "deafening" fortissimo in the finales of his larger symphonic works, particularly in the *Extase* and the *Prometheus*.

Skryabin who had become the idol of the "left musical front" in his lifetime, and was canonised soon after his death, later began to undergo the queer and unexpected, yet rapid process of growing obsolete. Of course it is hard to dispute the universal and historical significance of much that is contained in his works, even the early ones, let alone the last, but the flash of novelty, the unusualness of expression no longer seize the imagination. Many of his thoughts have become banal, much has lost lustre and withered. What was salon-like has become more noticeable and oddly enough has crept to the foreground just as have his numerous "commonplaces," in the abundance of which he occasionally vies with his disliked Chaykovski.

The most difficult and most terrible thing for a composer is to pass the dreaded "test of time." There have been so many who in their time had shone as stars of the first magnitude only to dim prematurely.

But Skryabin had, in addition, to cope with extraordinarily unfavourable circumstances in connection with his romantic world feeling and the collapse of this school in the

West and in Russia under the influence of the latest historical events. At present the musical world does not accept romanticism and Skryabin is already a stranger in the "left" circles, nor is he regarded as their own in the ranks of the "rights" whom he had neither managed nor wished to join in his own time. Contemporary music, wise, business-like and calculating, is most wildly antagonistic to Skryabin and his old-fashioned romantic dreams. "Music for music's sake" has become the generally accepted motto, while with Skryabin the most important point was that his music was meant for something else, but not for music. Unrecognised in the West where they have not as yet digested his fine qualities, he is beginning to grow dim in Russia, crowded out as he is by the victorious esthete psychology which was as alien to him as the faddist love for antiquity. And Prokofyeff, so antipodal to Skryabin, at present promises to crowd the creator of the *Poème d'Extase* from the heart of the forgetful musical world.

But of course, "tests of time" are not passed so quickly. Perhaps just now circumstances are unfavourable for his popularity, for his way of feeling. At present we see the resurrection of former gods who seemingly had been buried forever under historical rubbish. Bach slumbered beneath piles of dust for a hundred and fifty years. Skryabin must rise from the dead, like a true "Messiah," and this resurrection will occur when the surroundings and social conditions will repeat to a certain degree the surroundings and the social life that had created him. At present such circumstances do not exist. But this does not mean that they will not in the future. It is exceedingly difficult to make historic prognoses of such nature. But to us musicians, who had once come close to Skryabin's creative art, who had once felt with him to the end, despite his being chained to the rock of his philosophy and its frailness,—it is clear that in his creative work there are elements of genuine immortality, of genuine genius; that these elements shall remain and will rise as had once risen Bach, disinterred by the far-sighted wisdom of Mendelssohn. And *vice versa,* it is very possible that many who are too alive now, and dispute Skryabin's rights to world recognition, will prove less lasting figures in history. This is the more probable because idea has always been more eternal than form, and that music with an idea, insane and fantastic though it be, always has better chances for renascence than music without ideas which at present is celebrating a premature victory.

Personally I have profound faith in a Skryabin renaissance, inasmuch as I believe in the inevitability of a renaissance of romanticism, the natural element of music. Either music in general will perish in the light of new achievements of civilisation, buried by the too "mechanical" age, or there will blossom forth on the same soil a mighty unparalleled romanticism. And romanticism will inevitably present the problems which Skryabin stated and which he naïvely endeavoured to solve. Skryabin proposed problems characterised by genius, occasionally in his judgments and constructive arguments there occurred notes of the ingenious intuition of a born religious philosopher. But he lacked the powers of systematically executing the enormous tasks which he met at every step. Skryabin's insanity did not lie in his ideas, but in the central rôle which he wished to play himself, in his self-opinionation and self-love. His insanity consisted in not knowing his own powers. Here was the root of the evil. Taken apart from this "evil," Skryabin is neither insane nor monstrous, but a man who was painfully absorbed in thinking and wished to arrive at a joyous solution of the problem of the world. And in his music was reflected this joyous and impotent urge towards something "absolute."

We cannot say that the "salon" elements, of which there are so many in his piano compositions, will forever appear in the same light. Such they seem to us at present, for they have been too numerous, and we have been too absorbed in this intoxicating hothouse crowded with poisonous flowers. But Skryabin's musical achievements possess elements of eternal beauty, elements equal in genius to the best pages of Chopin, Wagner, Liszt. The last named authors were more intact, more consistent, were simpler and healthier than Skryabin, whose spirit was afflicted with the disease of megalomania. This mania both gave birth to Skryabin's creative art and partly destroyed him. I am convinced that without this "mania of the grandiose" Skryabin would not have written anything, or else composed badly and little. For his creative work he was in need of the constant narcosis of self-deification. Like the drunkard, the alcoholic Musorgski, he needed to go off upon insane planes for his creative work. Musorgski would reach this insanity with a good dose of cognac, like his genius-gifted colleague in moods, Edgar Allen Poe. Skryabin needed intoxication by means of occult fantasies, by faith in the beyond, in self-deification. It was a narcoticising that roused him to creative work. Without it, he would have fallen into gloomy despair and would have grown silent in the drab everydayness.

There is a hidden tragedy in Skryabin, a tragedy which he carefully concealed in the folds of his theory of "joy" and "intoxication by ecstasy." Skryabin used to say that one single grain of the joy that filled him was so vast that "myriads of universes could sink in it without ruffling even its surface." This terrible hyperbole recurs several times in his *Diary*. But behind this hyperbole is felt the tragedy of contrast. If this joy does not exist, if it proves a dream and a fantasy, what then? Then darkness without a break, and despair. . . . Skryabin's extreme joy is forever balancing on the edge of an abyss into which it is constantly in danger of falling. And fully aware of this it is full of forced cheer, intoxicating itself with hyperbolic utterances.

This joy does not possess the characteristics of endurance. Perhaps it is a "sincere make-believe" of which the author himself was ignorant. But in Skryabin the will towards his own genius was extraordinarily strong. And had he, like Wagner, been able to limit himself and applied in the sphere of music all the energies of his spirit, he would perhaps have been among the very greatest. But this very spirit of self-limitation was lacking in his typically Russian nature. He would diffuse illimitably and he unavoidably came to self-deification. This destroyed his creativeness.

The insane maniacal element does not exclude genius. We remember maniacs of genius,—Hoffmann, Novalis, Nietzsche; we remember the greatest romantic of all, Edgar Allen Poe. Perhaps excessive delving into questions of the roots of art leads to partial insanity. At all events Skryabin is one of those persons about whose creative art and personality one can and must say a great deal. One may even say that the creative work of such persons is not so interesting as the personality reflected in this creative work. A personality of genius does not always find within it an outlet for adequate expression of genius in art or science. There are geniuses who never at all find "points of application" for their genius. Skryabin had a musical point of application, but somehow or other made no use of it, having succumbed to the lures of the dream of many or of all points of application. We may dispute the attributes of greatness of this personality, we may say that Skryabin possessed little of the greatness of spirit, little of genuine profundity, a mass of narcotic self-intoxication, but it is impossible to deny that it is a profoundly interesting personality.

In his diaries occur thoughts of which philosophers might be proud, but unfortunately these ideas have not been deeply plumbed and fully expressed. In his poetic creations and in his unfinished text of the *Preliminary Action*, there are moments which prove that the inward experiences often carry

one past the limits set by insufficient external gifts. Skryabin, essentially a poor and "talentless" poet, nevertheless
somehow conquered this lack of talent and produced poetic
achievements that oddly agitate and powerfully affect. . . .
One may laugh at the fantastic idea that overwhelmed him
in his *Prometheus,* to accompany the symphony of sounds
with a symphony of coloured lights, but it cannot be denied
that in this naïve idea there was also some queer attraction,
some inner justification of it. But all this was suspended in
mid-air, all of it was left unfinished, Skryabin went helter-
skelter in his fantasies and his plans, having neither time
nor patience to work out one part of his plan. And his
symphony of light hung in the air unfinished, enigmatic,
undeveloped. And his Mystery remained a weird sphynx
of pathological talent,—simultaneously the joyous and gloomy
fantasy of a man who, like a mediæval believer, awaited the
immediate end of the world; with this difference, that the
latter had awaited it from without, awaited it with meekness
and fear, while the former expected it as one in power, from
himself, haughtily deeming himself the very one that was
"to come in glory to judge the living and the dead." Russian religious reality is manifold and conceals terrible secrets
within itself. In his queer spiritual make-up, Skryabin possesses something in common with the Russian fanatics of
the old faith, sectarians of the ecstatic creeds. In his theory,
too, an important rôle was played both by the ecstasy of love
and extreme eroticism, in which the spiritual and the most
carnal fused into a gripping chord; it, too, possessed its
messianism, its haughty self-garbing in divine vestments, its
consciousness of its own sanctity and bountifulness. There
is in him both the dark and the radiant which is so characteristic of Russian rambling religious thought, the demonism
and the being possessed, in connection with the urge towards
the highest enlightenment. He is the first Russian sectarian
who became a musician to his own sorrow and who wished

to make music the handmaiden of his religiousness. But even if Skryabin's personality, which unquestionably deserves studying, can be separated from his music and be considered by itself, there looms before us a great musician with the characteristics well-nigh of genius. As is frequently the case with composers who think too much about their creative art, so also with Skryabin the intuitivism grows weaker in the course of time and a rational schematism takes its place. Simultaneously mastery grows stronger, a firm manner develops and intuition disappears. Skryabin's first compositions are more intuitive than the last, but the last are nearer perfect, more refined and rational. He was a lyricist of the tragic type during the earlier half of his life and became an ecstatic during the latter part. During both of these periods he was a nuerotic, and in this field one must say Skryabin really was a genius and has hardly been surpassed. His eroticism is not the elemental eroticism of Wagner, it is a tender, refined, tonal caress that possesses an almost physiological meaning. Skryabin was a true poet of tonal erotic caresses and he can torture and sting and torment and fondle and tenderly lull with pungent sonorities, there is a whole "science of tonal love" in his compositions. This eroticism is his most delicate and most unseizeable trait, and the most difficult to communicate in performances. Hardly any pianist can communicate this world of Skryabin's which he alone could communicate so ideally. Both pianists and conductors (with exception of Kusevitski alone, the inheritor of Skryabin's tonal secrets) coarsen Skryabin and deliver him to the public in unrecognisable form, whence comes the odd comparing of Skryabin with Strauss and similar misunderstandings, and hence the best in Skryabin has in reality remained unknown to the world so far. This perhaps explains also the indifference towards him, for Skryabin coarsened, his flaws emphasised, his rapidly evaporating and tender qualities having been lost, can be absolutely unbearable. This exquisite flower of the musical hot-house loses its aromas on being touched and carried out of its atmosphere. Unfortunately so far, pianists have not grown genuinely enthusiastic about Skryabin and there are few who would be capable of this. It may be said that Skryabin is almost unknown to the world. And we are the more justified in our hope that in time he will become known.

His First Symphony may properly be regarded a milestone in his art, the border of his enthusiasm for Chopin and the border of his epigonic period. In this Symphony he sets himself an "extra-musical" problem for the first time. Then comes his Third Symphony, the most central of his compositions in which both his personal qualities and its heredity from Wagner and Liszt have been combined in a form most advantageous to him. Finally the *Poème d'Extase* and *Prometheus* represent the last stages of his development, after which was "destined" the Mystery, which was shattered against the two enduring laws of the physical world. Of these last two compositions, *Prometheus* is more severe and somewhat drier, the *Poème d'Extase*, warmer and more harmonious. In his last compositions the schematism of thought, the rationality of constructions may be discerned more and more clearly. Musical intuition yields its place to reasoning combined with considerations of non-musical nature. Nevertheless, even during this period he created works of genius, among which the Sixth, the Seventh and the Ninth Sonatas are the most striking. But as time went on it became clearer that Skryabin's musical genius was somewhat "possessed"; his rhythms acquired a spasmodic character, the musical web a jerky structure. Whether these were "real consequences" of his incomplete psychic normality or the true direction in which such queer talent develops is hard to say.

Skryabin did not found a school and he could not create one. Too intoxicating was the atmosphere of his creative art; it was too hard to bear lingeringly, and school means lingering residence. There were many "Skryabinists" and nearly all of them were in Russia, for Skryabin has not succeeded in gaining even a tolerably firm footing abroad for his art. But all these Skryabinists were Skryabinists by half, for the most essential thing in Skryabinism, his "general psychological tone," is too bound up with the "non-musical make-up" of Skryabin. One had to be a follower of Skryabin in his queer religion in order to become a genuine Skryabinist. There proved to be none such even among his musical friends and admirers. On the contrary, rather among the non-musicians Skryabin found partial adepts of the mystical doctrine of his messianism. It is difficult to pronounce judgment on the sincerity of these adepts, but it is true that they existed. But however the case may be, the Skryabinists confined themselves only to this: they acquired certain methods of Skryabin's harmonic and melodic writing which but embarrassed them, because these methods were so characteristic that they immediately "convicted" the one who made use of them. And the musical Skryabinism evaporated as quickly as it was born. The atmosphere of the musical world has changed and it is difficult to expect the return of a love for "intoxications" and "ecstasies." Only a few epigonic composers and a certain group of composers of "Yavorski's School," of whom we shall speak later, have been impelled in a purely theoretical way, to circulate amidst the musical formulas created by Skryabin, and even so not always to the advantage of their creative work.

IGOR STRAVINSKI

(Born 1881)

THE name of Igor Stravinski is to-day perhaps the most brilliant on the world's musical horizon. He is the recognised master of minds and the supreme leader in the field of musical creative art, only Richard Strauss and Schoenberg, perhaps, sharing this hegemony with him. Stravinski has been fortunate; in his creative art he has found the synthesis of novelty and popularity which has been the most cherished dream of so many artists and which is the attraction that the career of a composer exerts "fame in one's lifetime." Creative musical art works in a field of darkness; the musician-composer labours for a circle of persons unknown to him, while he is guided only by the obscure directions of his genius. We know cases where this gift of genius dictated to composers creations that had no chance whatever for recognition among their contemporaries and the creators died unrecognised. Their descendants admired in these compositions, not only the beauties of art, but the courage of the spirit that could so heroically withstand the calls of fame and labour for the future. Perhaps our times in general are not conducive towards the appearance of heroism of this kind, and heroes of this type become anachronisms as bad, if not worse, than some Hercules who deals with lions and highwaymen in the most primitive homespun fashion. The idea of eternal fame fades not only in the mind of the denizen who has been disillusioned in his romantic dream of a "future life," but even in the mind of the artist himself. The artist who formerly still bashfully cloaked himself in the phraseology of idealism, now dreams very frankly about recognition "coming in his lifetime." And this is not some ordinary artist-tradesman who supplies wares to the market of demand, but a genuine artist. We see the strongholds of idealism tumble, one after another, and life's prose peeps out from behind the artistic draperies. And those who are now marked with the stamp of genius in their narrow musical sphere, are now, alas, no longer prophets nor "priests of the sacred art," but plain manufacturers of values, and their genius does not reach the sphere of genius of the spirit.

This is the sign and stamp of the age, and if our discussion of Stravinski touches upon this sphere, one must admit that Stravinski is in the highest degree a contemporary phenomenon. He is the liveliest reaction to the keen, refined, sated taste of our time. This master of contemporary musical thought, successor to the throne of Debussy and Strauss, who has succeeded in combining the highest tension of technical boldness with the highest and broadest democratism and power greater than Debussy's, has reflected in his creative art all that is lofty and base, banal and proud, which is characteristic of our age, and it is inconceivable to apply to him the same standards of appreciation that would be proper for any former phenomenon in music.

Stravinski's fame is based not only on his musical gifts (who measured it? and hard it is to measure it; perhaps it is not so great after all), but chiefly on his virtuosity in making full use of musical conditions and taking full account of fashions and fads, these two wavering and changing elements on which nevertheless, fame in one's lifetime almost exclusively depends. It depends least of all on the magnitude of endowments, but more on the composer's technical and even "commercial experience." Stravinski is immeasurably more a genius of musical business, rather than purely of music. He is truly sprung from the depths of the Russian National School. He was the natural in-

heritor of the interest which Russian music had aroused in
Paris, the centre of the world. One fine day, on the border
of the last century, France, beautiful and full of the joy
of life, to her own amazement, suddenly "understood" the
sombre and tragic language of Musorgski, that wanderer-
genius, who had started with positivism in music, only to
end with psychologism and mysticism. But if Musorgski,
in the age-long conformity with the strivings of the Russian' spirit to "antinomies," strove to combine Darwin with
Dostoyevski, I do not think that "beautiful France's" fondness for him was due to this. Our Russian National School,
also called the "mighty coterie," had struck the fancy of
France and her thousand year-old culture, not with epilepsy
served up in artistic form and in a positivist psychological
shape, but with those terrible abysses towards which Musorgski's Russian spirit, like all Russian spirits, had a particular
tendency to approach. We do not think that this sphere
became comprehensible in feminine France, in a land where
the commanding heights of art belong to taste. The unusualness, the immediateness of inspiration, the novelty and
sharpness of the external means, the barbaric primitiveness
of the Russian and Oriental melodies,—this is what lured
the descendants of Rameau and Couperin, and lured so
forcibly that Musorgski's influence is extraordinarily strong,
even upon the greatest genius among the French, Debussy.
We may add that here there was a hidden kinship of cultures. For it is no secret that the Russian nobility, to which
class all our composers of that time belonged, were half
French, if not in origin, at least in culture and even in
language. Glinka and Musorgski both usually conversed
in French and in the seignorial estheticism of their music,
and in their collection of colourful types, French estheticism,
discovered "kindred traits." Unquestionably, all the ethno-
graphism of the "mighty coterie," the somewhat dry and
cerebral elegance of Rimski-Korsakoff, does not come from

typical romanticism but from the enlightened estheticism
of the nobility.

We know also that the faith of the Russian *Koochka*
(coterie), was such that gradually estheticism overcame romanticism and unrestraint, the former barbarians and an-
archists became decent people, and like Lyadoff and Rimski-
Korsakoff, frequenters of salons, retaining as much of their
barbarism as was necessary in order not to appear commonplace and uninteresting to these salons. In the list of the
Russian esthetic menu this same "pleasing barbarism" was a
spice about which one could grow enthusiastic, a sharp con-
diment after the flapid European cuisine.

I should not wonder if our "Koochkists" were esteemed
in France from this very point of taste. The sharp traits of
"oriental barbarism" were acquired by and became the
musical property of the most cultured of nations, and here
they were recreated almost to the point of becoming unrecognisable. But after all, this unrecognisability is explained
by the fact that the Frenchmen "comprehended" the Russians erroneously if strikingly and forcibly after their own
fashion. The story of Richard Wagner repeated itself;
he, too, originally was the object of excessive and unexpected
enthusiasm on the part of the French, until it became clear
that they saw only "Wagner's pedestal" and not his whole
hugeness, and it made them comfortable. As soon as they
began to discern the proper size of his genius, their enthusiasm gave way to horror. Just so Russian culture passed
through France, laying hold of it somehow and even fructifying it with something, but misunderstood to the very end.

As I have said, Stravinski was the natural and "ready to
hand" successor of the influence of the Russian National
School. But in him the estheticism observeable in the
"coterie" is decisively predominant. Stravinski is a typically
esthetist phenomenon. He is not Wagner or Skryabin who
had expected from music and from art a transformation of

the world. Stravinski could write an impressive chorus to the mystical text of the "star-visaged Balmont," he could be externally imbued with the apocalyptic moods of the poet, but his conviction in the apocalyptic visions will hardly be greater than, say, Lyadoff's, who in his time also toyed with the Apocalypse. Stravinski can compose a mystery, *Sacre de Printemps*, but he has just as little faith in his "ancestors" and the rites of "kissing the earth" which appear there, as the skeptical and wise old man Rimski-Korsakoff had in his musical fairy-tales. But I would say that Rimski-Korsakoff was more naïve and therein, more "mystical" than Stravinski. He could be a convinced "pantheist" and feel the proximity of *nature* as an animated being. Stravinski, on the other hand, does not believe in anything at all, he only pretends that he believes. And he does not possess the evanescent naïveté which is altogether typical of the narrator. Stravinski makes believe in earnest: occasionally he definitely sets himself the task of "scaring his hearers." Rimski-Korsakoff was a naïve, kindly grandfather with fairy-tales, Stravinski is a wicked magician, but both use "children" to work on and they fool them without believing themselves.

Herein lies their essential difference from Wagner, Skryabin and others who themselves believed and were exasperated when others did not, regarding these others not as "children," but "fellow-beings" who were to be shepherded and guided by them and generally predestined to follow them.

The rationalism which we observe in Rimski-Korsakoff manifests itself in a still more categorical form in Stravinski. He is a genuinely great master. We shall never find dilettantism in him, even in the slight degree in which it occasionally crops up both in Skryabin and Prokofyeff. He is in the panoply of his trade and his technique. There is nothing incidental with him. Everything has been thought out and the most modernistic elements are more conditioned by the "play of mind" and ingenious calculations than by so-called "immediate inspiration." Most probably also Stravinski became an innovator for reasons of a "rational" nature. It was not at all some insane attraction or a lamentable seeking of new sounds. For such things he is too modern. Like any experienced magician in the manner of Cagliostro, he himself will, perhaps, spread legends about his being possessed, about supernaturalism if need be, but the process itself of his creative work lacks the irrational element and to a greater degree than any one of the great composers. He does not, like Beethoven, listen to the "voice of the soul whispering melodies." He does not burn up in the intense fire of his musical visions, like Wagner. He is not tortured, like Chopin, with an insane thirst to seize and grasp the flitting fragments of inspirations as though heard in other worlds.

He firmly knows that one must be an innovator, or one would not make one's way, or one would miss the precipitous train of modernism, would not attain the reward which one's gifts promise. Gone are those times when a creative artist created "quietly," obeying but the inner urge and believing that some day his tones would find their way to understanding. "Quietude" exists no longer. Now, one must first of all attract attention to oneself. And this is impossible without distinguishing oneself with something extraordinary. In our period, an innovation becomes a sort of inevitable advertisement. By means of the extraordinary the composer attracts attention to himself as though by a shrill shout or the penetrating toot of an automobile. And it matters not whether people discern the "quality" of this innovating modernism. All that is needed is that the composer should be noticed. And accordingly, entirely different demands are made upon this contemporary innovationism; it need not at all be fine to the experienced ear of the specialist, it need not be profound, complex, flowing in spheres which the ear of the throng fails to reach. It must be glittering, sharp, shrill-voiced, like the electric signs, flickering and blinding. It must have "rapid action"; otherwise in the insane rush of modern life the composer would "come too late."

Modernism of this kind is of course dictated to a considerable degree by considerations of a mental sort. The composer's very path begins to resemble not the path of a creator, but rather of an inventor. The first requisite of novelty is lack of similarity to what has preceded. Every trait of epigonism must be wiped out, if possible, and everything is wiped out which is felt in a familiar manner. The most destructive and accursed thing for the new composer is to be convicted of "similarity" to some one else. The physiognomy may be utterly monstrous, deformed, but it must be "his" unlike others'.

When we examine the path taken by Stravinski, we immediately find all the traits which we have just sketched. First of all we shall recall how Stravinski made his début in the composers' world immediately on leaving Rimski-Korsakoff's acedemic tutelage. His First Symphony possesses nothing characteristic. Not one of those striking features which distinguish the present creative art of Stravinski. This Symphony shows the typical average epigonism. It is even impossible to say much about the author's "musicianship." Average, even music, decently orchestrated, resembling both Glazunoff and Rimski-Korsakoff. Thus had written and still write the numberless composers who in their time gathered in Byelyayeff's academic circle and created the very conception of the "St. Petersburg mechanical production of music" (see Appendix).

Stravinski did not find his path and talent at once. Music is a dark field, and being talented in music does not at all mean being gifted in all its manifestations. We know that there have been specialists in "melody" like Schubert, specialists in harmony like Skryabin, that there have been some like Berlioz, who concentrated their innovatorship exclusively on sound itself, on colour. Berlioz, that strange musician who combined the traits of a genius gifted in the field of colour with the traits of definite lack of talent in a number of other musical elements, resembles Stravinski to a certain degree, though his opposite in the romantic pathos that swayed him and his complete helplessness in ordinary life. In contrast to this last, Stravinski appears a commercial genius, a kind of musical bank director. Stravinski, is poorly gifted in the most musical field of all, the field of melody and here his similarity to his teacher Rimski-Korsakoff becomes apparent. But he is infinitely gifted in invention which has enabled him to discover new worlds in the field of rhythm and orchestral colouring.

Stravinski came in the epoch of the dissolution of the Russian National School and at a period when the very product of this dissolution, academism, also began to decay. As a net result, he effected, as it were, a return to the traditions of the Russian National School, to her estheticism and her connection with folk melody. Naturally he could not long remain in the academic atmosphere of "Byelyayeff's circle" and of course he followed those that were nearest to the "coterie," the French impressionists Ravel and Debussy, who had themselves sprung up from the soil of the recreation of Musorgski's creative art.

Stravinski marches with firm step in the sphere of orchestral colouring, combining as he does the achievements of the composers of the National School and the achievements of the French neo-impressionists with his own. Extraordinary gorgeousness of orchestral hues, was the first thing with which he began to astonish his contemporaries. His *Fireworks* already breathed inventiveness in spite of the scantiness of the purely musical lines. The author's estheticism already manifested itself in this composition and the Fantastic Scherzo which appeared simultaneously. He is not at all interested in giving expression to himself, his spirit; he conceals himself in his music, remaining extremely objective and openly picturesque in the extreme. The composer will have nothing to do with the tragic, nothing with lyricism, he is brimful of plans and projects of entirely new revolutions in the world of colouring. This estheticism draws the author to his spiritual fatherland, France, and here, too, he correctly divines his style; he begins to cultivate the ballet, choreographic music. Stravinski correctly realised, and realised before others did, that Russian opera had been exhausted, that it had become old, that its national lyricism was now out of place. He realised this at the time Dyagileff's Ballet was making its triumphant march through Europe. Indeed, the Russian conquering choreography, one may say, towed behind it all Russian music to the public at large. And Stravinski, too, joined in the procession. He became an active collaborator in the ballet business. He specialized in the music for the complicated and modernized choreography.

Zhar-Ptitsa (_Fire-Bird_), his newly conceived ballet, was musically written by him in decently ordinary Russian national tones, after all. And it strongly recalled Rimski-Korsakoff. The only new thing here was greater splendour and greater boldness in colour. Simultaneously, a fact of extraordinary importance took place; definitely and once and for all, Stravinski bound himself to fashion in the sphere of art, he became a "new" composer, not only in the methods of embodying the artistic, but also in the stimuli of creative art. He definitely desired fame and achieved it and thereby he drew a sharp border-line between himself and the former Russian composers who in general had never composed "for the sake of fame." The spirit of Paris manifested itself here too, in the figure of Meyerbeer, who now became extraordinarily near to Stravinski. Also a composer of genius, Meyerbeer nevertheless had sold his music, for the potage of fame and recognition in his lifetime.

Stravinski felt correctly and subtly the pulse of contemporary life, he noticed the death of opera, the current fad of the ballet which was now blossoming forth in the capital of the world as a gorgeous flower of contemporary artistic culture. The Parisian fashion market demanded new ballets and demanded them exactly in the style which had just conquered the hearts of the Parisians, the style of extreme exquisiteness combined with acute "barbarism." The attributes which the French spirit had rightly or wrongly read in Musorgski's and Rimski-Korsakoff's scores, were now demanded also of new music in a still more acute and striking form, in a "double-strength dose."

Stravinski became the purveyor of the wares demanded by that musical barbarism, by this Russian style understood as a style oriental and highly spiced, wild and anti-European, but fully armed with European methods. Did this mean catering to the tastes of the throng? Not quite, for it must be remarked that the tastes of the mob and the law-making of fashions are not one and the same concept. Stravinski did not become caterer to the throng, he was too clever, but he became the law-giver of musical fashion first in the world's centre, Paris, and later well-nigh to the whole world.

The structure of fashion is a very complex affair and will surely find its investigator some day. The truth of the matter is that some secret and elusive group, something like a "masonic organisation," always small and never belonging to the "crowd," but rather always to the cream of society, dictates and invents these unwritten but inexorable laws of private and public life, and determines these waves of demand and call for things. In the field of art this hierarchism of the fashionable law-givers is still clearer. Stravinski succeeded in a remarkable way in mastering the secret of this odd and powerful mechanism which to his predecessors was a sort of mysterious lottery. Gradually he became the head of this organisation. If the *Fire-Bird* was still written on epigonic lines and was, as it were, interest on the capital once upon a time invested by Russian composers in the treasury of French music, one can nevertheless trace in it the beginnings of the curious departure of Stravinski from Russia and from Russian perception of Russian events. It is a very odd story. Undoubtedly, our "Koochkists," too, had had moments of "looking askance" on Russian life, and it is possible in general, that without such an approach even Russian romanticism embodied in the National School would have been inconceivable. But in Stravinski we begin to observe not only the glances askance, but even an ironical, half-satirical attitude toward this Russian life. With him, the Russian and Slavic elements are but a commodity to export abroad, to satisfy the demand for Russian barbarism and orientalism. And the composer strove with all his might to present his nation in the most barbaric, in the most oriental and savage form possible. Here there was no longer a question of naïve love for the fatherland which, after all, had been undoubtedly present even in an "askance-looking" *barin* (nobleman, estateholder) like Glinka or Rimski-Korsakoff. Here was, instead, the attitude of making despicable sport on a commercial basis. These features gradually growing stronger, reached their point of culmination in Stravinski's last compositions, in his *Little Wedding,* his *Mavra,* in his *Adages,* which constitute definitely the quintessence of an ironic attitude towards his own people and life.

In this sense the line of Stravinski's nationalism proves to border on anti-nationalism, in a caricature-like exaggeration. The old composers' fondness for collection-making gives place to a caricature drawn to please the "enlightened West" which loves things to be as funny as possible. In the eyes of Stravinski himself, who has become a genuine Parisian, Russia becomes a caricature of a land, where "Cossacks" ride, spear in hand and flog the people with *nagaykas*, where white bears promenade through the streets, while the Russian good folks in *papakhas* (tall fur caps) sit in the shade of a "heavy foliaged cranberry tree" and sup "in a *troyka* team and have *samovar* for dessert," gazing the while on the mottle-coloured cathedral of St. Basil the Blessed.

Stravinski's central creation, his *Petrushka*, a ballet on an original grotesque theme of Benois, reeks with caricature. At the time Stravinski had to hurry to catch the "train of fame." The slightest traits of epigonism had to be blotted out in his creative work. In the *Fire-Bird*, too many things recalled too many and too recent other things. Fashion demanded new sensations. In Russia, Skryabin was maturing and "innovating," in Germany Arnold Schoenberg had made his bold appearance; the old world of harmony and melody was manifestly tottering, a new abyss presented itself to the gaze and this abyss was to be overcome by him who wished to play the first fiddle in the orchestra of the world's music.

"Boldness conquers cities" and in this field, first and above all, one must not fear boldness. Perhaps in every creator endowed with genius, one-half is made up of boldness, which is beyond the ordinary human chained to tradition. The limits of this boldness are theoretically inaccessible, but frequently even the boldest break certain invisible but very firm bonds which fetter their art to the past.

It is from *Petrushka* that the period of boldness dates with Stravinski. There was boldness in the very theme, it was at all events an extraordinary theme for a ballet. Here we see a transplanting to Russia and St. Petersburg soil of the fantasy of Hoffman's doll-world come to life. The old ghostly, weird and terrible St. Petersburg, the gloomy city of The Bronze Horseman, was reincarnated in its private and social life, into which were woven in a masterly fashion, features of the *Comedia del Arte* in Russian exposition; Pierrot-Petrushka, Arlekin-Moor, Columbine-Ballerina, surrounded by "tinfoil" magics, and if the libretto was highly talented, its musical embodiment must be acknowledged to be truly that of genius unique in its kind. Stravinski for the first time looms before us the genuine Stravinski in full size.

Of course all this was "planned" for the market of demand in fashion. It presented precisely the Russian fairytale and barbaric fantastics which the enlightened snobs of the West had hungered for. Clamped in the vise of a doll's world, the tragedy of Petrushka and the dancer and the grotesque life of St. Petersburg in the early nineteenth century with its dances of the nurses, and its devil-may-care merchant, shifting as though in a kaleidoscope glittering and thoroughly barbaric against the background of a noisy fair, were bound to produce an overpowering impression by the novelty of approach and theme. Here we find in Stravinski for the first time a revelation of his fundamental quality, his genius for tonal wit, and his capacity for musical characterisation, while the music flows without constraint, without for a moment tiring the hearer, for all of it is but delighting him continually by contrasts and ever new inventions in colour.

The author's wit is shown in the masterly use he had made here of the elements of musical irony. Ominous instruments like trombones and tuba revealed here for the first time their humorous nature; these gloomy companions of tragedies and majestic events proved capable of eliciting laughter even from an untutored hearer. But that is not all. Stravinski makes use of popular and street tunes of the time, being perhaps the first to enlist their aid in "serious" music. He inserts hurdy-gurdy tunes, making use of them with purely musicianly irony which perhaps is lost on the "non-musician" owing to its finesse. Devoid of the gift of his own melody, this musical inventor fully compensates for his lack with the masterly use he makes of somebody else's tunes. The false notes of the hurdy-gurdy, the traditional "untutored" hand-organ harmonisation, these gems of irony and wit are scattered everywhere and while delighting the uninitiated with the sheer horse-shoe luck of "realistic embodiment," they nevertheless are to the musician a source of delight from the contemplation of this profound and almost bitter irony they contain.

Stravinski's objectivism reaches its limit here. Here we do not perceive at all either sympathy or non-sympathy on the author's part for any one of his *dramatis personae*. With a sort of rapturous frenzy he trots out the musical figures of his "misshapen beings" exhibiting before the hearer an unparalleled gallery of "monsters" and lovingly painting with the idealistic art of sounds certain extreme types out of the lower depths, as for instance in the *Coachman's Dance*, which stands absolutely alone, with an acute sense of contrast between the most ideal of arts and what it pictures.

The brightest place among Stravinski's compositions belongs to *Petrushka*. Both his opponents and those whom he subsequently alienated, were unanimous in admiration of this composition. Perhaps this very "woodenness" of the theme itself gave him an advantage, for one does not ever sense Stravinski's soul in his music; he hides it painstakingly; perhaps he is a sort of Petrushka himself, and instead of a life of the soul, he has only tricks and tin-foil magic. Perhaps, like Petrushka, instead of blood he has *klyukva* (variety of cranberry) juice, and instead of entrails, sawdust. All his creative art strongly recalls this doll's world pictured in *Petrushka*, which magically and trickily comes to life. This magician can occasionally make one believe that he is a great musician and make one overlook the inner chill of his creations, which have not been composed by thought and heart but by cold calculation and a hellish technique and the inventiveness of its "inventor."

From the purely musical point of view two elements are of interest in *Petrushka*. First, the cultivation of street tunes which until then had never been admitted into "decent musical company," next the decorative methods of orchestration, first introduced by him. Stravinski is an experienced tonal decorator, he knows full well that much which appears impossibly cacophonous, acquires a *raison d'être* in orchestral garb. There is music which must be heard from a distance just as one scans scenery, and the old norms of composition 'and "part writing" are no longer applicable to such music. On the contrary, when heard so "from a distance" the ordinary former manner of composing proves as much out of place as a detailed painting of scenery in the theatre would be out of place. In *Petrushka,* Stravinski makes the first use of these decorative methods of orchestral composition so opposed to the methods of Rimski-Korsakoff and the French. Here begins his departure from the past and his break with old music to which he still partly clings in *Petrushka,* for if we discount decorative elements, neither its harmony nor its melody shows any particular attempts at innovation.

The cult of harmonic audacity became a sort of epidemic at that time. Musicians of the most diverse tendencies strove to surpass each other in the "invention of new harmonies." Ravel and Debussy as well as Skryabin worked in one direction of finesse, Strauss worked in the other decorative direction, and Stravinski began to work, too. Harmonic tradition collapsed; everything became permissible and it was but necessary to find one's bearings in these riches obtained by this unexpected "license." As a harmonic innovator most likely he came into the field not unmindful of the fact that others might outstrip him, but being bolder he did not stop at half-measures.

While the neo-impressionists and Skryabin worked timidly and in accordance with tradition, rearing their "new" harmony as "superstructures" above the old; as an evolutionary unfolding of established principles, Stravinski broke down everything old at one blow. In this spirit of complete harmonic anarchy were written his *Japanese Lyrics*, which people did not know for a long time whether to treat as the wild antics of a futurist or as the serious attempt of a musician. But Stravinski's harmonic innovations stood out in still more striking form in his ballet, *Sacre de Printemps*.

In this theme barbarism was still more strongly emphasised than before. The antique or modern "Russian life" seemed no longer sufficient. Stravinski returned to archaic Scythian times, resurrecting figures of "ancestors." Pantheism which with Rimski-Korsakoff is painted in soft, almost salon-like tones, was served up in all its brutal and lapidary ferocity. Something ancient and out of the mound era, something out of the stone age, of cave-men and their psychology still linked to brute nature, breathes from this composition and its conception. It is music's counterpart to the Russian painter Roerich (no wonder, for Roerich indeed painted the scenery for this ballet), but this is Roerich raised to a higher degree in his stoniness, in his lack of finesse. In order to embody this savage and ferocious conception, the composer made use of an utterly unparalleled musical palette, made up of the same stony, ferocious, unconquerable and unbreakable colour harmonies and the same ferreous, almost soulless and spasmodically elemental musical rhythms, recalling the rhythms of earthquakes and cataclysms. The orchestral palette in this composition is just as lapidary, the music resolves itself into a series of explosions and for the first time 'in all its fullness Stravinski's aloofness stands out from previous musical compositions and tradition. Beginning with this *Sacre de Printemps* we may consider Stravinski, if you please, no longer a musician in the former sense of the word, his art no longer music but some new "tonal art" which has its own laws, its own new expanses, perhaps more kindred to the laws of painting than of former music, and into which former music enters only as some particular incident.

At the same time, this composition contains organically also some of his former achievements, elements that had become his style. Stravinski's melody, feeding on alien sap, and devoid of individual colouring, as of yore, stands out as a certain ethnographic datum. Russian, or more precisely Slavic melody and Slavic rhythmics, loom against extraordinary tonal ranges and masses of sounds which impart unusualness to the simplest designs. If in *Petrushka,* Stravinski wore the panoply of wit, we are face to face here with the composer's endeavour to be "serious" and, more than that, mystical and terrifying.

He desires to frighten, he wishes to achieve the impression of mystical and elemental horror. Does he succeed? For in reality the innermost essence of the composer remains calmly esthetic. His desire to harrow is rationalised, a "mental conclusion," not an emotion. Of course, with the colossal arsenal of means which he possesses and wields like a virtuoso, he may frighten in earnest. And yet, the *Sacre de Printemps* leaves the hearer cold. Behind the terror of its exterior, no terrible spirit is felt, behind the unbridled emotions one does not feel their contact with the author; it is a stage earthquake contrived in a masterly and virtuoso fashion, and if the author had the intention of here imitating a tonal Roerich he did not achieve it, for Roerich is infinitely more profound and more genuine. This stage earthquake really breathes the fullest harmlessness of the museum. Stravinski did not fully succeed in the grandiose gesture of this composition, and perhaps the author himself felt that he had strayed from his path, that this field of mechanically perceived grandiosities was not his sphere. He is an ironist, a satirist, a gorgeous decorator. The hearer remains cold towards Stravinski's mysticism and pantheism in which he doesn't believe himself, just as he is cold to the author's "eschatology," in his cantata *The Star-Visaged*, also a splendid composition but cold in its abstract splendours.

The opera *Rossignol* (*Nightingale*) which Stravinski wrote subsequently, shows the composer's departure from the ballet which, having made a great stir, apparently ceased to be such an indispensable part of fashion. Stravinski sensed this and tried his powers in opera, but this essay of his must probably be classed as a mere "trial," for in the style of this composition may be discerned too great variety, and the author's methods themselves are inconsistent. Stravinski is seeking, stubbornly and persistently, something wherein he may once more flash and strike the imagination. Little by little we observe the composer's departure from Russian traditions, little by little he ceases to draw his themes from the Russian well-spring exclusively. The Russian element in his creative art now begins to play a rôle equal to any other "exoticism," whether it be exoticism Chinese (in the *Nightingale*) or Japanese (in his songs) or any other whatever. Fearing to remain at a standstill, Stravinski is trying to rejuvenate his creative art with various glands and inventions. He keeps to the "rational path" well tried by him; he endeavours to fructify his creative art by contact with the sphere of modern dances, the city dances, instinctively feeling that in their characteristic rhythmics he may achieve contact with contemporary life. In this spirit he writes his *Ragtime for Eleven Instruments* and his *Piano Rag Music* essays for artistic fox-trots. Turning to the field of city dance was a rather common method of many composers for refreshing creative art. Once Schubert and Chopin and after them Liszt in this way created fresh works of genius. Perhaps this consideration played an important part in this case, too, the more so since it grew clear that the old dances had died simultaneously with the birth of the new city and that new themes were to be sought now.

True to his principle of contrast with the past, Stravinski simultaneously begins his researches in the field of colour in another direction. The huge orchestra introduced by Wagner and developed by Strauss and Skryabin and raised to the limit by Stravinski himself, now becomes a banality. People are used to it. Besides, it does not pay, owing to its enormous number of performers. Stravinski begins to cultivate small ensembles, small but always original, unusual in the choice of instruments, departing from classical traditions. Already his Japanese miniatures were written for an unusual ensemble of piccolo, flute, clarinet and strings with the piano, but subsequently he goes still further. His mastery in handling orchestral sonorities enables him to create freely in the oddest combinations, the more so as the composer's task is the creation of new sonorities, and in this, the old appreciation of the beauty of these sonorities, the degree of their euphony is completely disregarded. Innovators in the field of harmony yield their place to innovators in the field of orchestral ensembles.

With this purpose in view, he wrote the above-mentioned *Ragtime,* the *Renard,* a sort of ballet for chamber ensemble, a one-act comic opera, *Mavra,* on a theme taken from Pushkin. There is a probability that even purely economic considerations were at the bottom of this unexpected "chamberness" that had seized the composer after his terrible experiments with huge ensembles. Performances are easier and more frequent in this way and the cost of scores and materials is reduced. It is amusing, but in the biography of so modern a composer as Stravinski even such a detail must be considered.

Stravinski kept to the path of chamber music but these chamber organisms are woven of such extravagances that none would recognise the old quartette consecrated by the sacred tradition of Beethoven and Brahms. In the early chamber ensemble musicians valued first and foremost "the equal rights of the instruments." It was a sort of a musical free republic without even a president. It was prized as well for the austerity of its resonance, the abstract aloofness of sound. Stravinski values just the opposite. With the mastery of an experienced gold-digger who extracts gold from barren sands, he can find in modest ensembles the splendour and variety of the colours he needs. He values them exactly for the refinement of colour, for their finesse, in comparison with which orchestral colours cannot but appear coarse. The violin, the cello, all this no longer appears the conception of a "single timbre," but falls into a multitude of diverse timbres, and Stravinski makes the maximum use of the diversity of sonorities locked up in these instruments, resorting as he does to the most extravagant methods of sound-extracting, that have never been made use of. Thus, Stravinski ushers in a new era, an era "of intensive colour cultures," if one may use this expression. On a small quartette parcel of land he cultivates musical fruits which the possessors of enormous orchestral worlds had never dreamed of. This new culture comes in the stead of Strauss' "extensive orchestral cultures."

Most likely, even this would soon grow stale, because the musical Edison, weariless in his inventions, suddenly conceives a tender feeling for the old. He overfed himself on the achievements of new music, and suddenly was drawn towards the old and naïve Pergolese, whose music he works over in his own new spirit, with his usual wit. Of course the old Pergolese would never recognise himself in this new remodelling (the Ballet *Pulcinella*). But no such things are expected of it. The senile virtues of these composers came here exclusively as the objects of rejuvenating pharmaceutical means. However, not the decrepit Pergolese proved to be rejuvenated but Stravinski himself, he who in our palpitating age, is at forty older than Pergolese at three hundred.

Fashion changes like the revolving stage of a theatre. And its law-giver must forever be on the alert to invent something new in order to remain in the public eye and not to lose the affections of this fickle sweetheart. Even in Stravinski's attitude towards "Russian barbarism" there has come a change. He is almost no longer a Russian, but a European. The ironical attitude begins to predominate in him when once again he attempts to reproduce Russian life in the *Little Wedding* and in *Mavra*. In his search of the new and the pungent, he returns not only to Pergolese, but also to the old Russian song primitives (in *Mavra*), as well as to the tonal primitives in his children's pieces and songs. And we see Stravinski industriously composing "clever" little pieces, on five notes, for spoiled children of to-day. Truly only the unfortunate children of the twentieth century can study these musical falsities in which the experienced hand of a painstaking and great master has eradicated all the elements of lyricism and musicalness. The nervous, prematurely aged, too clever and too dry children of our European confrères cannot have a better mirroring of their degenerating psyches.

The call "back to antiquity" proves the strongest in Stravinski. He correctly noted that in our chase of the new we have too long ignored and forgotten antiquity. And during this lapse it has perhaps itself acquired all the attributes of "novelty." And so Stravinski makes his "face about to the classics." True, it is difficult to recognise the classical world in this reflection in his crooked mirror, but the fact itself is of interest. In this queer style of "false" Bach, Stravinski wrote his Piano Concerto and his Sonata. Wicked tongues assert that the causes of this last departure are to be sought in the fact that Stravinski himself wishes to become a pianist and has prepared these compositions "in keeping with his own technique." Granted that this is more witty than true, nevertheless this queer conclusion of the colouristic and resplendent musical career of our composer, though undoubtedly called into being, like all of Stravinski's acts, by considerations of an inexorable logic, cannot after all help producing a queer and somewhat pitiful impression. Involuntarily there comes to·mind the analogy with a man who had been overeating on too magnificent dishes during the course of his opulent life and has settled on a diet in his old age "by physicians' orders." At any rate we, the hearers, are not so particularly interested in being present at these dinners "according to diet," with which Stravinski now regales his admirers. But times change; perhaps our composer's stomach will grow better, the term of dieting will be over and we shall have served up to us some more interesting dish again.

For the time being, we find Stravinski exactly in this pitiful condition of one undergoing a cure for the indigestion of his musical stomach. What will happen later on we know not, but what he has already accomplished is perfectly sufficient to grant him the title of a *very great Russian composer*. This figure undoubtedly possesses elements of genius which at times appear odd, because they manifest themselves in a sphere that has been unusual for a Russian musician. Stravinski has accomplished what he desired, he became master over the minds of his contemporaries, he became the commander of the musical heights and the law-giver of fashion. Whether he will be able to maintain this position of his, which in its very essence cannot be stable, it is difficult to say, but among the assets of Russian music, and this is indubitable, such things as his *Petrushka* and even his *Nightingale* and *Sacre de Printemps* will doubtless remain and occupy a firm place as the classic creations of an incomparable artist and master, endowed with enormous wit and gorgeous fancy, if not a great soul.

To speak of his influence is even strange, for there are very few composers who have not fallen under the influence of this powerful, though in its sources rational, creative art. However one might evaluate Stravinski's repeatedly and bizarrely changing style, he undoubtedly constitutes an era in musical art. With his mighty and masterful hand he has frequently turned the course of his creative art and together with it turned the whole musical world. At present he is undoubtedly the most resplendent and significant figure of contemporary life.

SERGEY PROKOFYEFF

(Born 1890)

SERGEY PROKOFYEFF came into being in Russia at the time when Skryabin's genius still shone with the brilliant light of the recognised master of the "left wing" of the musical world. In order to understand Prokofyeff's importance and the destinies of his rapid and firm popularity, one must know the co-relation of the musical forces existing at the time. This, like the general historical situation, proved favourable to the young composer in the same degree that it was "unfavourable" to Skryabin.

By nature Skryabin was an innovator, but his love of innovation was tempered with a certain "timidity." It was incomplete in the first place, for it did not embrace all the spheres of musical form but only one sphere of harmony, and in the second place, it was ever accompanied by looking backward, for in Skryabin there lived simultaneously the academist and partisan of tradition. In the final balancing, Skryabin lacked that boldness, that coarseness, if you will, which is the concomitant of every revolutionary act including the artistic. At the same time Skryabin, as an innovator, denied certain postulates proclaimed by the preceding era of Russian music. He was the reflection of symbolism in literature, he was a protest against "brainless" art, and he was a living negation of "music for music's sake." Hence, he was antagonistic not only to the conservatives, but to a part of the left wing, and in particular to the group of "esthetes" for whom music existed for music's sake and ended there and then. Skryabin was a living negation also of nationalism in Russian music, he was antipodal to the *Koochka* and at the same time antipodal to Chaykovski in his everyday, drab view of the world. Such is the fate of every outstanding figure, that by its creative work it always denies the preceding day of art.

But the tragedy of Skryabin lay perhaps in the fact that he did not deny all this so strongly. At the time, a group of musicians could by no means apperceive him for they had become too much a part of the ideology of the preceding epoch, for instance, the ideology of the "mighty *Koochka*" or that of Chaykovski. On the other hand Skryabin came somewhat too late, and at all events he never took account of the fact that he operated with a material and a tendency that were not very grateful. Impressionism cultivated harmonies, it ignored the more living forces and more stable sphere of melody and rhythm. Impressionism dissolved itself in tonal aromas without noticing that these aromas begin to cloy and poison, that they are incapable of sustaining a lengthy existence. The whole musical material with which Skryabin operated with all his high-class qualities of genius was of the "perishable products" variety. It was stifling in this hot-house polluted by mystic poisons where the cruel composer of *Prometheus* and the creator of the unrealisable *Mystery* locked up his hearer. In its very essence this music prepared against itself an active protest. In the very nature of these intoxicating harmonies, in these caressing, drugging rhythms, drowsy as visions, in this absence of simplicity and buoyancy, lay concealed the destruction of Skryabin's entire life's work.

Even in Skryabin's lifetime symptoms of protest began to crop up. Already in his lifetime, we see the appearance of Metner, as the living personification of a protest against the lotus spell, which Skryabin cast over music; Metner with his rectilinear rhythms, his negation of all colourfulness, and enchantments. Many had not managed as yet to see through the spirit of Skryabin, when the time came for those who had seen through him to feel a peculiar need and yearning for fresh air.

Sergey Prokofyeff was such a reaction against Skryabin's sorcery and incantations. He was a perfect antithesis to the creator of *Prometheus*. Not a trace of the mysticism and witchcraft which Skryabin employed; not a trace of diffuseness; on the contrary, the enthronement of clear-cut and even coarse rhythm. No attempt to complicate and refine the harmony; on the contrary, the harmony becomes primitively simple, primevally dissonant if need be. Prokofyeff was, as it were, the negation of "Skryabin's artistic day," he came out with a series of completely opposite recipes of creative art. This was, above all, a definitely reactionary phenomenon as regards refinement and complication, it was a phenomenon definitely retrospective in the sense of "return to antiquity," even to classicism, if you will. For in Prokofyeff's rhythms and his constant "scherzandos," in this eternal jest which had disappeared from the musical language of the impressionists, there is much in common with the eighteenth century, with the epoch of Scarlatti. The impressionists had forgotten how to joke musically, music had become boresome and wearying, everybody had wrapped himself in a magician's cloak and began to officiate as a high priest and now the "street gamin" makes his appearance and hurls a stone at these sacred figures. And he is encouraged, because the hot-house atmosphere had begun to weary and bore. But Prokofyeff's position was doubly advantageous; he was joined also by those who had not as yet fathomed Skryabin and to whom Prokofyeff as a phenomenon nearer the past (say even to the Russian National School) was more kindred and close. He was also joined by those who had overfed on Skryabin and therefore left him. Prokofyeff restored to Russian music the jest and irony, the satire and laughter. He rid it of the eternal sacred pose which may not be so pleasant to all. He was taken to the bosom by both the enemies of Skryabinism and those who had abandoned it. Mischievousness and youthful vigour gushed from his music, and at first it was enjoyed, although many noticed even then that in this quality the composer must observe the same precaution in order not to call forth a perfectly similar reaction.

By those faithful to Skryabinism as a sacred tradition, by those to whom music continued to mean a sacred act, to whom its old-time connection with thought and mysticism was dear, the appearance of Prokofyeff could be classed only as vandalism and a return to barbarism. But history was not on their side. Events completely turned sympathy away from mysticism, from sacredness, from problems of profundity. A militant and cruelly merry era was coming on. And in this era the creative work of the life-brimming, vigorous Prokofyeff was far more in place than the sacred incense-burnings of the aged Skryabinists.

In his make-up as a composer, this "youthful conqueror" (and, as is well known, "conquerors are not judged"), is a bent to restore the classic musical view of the world. Music is a pleasure and not a heavy cross or a doom. Vigorous, clear-cut rhythmics, and naïveté of melody are raised to a cult, the technical methods themselves become a negation of those that had just been in vogue. Prokofyeff declared war upon the romantic piano style and resuscitated the cruder style of the classical era, the lingering broken arpeggios introduced by Chopin and Liszt disappear from Prokofyeff's music and are replaced by the technique of Beethoven and Hummel. Playful and satirical rhythms inundate music. Savagery and barbarism also become something needed and desirable as a reaction against the refinement of the preceding epoch. Diatonism replaces chromatism, the melody becomes childishly simple. To harmony is restored its lost right to be pleasing or displeasing. In this way a completely "positive likeness" of Prokofyeff is the result of negative characteristics.

True, we cannot conceal the fact that the figure obtained in this way does not possess sufficient depth and variety. But these qualities are not in demand nowadays. Prokofyeff's music occasionally seems some continuous tonal joke, some "cruel sport" in sounds at the expense of the hearer. It is not without reason that our author is inspired by such themes as *The Jester Who Had Outwitted Seven Jesters*. This "jester" will outwit others besides the seven jesters. But we fear that he may outwit his own truly enormous musical gifts. And there are both symptoms and dangers of this. All music expresses, willy-nilly, the psychics of its creator. There can be no insincerity here. It is inconceivable to pretend in music, sincerity comes as a result *per se*. One cannot conceal the fact that Prokofyeff's talent may be really dazzling, his musical apparatus that of a genius. But what I cannot see is that with his apparatus of a genius he proclaims genius-fashion the poverty and penury of his soul which is ready "to lose all, jesting." And the more the method of expression shows genius, the more convincing the proof in which the author is hardly interested.

Unquestionably as a phenomenon, Prokofyeff is extraordinarily brilliant. Unquestionably much in his music is a genius' prevision of the utterly new in tonal art. But unquestionable is also the fact that his soul as such, is indigent, that it is monotonously poor, that the scope of his moods is not only not exquisite, but even coarse and primitive. It is impossible to be a composer of scherzos only, it is tiring and even harmful to the composer himself.

And in his music we really observe something like the phenomenon of a composer being obsessed with certain moods. These "mischievous" rhythms of a street urchin become annoying, they scurry forth like little devils and apparently at a moment when the author himself does not want them at all. Skryabin, too, was possessed, but in an entirely different way. He was possessed by salon-demons who afterwards grew into some sort of genuine demons. But in Prokofyeff's case, they are mere little devils.

And occasionally one feels a desire to liberate the gifted composer from these obsessions. Deep down in Prokofyeff, it seems to me, there lies hidden something incomparably more profound and genuine than what he gives expression to. As a genuine gamin at the age of transition, he seems to fear in music his own better feelings, he prefers to cloak them with assumed mischievousness, he is possessed by "false shame." There are composers who, if one may use the expression, have their own "mystic" age. It determines their musical being. We picture Beethoven as a mature man, Mozart as a child, Bach and Brahms as aged men. Prokofyeff is a youngster and it is difficult to say whether he will ever outgrow this age. Mystic ages are very enduring; people are born and die with them. Skryabin was and lived and died a youth and Prokofyeff is apparently not destined to get out of his youngster-estate and the false shame connected with it.

And withal, these "deep" feelings exist in our "jester"; they ring in the sorrowful notes, in the melody occasionally suffused with genuine anguish, just as Musorgski's before his death was occasionally filled with an unexpected limitless tenderness. Such are his *Fairy-Tales of Old Grandma,* his *Grey-eyed King,* his *There Are Other Planets,* such is the Adagio of his Fourth Sonata for the piano, such is the Theme and Variations of his Third Concerto. Unquestionably, Prokofyeff does possess these qualities but some mischievous power and buffoonery compel him to hide them as deeply as possible. This nature Prokofyeff possesses in common with his literary twin, Sergey Yesyenin. The latter, too, from behind the hooliganism of a mischievous exterior, occasionally and unexpectedly would reveal a tender and deeply bashful soul, at other times tucked somewhere far away.

So far, life has treated Prokofyeff kindly and even lovingly. He has been spoiled by early recognition, world-fame and success. Amid these attributes of artistic happiness, he has had no time to think of the more necessary and more important. Hence the tempo of his inner growth has been slackened, hence his genius has been inwardly growing poorly, although "his recognition as a genius" has managed to grow up long ago. He is fertile and prolific as an author; more than that, there is observed in him a certain superabundance of "professional enthusiasm" and occasionally he writes more than necessary, making use of his acquired habit and the manner that has formed with him. As a matter of fact, Prokofyeff is an established composer. He belongs to the species of those who do not go through an evolution, but find themselves once and for all, successfully and exactly, and after that evolve their own manner and inevitably repeat themselves. We can hardly expect anything new of him; though he may write still many beautiful and interesting things, there cannot be anything unexpected. Only there may suddenly unlock itself that "holy of holies" of his inner essence which at present he so labouriously screens with all manner of "jests," and then we shall witness a transfiguration analagous to the tragic transfiguration which took place in the poet Yesyenin.

If we wished to establish Prokofyeff's genealogy as a composer, we might probably have to betake ourselves to the eighteenth century, to Scarlatti and other composers of the good old times, who have inner simplicity and naïveté of creative art in common with him. Prokofyeff is a classicist, not a romantic and his appearance must be considered as a belated relapse of classicism in Russia, which had so far been spared this "children's disease" by Fate. But occasionally people fall ill with children's diseases even in mature age and then its form is usually particularly severe. This very thing happened with Russian music which fell "severely ill" with Prokofyeff after its romantic era. This classicism is made complete by the very image of Prokofyeff as a creative artist, who belongs to the type of musicians now forgotten, but frequently met with in classical times, musicians who "sing like birds," compose with no thought but naturally, thinking neither of esthetic problems nor of philosophic depths. This typical "musician" is a musician of the purest water. Of course, there are birds of various kinds and their songs are also of various kinds, still every one of them will not suit everybody's taste. But the thing of importance here is the cardinal difference of this type of creator from the others, geniuses of sustained power, conscientious, reasoning creators who, in the process of the painful labour of thought and feeling, go through periods of pregnancy with their works and not infrequently must be the smiths of their power on the anvil of their genius. Such were the Titans of music, Beethoven, Bach, Wagner, Brahms; such was partly Skryabin and even Musorgski. The profound seriousness of their creative work is to a considerable degree determined also by the insufficiently yielding nature of the material itself, by the fact that the tonal web is stiffened with thought.

As we have seen, Prokofyeff's classicism has been determined by his having instinctively divined his own generation's yearning for a change of moods, for an esthetic change, for a contrast with the preceding day of art. Indeed, if every musical composer individually, in each of his compositions, is always guided by the keen feeling for contrast among the individual parts of a composition, without which creative art becomes wearisomely grey and monotonous, if every composer feels this insuperable need for the appearance of the contrasting episode, approximately the same is observed also in the life of the collective organism, in the life of musical epochs. Styles change, also guided by the feeling of the inevitability and necessity of contrast. And the more striking the expression of any style whatever, the sharper the feeling of protest against it. The musical

style of one period absorbed and made its own by one generation, begins to call forth an insuperable impulse towards its
opposite, towards the creation of a contrasting style. This
easily explains the changes of styles and schools known in the
history of music, and the attentive observer will without
effort distinguish in them a definite periodicity of deviation
and recurrence which possess all the marks of a rhythmic
figure. And it is not difficult even to observe that the period
of these oscillations of style is approximately equal to the
life of a generation, about twenty-five years.

Prokofyeff's classicism originated as an antithesis to the
style of the impressionistic epoch and Skryabin. Of course,
this is relative classicism, but it would be difficult to class him
also as a typical romantic. Prokofyeff is the living antithesis
to "Skryabin's time," and even his artistic mischievousness
itself, which passes into a sort of esthetic hooliganism, is determined by the feeling of contrast with the overdose of
salonishness and impressionistic propriety of Skryabin's music.
Characteristic of Prokofyeff's is this denial of his, in music,
of the transcendental elements, his locking himself up in a
purely tonal world. And in his very manner, as regards
for instance the "subjects" of his musical compositions, there
has remained something from the dear artisanship of the
happy classical age. With him, as with Mozart, it really
makes no difference on what theme to compose music. His
enormous talent saves him in his unthinking and merry creative work. But occasionally one gets wearied by this music
which possesses too many sounds and too few "values." Occasionally the question comes to mind, why does this magnificent apparatus of expression in tone go for naught, when
its owner has "nothing to express," when his soul is empty
and gay and shallow? And then one ponders: what is better,
to express in the manner of a genius the poverty of one's
inner world, as Prokofyeff does it, or in the fruitless impulse,
in the ardent desire to take possession of the unyielding

apparatus of external musicalness, to be constrained to guard the treasures of one's own spirit in the dungeon of one's inner life?

Prokofyeff's classicism expresses itself both in the simplification of his musical fabric, which in comparison with the fabric of the impressionists and Skryabin, presents an indubitable step backward, and also in the "colourlessness" of his music. Taken all in all, Prokofyeff is a graphic artist, and his music is devoid of tonal colourings. In his orchestra, too, he is single-hued and grey; he does not possess in any degree the gift of the orchestral palette. Even the jest so peculiar to him, proves entirely graphical; the instruments of his orchestra cannot joke, as they can for instance, in the masterly fashion of Stravinski. In Prokofyeff's creative work, as with every "classic," the design is in the foreground and it dominates so far that no room is left for the other components of the whole. In general, this creative work stands under the huge sign of "return to the old." There comes back the old world of jest which had perished in music with the romantic era, there comes back the simplicity, there returns the periodicity and the squareness of rhythmics. The very manner in which he treats the piano is classical; from the romantic harp instrument the piano once again becomes "the cembalo" or the "clavichord" of the good old times. And simultaneously there is resurrected in him the "ecstasy of virtuosity," of naïve, tonal equilibristics. Prokofyeff brings back to life the fleetness of passages, long leaps of the hands in the piano technique, and in general, all that old-fashioned technique of the times of Kalkbrenner and Hertz.

The classicism sensed in Prokofyeff was the cause of his being accepted and recognised not only by the "left-wingers," but also and principally by those of the right. He pleased also the masses who once more heard with delight in modern music the rhythmical precision and vigour of march-like and gallop rhythms. The masses do not need so much, and rhythmical precision is one of the most primitive require- ments, for it is well known that the ability to distinguish rhythms develops first of all. His audacities and the veneer of innovation were the more acceptable in that they came "not in earnest," but under the sauce of a jest, and one can jest with anything, as is well known. After our references to his classicism it will be of interest to mention the names of his compositions, especially of the early period. Prokof- yeff wrote a Classical Symphony, minuettes and gavottes, preferring to express himself in these classical forms and not within the romantic frames of nocturnes and "poems." The enormous services of Prokofyeff, who had once more gone back to cultivating the classical field, consist in his having proved that this realm, and in general the realm of simple musical means, has not been exhausted by far, that here is possible not only a banal and traditional return to antiquity, but also a creative return, embodying a movement forward. He has proved what people had not believed in the epoch of impressionism, that a "new freedom" was possible in the scheme of these old means of expression, and that vigorous rhythmics harbour more enormous resources than the rhyth- mical stream of impressionism flowing indefinitely in a single hue. Music, which has been fused into some single being by romanticism, is once more dissolved into its separate com- ponent parts, and the hearer discerns in it with pleasure all of melody and rhythm and harmony.

All this music operates with "the unexpected," with those elements which being in their nature classical, had neverthe- less not in their time received the rights of citizenship in a classical world, but were left unfinished by the classicists. And all of this now at its appearance, glitters with freshness and novelty, and at the same time reveals something long forgotten, something which is both familiar and natural. Together with Stravinski, Prokofyeff paints for us the living image of contemporary life; in its tendency for the simplification of experiences lived through, for the "unloading of the inner world," for the minimum "psychology," for the desire not to remain too long on the same spot, "to walk around and by" in the chase for new superficial sensations. In this psychology there is something that comes from the moving pictures. And really, Prokofyeff's music is cinematographic to a high degree.

Many students of Prokofyeff's creative art desire to see in it a reflection of the Russian Revolution and the experiences of the grandiose war. In his music they wish to find the barbarisation which has come as the result of the coarsening of morals therefrom. However this is hardly just. With all its attributes of barbarism, Prokofyeff's art is devoid of the attributes of might, majesty, monumentality. And his very "barbarism" is relative. What is typical in him is not barbarism, but mischievousness, and jesting, manifestations which are in reality of a civilised, not a barbaric variety. On the contrary, we cannot deny Prokofyeff a certain degree of specific refinement, although it is the opposite of the refinement of the impressionist world. And besides, Prokofyeff's creative art had taken shape before the War and before the Revolution, with which he in reality had no connection at all. Accordingly, this version of the influence of the War and Revolution must be abandoned. Prokofyeff did not come as the result of these events, but as the result of a purely musical contrast with that which had gone before. And fortunately for him, historical tastes had veered exactly to the side of a certain coarsening which naturally contributed to his popularity.

Prokofyeff had paid tribute to "barbarism" in its narrow sense, in his Suite for Orchestra *Ala and Lolliy,* and in his Cantata *Seven,* set to words of Balmont; but these are not so typical of the composer, they are rather the tribute of imitation of and competition with Stravinski, the true owner of the secrets of barbarism. Characteristic of Prokofyeff is his turning to opera. One must be, if anything, naïve and a naïvely classical "artisan" to write operas now, when stage experiments have placed the entire operatic art under a heavy sign of doubt. But Prokofyeff's attitude towards opera is exactly that of a classic; doubt does not concern him. He has no favourite forms of clothing his ideas. He writes with equal mastery and enthusiasm, both piano miniatures and symphonies and symphonic poems, and operas and ballets. He is a typical eclectic in form. And he conquers with this naïve attitude of his. It is exactly his operas that have proven exceedingly interesting contributions to musical literature, and perhaps exactly for the reason that they have been composed without any *a priori* theories, with no desire to prove something. *The Love of Three Oranges*, set to music on a theme drawn from Gozzi's dramatic novel, is a splendid and exceedingly witty composition. The symphonism of operatic style, first introduced by Wagner into opera and firmly established there, calls forth a reaction on Prokofyeff's part; and he strives for a decrease of symphonism, and in this again he manifests his classical nature. Prokofyeff's opera is full of peculiar theatricalism, but remains musical at the same time. The composer has successfully, though on a wholly different plane, found the synthesis of stage and music, which had so long been sought by theoreticians. Prokofyeff's opera is brimful of scenic and theatrical qualities; it is equally removed from the oratorio style of Wagner's music-drama and the static lyricism of Russian opera. This opera is the only one on the operatic horizon of the present day to give incidentally a striking solution of the riddlesome operatic problem.

Prokofyeff is no symphonist, first of all owing to his colourlessness, and then because a true symphony is the child of a romantic era. Prokofyeff, the classic, though he has written one "classical" and one "mere" symphony, nevertheless lacks the inner dynamics necessary for a symphonist. His orchestral compositions are too graphic and too colour- less to become at the same time symphonic poems as well. Even his essay in ballet form, *The Jester Who Has Outwitted Seven Jesters,* turns out to be graphic, though it teems with purely Prokofyevian wit and mischievousness. However odd it may seem, Prokofyeff, the cut-up, proves more "cutting- up" than puissant in the final analysis. He is not an eaglet destined to grow into a big eagle. He is a "stabilised" eaglet who will die such. And hence in the features of this cut- up, there unexpectedly appears more intimacy than could be expected.

For this reason, Prokofyeff's lyricism holds so central a position in his art, just as does his "piano world" to which he belongs himself, as an excellent though somewhat rough pianist. Those "gaps" to which I have referred before, are scattered in the greatest quantity in these lyrics, which gives us a glimpse of Prokofyeff's inner world, proofs that behind the veneer of mischievousness and roughness, he possesses a tender and perhaps profound subconscious world. Here he loses his ties with the classics and comes rather closer to the great Russian romantic Musorgski, with whom he has in common both the tragic turn of melody and the contours of tunefulness which unexpectedly betrays traits of kinship with Russian creative folk-art.

These traits of seriousness transpire also in his piano sonatas of which the Fourth is distinguished by its Adagio, overflowing with the gravity which occasionally assumes purely Beethovenian outlines. Prokofyeff the "jester" is so obstinate in his buffoonery that somehow one has no faith in this seriousness and it seems put-on. It seems that the author pretends, that in reality it is only a pseudo-serious mien care- fully prepared in order to make people laugh the more un- expectedly. But we should dearly like to think that we are in error and that this seriousness is genuine, in spite of the "quantitative majority" which the "jocular shades of opinion" have in the parliament of his moods. This same unexpected lyricism and even sorrow enshroud certain passages of his piano concertos in which Prokofyeff, true to the traditions of his classicism, once more transfers the centre of gravity from the orchestra to the piano. Just as weird and even uncanny in their unexpected sorrowfulness are his *Fairy-Tales of Old Grandma.* Prokofyeff the mischief-maker, turned into an old grandma and sighing about the past, is a picture that would make one ponder, if one did not know that in the psyche of our composer everything is much simpler and that there is no room for "problems of depths." These beautiful miniatures breathe suppressed sorrow, psychologically they fairly reproduce the uncanny and epic feelings of profound old age. Whence come these moods in Prokofyeff, the youthful and vigorous? Or perhaps here, too, his keen sense of musical contrast finally revolted against his own monotony of moods? If it is so, it gives reason to expect a great deal in the future.

Prokofyeff is not a Russian composer only. He is already a world composer. He has been recognised, and has outstripped in this recognition not only his contemporaries but even a number of predecessors including Skryabin, who is still awaiting recognition. At the same time he has proven also more fortunate than Skryabin even in the matter of founding a school. There is already a Prokofyeff school, there are already imitators of his, and there are "followers," which is still more important. Prokofyeff's good fortune lay in the fact that his musical style is far more suitable for forming a school than was the style of Skryabin. The latter was too specific, too monotonous in his methods. And imitating him, degenerated into sheer cribbing. Prokofyeff is more multifarious in methods, his method of composition is not so schematic as Skryabin's, it is not so easy to lay hold of his ways, and hence his epigones may have characteristics of their own, and be composers of importance. And already we see his followers, especially in Russia, where Prokofyeff's influence and popularity are enormous, and abroad, where under his influence is being developed the talent of Alyeksandr Cheryepnin and even of a group of foreign composers. Phenomena which call into existence a school are in themselves a testimony of importance. And there can be no two opinions with regard to Prokofyeff. There may be difference of opinion about the depth of his inner world, about the value of that world, one may not agree about the too monotonous style he has selected, but one cannot deny that in his person we have one of the most important Russian composers, the first Russian classicist with musical gifts of exceptional intensity. Nor can it be denied that in spite of his seeming severance from the national line of the development of Russian music, and his outward cosmopolitanism, in reality Prokofyeff is a profoundly Russian composer, more Russian than, for instance, Tañeyeff or Skryabin, or Metner. The elements of Russian style, deeply hidden in the essence of his melodies, are nevertheless revealed by both inward feeling and analysis, and here discloses to his advantage, a kinship with the greatest genius of Russian music,—Musorgski.

SERGEY RAKHMANINOFF

(Born 1872)

RAKHMANINOFF belongs to the same generation as Skryabin and Metner and a number of other prominent Russian composers. A whole pleiad of brilliant musicians were graduated with him from the Moscow Conservatory in the early nineties of the last century, the Conservatory's golden years. The youthful pianist-composer was one of the few who received a gold medal at graduation, one of those who graduated in two specialties. Even in his student-days, the most brilliant hopes were entertained for him, a composer's career *par excellence,* as a worthy successor to the already famous and acclaimed Chaykovski, the idol of Moscow.

In drawing Tañeyeff's portrait, we have already spoken of the specific conditions and sympathies in the Moscow musical world, of the peculiar "local patriotism" of the Moscovites and the undercover competition between Russia's two capitals, Moscow and St. Petersburg. In many respects Moscow was more backward than St. Petersburg and it was interesting that at the time when novel ideas were fermenting in the musical world of St. Petersburg and produced such potent phenomena as the Russian National School (a group of five great composers, unparalleled in the intensity of their talent, three of whom, Musorgski, Borodin, Rimski-Korsakoff, may be considered geniuses), peaceful conservatism reigned in Moscow. It was explained by the enormous authority of the naturally conservative Chaykovski and the Conservatory's director, Nikolay Rubinstein, himself hardly partial to the contemporary seekings of new paths. Here there was no strife between left and right, between the old and the new.   Here the catechism of Chaykovski and Nikolay Rubinstein held absolute sway, and following this catechism which was not always consistent, and did not reflect so much the "tendency" as the personal sympathies of these great musicians, the Moscovites hated and did not know Wagner, disliked the Russian National School in the persons of Borodin, Rimski-Korsakoff and Musorgski (especially the last), maintained a skeptical attitude toward Liszt and Berlioz, considered Brahms a nonentity and worshiped Chaykovski as the people of St. Petersburg never worshiped him either before that or later.   This catechism was so universally recognised that nobody ever got it into his head to argue or fight against it.   For a composer of that epoch to be a seeker of new paths, or innovator, was considered well-nigh a disgrace, at all events an infraction of the *bon ton* of the Conservatory.   It was considered the greatest piece of good fortune for a young composer if he could write like Chaykovski or Anton Rubinstein, and everybody strove to attain that goal.   In this odd atmosphere, which smacked of provincialism, Rakhmaninoff's talent grew up and in his earliest years developed that spirit of "moderation" which has distinguished him all his lifetime: a lack of sympathy with anything striking, sharp, pointed.   Chaykovski's enormous authority and gift of genius laid their ineffaceable stamp on him and Rakhmaninoff's entire esthetics developed under the influence of this, after Musorgski, possibly most "Russian" of all Russian composers.   These esthetics, if one may use the expression, were also to a certain degree Moscovian; at any rate, the Moscow life of that time found its reflection in it and in the tones which were subjected thereto.

It was an artistically Bohemian milieu with a strong bourgeois colouring. Moscow musicians gave themselves up to life's amusements considerably more than the musicians of St. Petersburg. The famous Moscow restaurants, the no less famous gipsy choruses, the atmosphere of continuous dissipation in which perhaps there was no merriment at all, but on the contrary, the most genuine, bitter and impenetrable pessimism,—this was the milieu. Music here was a terrible narcosis, a sort of intoxication and oblivion, a going off into irrational planes. Drunken mysticism, ecstatic sensations against a background of profound pessimism permeating existence. It was not form or harmoniousness, or Apollonic vision that was demanded of music, but passion, feeling, languor, heartache. Such was Chaykovski's music and such also the music of Rakhmaninoff developed into.

Of course, time did its work little by little. And even a musician, stoically devoted to the traditions of the conservatory, could hardly fail to see the beauties revealed in certain compositions of the innovators. Even in the earliest creative works of Rakhmaninoff, his student opera *Aleko*, for instance, or his Symphonic Poem, *The Cliff*, something in common may be found with Borodin, occasionally with Musorgski, a few traces of Liszt or even Wagner.

But time worked, and Rakhmaninoff, the convinced follower of conservatory traditions, unconsciously drew into his creative art a number of features from the repertory of the mighty *Koochka*. He was carried away by the orchestral colourings, waxed enthusiastic even over programme music, over the symphonic poem on the poetic text, and over certain new effects from the harmonic palette of Liszt, Wagner and Borodin.

True, all this was by no means intentional, or emphasised, for Chaykovski "himself" wrote programme pieces for the orchestra, such as *The Tempest* and *Francesca Da Rimini*, in these paying no small tribute to Lisztianism. And "quasi-innovating" attempts of this kind in reality did not alter the character of the youthful author, a true offspring of Chaykovski. His first compositions do not produce the impression of anything original or peculiarly his own. It is Chaykovski with a certain complexity of tonal fabric, but the same familiar elegiac mood which deploys into impenetrable darkness, adding a dizzy, passionate erotism, something kindred to that same "gipsy" spirit of music against the background of which his talent developed.

Rakhmaninoff's creative work, like his whole artistic life, did not constitute a straight line, or an uninterrupted, unswerving, striving for a goal, early set for himself. On the contrary, this profound and passionate, self-enclosed and pessimistic soul was will-less, just as was his great teacher, Chaykovski; his genius was not shaped by efforts of will-power, but tossed about among ephemeral moods. Life had called him with mighty calls in his excessively tempestuous youth. And perhaps this very life with its temptations, and the dissipation of the typical artistic Bohème was the cause of the spasmodic nature of his creative work. Evidently the composer himself felt that two paths lay before him, either the path of sensations, of enriching himself with life's experiences, but without hope of shaping them artistically, or the severe path of an artist-creator, attained only at the price of sacrificing the former.

Apparently the choice was made after one of the most powerful interruptions in the creative work, when the composer who had always been inclined towards reflexion and pessimism seemed to think that his creative gift was deserting him. Evidently this struggle, this heavy inner tragedy, had cost Rakhmaninoff dearly, but after that there once more came into his creative work an active streak, a new access of inspiration, as it were.

This first early period of his is occasionally characterised by a too slavish imitation of Chaykovski, by a too low amount of originality, as though even the thought of originality had never come into the author's head. Perhaps general conditions enhanced this phenomenon, but in particular it was the effect of the lack of general culture which generally weighed heavily over the life of many of the Russian musicians of that and the preceding generations. The conservatory supplied one with a musical trade, but it gave no general education and the conservatory students could not boast any degree of culture whatever. Their artistic horizon itself proved inordinately limited and only truly fiery natures of genius like Skryabin or born thinkers like Tañeyeff were capable of emerging from this atmosphere.

At this time Rakhmaninoff wrote his smaller piano pieces, among them the C-Sharp Minor Prelude which made him famous the world over, and in which clearly rings the fundamental leit-motif of his life, the facing of the terrifying and unconquerable power, fate or destiny. The helpless horror before it, the impossibility of escape save in the arms of semi-consciousness, in the stupor of hashish, where in a world of spirits and dreams, man attains even temporarily though it be, the mirage of paradise. In imitation of his teacher Aryenski, he creates suites for two pianos in which he proves himself already a master of piano exposition. Chaykovski died in 1893 and in his memory, like a reflection of the Trio Chaykovski himself had composed on the death of Nikolay Rubinstein, Rakhmaninoff, with the touching naïveté of a devoted imitator, also composed a Trio in exactly the same form. His first essay at a symphony, composed for a large orchestra on themes from Russian ecclesiastical melodies, ended in failure. Symphonic style still baffled the youthful composer. Then came the spasmodic period in his creative art.

A renascence, connected with the decisive change in the whole mode of the composer's living, at once brought to the world Rakhmaninoff's best compositions. To the famous hypnotist-physician Dal', who had cured him of his Bohemian manner of living, the grateful composer dedicated his Second Piano Concerto which many consider his best composition. If not the very best, it is at least his "central" one, along with his Cello Sonata, which appeared simultaneously and has much in common with the Concerto both in colour and mood and even in themes.

Now the composer, deflected from dissipated and pessimistic moods, gained the perspective to speak of them in sounds. Previous to that life, that view of himself and his life experiences which comes as if "from the side" had overwhelmed this man who had felt in a morbidly profound manner, until he lost the objectivism which every artist must needs have in his creative work. Fortunate are such objective artists who can at any given moment become a dual personality and scan themselves and their inner world "from aside" after the manner of an observer and describer. But Rakhmaninoff in general is not of these and in general he does not belong to the type of "felicitous" composer. On the contrary, traces of profound effort and the terrible struggle and torments of creative art are inherent in his compositions. Each one has been achieved at a high price, it has cost him a part of his own self. It meant some sort of severance from himself. It is not the bright and cloudless creative art of Mozart, it is a gloomy doom, a heavy debt which he has bound himself by oath to pay.

In his Second Concerto, the world of Darkness seizes the hearer. This is no longer Chaykovski, it is far more gloomy and pessimistic than Chaykovski. In Rakhmaninoff's darkness there is still more impenetrableness as well as more majesty and solemnity. The *Moira* or Fate which had confronted Beethoven as an object of struggle and subsequently victory, which had confronted Richard Wagner as a fellow-warrior and his equal, which had confronted Chaykovski as a spectacle of unspeakable terror and deathly lonesomeness, confronted Rakhmaninoff as a terrifying and gloomy beauty, garbed in ineffable solemnity and sable majesty. This solemnity and funereal magnificence permeates the whole First Movement of the Concerto, that funeral march, semi-rapid yet without haste, which seems to symbolise the unswerving and fatal course of finite time to eternal oblivion. In the second theme, we hear the typical lyrics of Rakhmaninoff, after Chaykovski, the greatest Russian melodist of the lyric type. There is no impulse towards action in them: torpid, half slumbering, visionary. One would think a vision full of fascination and passion is sweeping before one's gaze, once more overwhelming with the torrent of darkness and then vanishing in the funereal clouds of eternity. The same dreamy, hallucinary, dazed character is possessed by the remarkable theme of the Second Movement (Adagio), the melody distinguished by a profile typical of Rakhmaninoff and lazily motionless, half slumbering, as though fearful of embracing a larger diapason. This semiconsciousness as a mood seized in tones, is exceedingly characteristic of the composer. It symbolises the volitional impotence of the author, who only sees what is disclosed to him but is not free himself to see it at will. As if in a torpid, hashish state, he, will-less and motionless, imagines visions full of fascination and beauty, and does not even wish to reach out for them.

And his impulses are just as strange, just as lacking in will-power. Occasionally something outwardly kindred to Wagner flits by in his crescendos and climaxes, but this is only momentary. Rakhmaninoff almost never reaches the point of culmination. The impotence of a fettered giant emanates from these climaxes, which weaken almost on the verge of their resolution into culmination. And above it all, darkness and death always. Whether he wishes to disclose to us the secret of his visions or not, it is all the same, for the meaning of this music is too clear and transparent in its obscurity.

Together with the rise of the creative art which simultaneously produced the Cello Sonata and the Second Piano Concerto, and soon afterwards, the Second Symphony akin with the Concerto, Rakhmaninoff revealed himself unexpectedly and strikingly as a pianist. Formerly unnoticed in this field, considered a composer *par excellence* by all, he suddenly disclosed such elemental technique and might of expression and rhythm, that he became at once the chief of Russian pianists. The ghost of Rubinstein came to life in this elemental interpretation, and the word "genius" which had been guardedly applied to his creative work, was here uttered immediately. Yes, this was the genuine performance of genius, that elemental execution with which Liszt and Rubinstein had once conquered the world. Rakhmaninoff appeared in a limited sphere, why, it is difficult to say, touching nothing but his own compositions, with occasional exceptions in favour of Chaykovski and Liszt. Later on in America he departed from this custom. But whatever he touched became filled with genius, just as all things became golden at the touch of the legendary king Midas. Whether he played his own Prelude in C sharp minor, or his less successful Prelude in G-minor, the hearer was ready to believe, and did believe for the moment, that he was face to face with a composition equal to Beethoven's in depth, and for the moment it was such. This extraordinary pianist with a rhythm of steel, with mighty and tender tone, with hands superhuman, like those of Liszt, and with the temperament that could engulf the temperaments of all the pianists of the present day, forthwith cast a heavy shadow over his own image as a composer in the eyes of the many. Whether the passive rôle of "performer" was more to the taste of his nature, will-less in its inner contemplative essence, for which creative work was a sort of torment, or simply whether the element of genius which unquestionably had lived in Rakhmaninoff reached the world more easily and by shorter route through execution than through creation, there is no doubt that wherever Rakhmaninoff *performed* he conquered unconditionally and more indisputably than when he attempted to enter the souls of others through compositions.

After his Second Symphony came his new large compositions. His two small operas, *The Miser Knight* and *Francesca*, his symphonic poem, *The Isle of the Dead* (based on Boecklin's painting which had been acclaimed until it was almost made banal), and his Third Piano Concerto made their appearance. Indisputably Rakhmaninoff matured in these compositions. Chaykovski's image vanishes little by little, obscured by the image of Rakhmaninoff himself. This latter image is not all-embracing, not broad, not multi-formed. Rakhmaninoff is by far "narrower" than Chaykovski. But psychologically he is greater than the latter. It is a mysterious story, a kind of clairvoyance, and the secret language of musical augurs is needed when we must speak of the measurements of personality, in composer and creative art. This "greatness of the man" is neither the merit of his creative work, nor the size of his compositions. One can be the author of huge symphonies and be little, and again compose preludes and be vast. One may compose poor music, yet be "great" in spirit, and in this poor music this greatness will still come to the fore in some mysterious manner. And *per contra,* one may compose pieces stamped with genius, on the basis of which it will be possible with special certainty to speak of the insignificance of their composer's spirit. Rakhmaninoff is a man of great spirit. I shall not undertake to compare his gifts as a composer with those of Skryabin, but my "clairvoyance" tells me that the spirit-Rakhmaninoff is greater than the spirit-Skryabin, regardless of my personal sympathies with Skryabin as a creator and a personality, regardless of the greatness of Skryabin's schemes.

By the same mysterious standard, Rakhmaninoff surpassed his genius-dowered teacher Chaykovski. He is a single-love man in creative art, and he is eternally confronted with one and the same terrible world. Always he speaks but of this world, and he says one and the same thing. Rakhmaninoff is not a composer of breadth. His musical palette is not varied and it is narrow. His methods of procedure are the same almost always. The profiles of his climaxes in his Third Concerto and the Symphony are nearly identical with those in the Second Concerto and in the Sonata. His melody, a drowsy, enclosed, stationary melody, full of drugged lyricism, revolves almost always in the realm of five or six notes, he does not like wide diapason and precipitous leaps. If he is rhythmical, his rhythm is nearly always the same, the hurriedly funereal rhythm of a sombre march, which occasionally gives the impression of the agitated call of a tocsin. It is even uncomfortable to compare this narrow, gloomy dungeon-world with the world of Chaykovski. And yet, Rakhmaninoff the man is felt to be greater in it than Chaykovski. He lives through his limited experiences with infinite, with Titanic force. Chaykovski's lyricism appears "commoner" than this gloomy lyricism. And Rakhmaninoff's language is more modern than Chaykovski's language, as is natural. In his new compositions he often resorts to Wagnerised harmonies and orchestral methods akin to Richard Strauss. His orchestra whose very sonority has, as it were, specialised in gloom, reveals a great master who always can extract from it what he needs. This sonorousness possesses the same gloomy magnificence as his music, the same torpid and will-less, paralysed contemplation of the beauty and magnificence and terror of death. Not everything created by him is equally good. The Third Concerto and the *Isle of the Dead* stand considerably higher than his Second Symphony, although this latter possesses pages of great power, in spite of being long-drawn-out, a characteristic common to his compositions.

Having conquered in the sphere of pianism, Rakhmaninoff immediately appeared as a conductor. This many-faced musical Proteus, similar to Liszt both in his pianism and the many facets of his gifts on the gloomy side, being devoid of the diabolic traits of the great "satanic abbot," appears inexhaustible in the manifestations of his genius. Yet one must say that if his manifestation in pianism is indisputably that of a genius, he has revealed himself only as a great talent in the sphere of conducting, while his path as a composer, the most interesting of all, exhibits odd combinations of traits of genius with traits of some sort of decay and doubt in his own powers.

At one time the Russian advanced critics fell upon Rakhmaninoff and harried him to shreds. He was also attacked by the musicians who belonged to the extreme left groups and particularly to the snobbish groups, of which there are so many to-day. His unquestionable spiritual succession to the old Russian gipsy spirit, permeated by inescapable pessimism and unspeakable hopelessness, gave occasion to reproach him with bad taste. Perhaps from the point of view of early twentieth century taste, Rakhmaninoff really lacked it. But taste itself is a quantity that varies greatly and rapidly. What at that time seemed "tasteful" and the height of musical gastronomy seems now, and frequently to the same people, the acme of tastelessness. Not so very long ago, scorn was the constant factor in the sensations aroused in musicians upon hearing the songs of the "fathers of Russian music," Gurileff and Varlamoff. And now they are considered the height of good taste, and the Russian National School, itself in turn, is, in the opinion of authoritative snobs, dangerously bordering on tastelessness.

If we recall the attacks of these little "pug-dogs" on the great "elephant Rakhmaninoff," a sense of the ludicrous rather than exasperation overtakes us. It is true that, thanks to his trained and inborn conservatism, Rakhmaninoff really was slow in his development. His talent in itself was heavy-footed and inagile, his creative process, sluggish, to which the small number of compositions during so long a life bears sufficiently eloquent testimony. But his greatest "crime" was the fact that he was born at the time when fashion and the musical masses had drawn people into seeking eminent novelty and in the epoch of the overthrow of old values. Skryabin's rising star obscured the star of Rakhmaninoff, obscuring it mightily and for a long time, but we dare hope, not forever. The star of Skryabin himself undergoes bizarre variations in brilliance; and it is hard here to be a prophet, especially since a mere decade separates us from Skryabin's death and his rival and competitor is still alive and labouring.

Rakhmaninoff is a representative of old music. None of the devices and forms of the new, especially of the newest, has affected his creative art. The partisans of the new art treat him with scorn, consider him a "living corpse," but do not we historians know full well that frequently it is the new which is the most ancient, that what is new for the moment often bears within it the elements of dissolution, and that a god of to-day will be unknown a quarter of a century hence and will perish in the forgetfulness of future generations? Within our memory, Brahms, Liszt, Bruckner, have been revived; forgotten authors of the antique centuries have been exhumed and, in the light of their taste and style, far more recent achievements in art have grown dim.

Accidentally and through no fault of his own, Rakhmaninoff got into the civil war of the Russian musical "Montagues and Capulets," the innovators and conservatives. The former won the day, but their victory was temporary, for the erstwhile innovators had already become conservatives unable to keep up with the demands of fashion. It is clear to the objective observer, that Rakhmaninoff is nearer to Skryabin, for instance, than the latter is to Stravinski, and that the line of demarcation between schools would have to be drawn in such a way that Skryabin and Rakhmaninoff would now find themselves on the same side of musical good and evil, and perhaps would become allies against their common new foe.

As a whole, the chain of events was shaping itself un-favourably for Rakhmaninoff. The fashionable critics pro-claimed him the "idol of the crowd," which he was, but without the disgracing shade of meaning of this word. It was considered that his creative work was too popular, too old-fashioned, which in reality it was not. Enormous musi-cal values lie hidden in his creative art and the musicianly quality shut up in Rakhmaninoff, "the idol of the crowd," would suffice many composers of modern times for fructify-ing their meagre and modest resources.

Lyric pathos and profound sincerity, the scarecrows of musical snobs of our times, reign supreme in his creative art. Rakhmaninoff is a typical romantic and in our age of the negation of romanticism in music he is not quite in place. But he is not alone. Nearly all Russian music, with few exceptions is the same. Nay more, to a dispassionate ob-server, it is clear that many "anti-romantics" of the present day, insofar as they are really composers of importance, only pretend to be such, yielding to the pressure of unmusical snobs, but in fact their music is just as romantic as is all music in general, which has not definitely forsaken the ele-ment of music.

Rakhmaninoff's lyricism has embodied itself with particular power in his songs, which may be considered a typical con-tinuation of Chaykovski's song lyricism. They have much in common with Chaykovski, but they are more monumental and less naïve than Chaykovski's songs. They are saturated with profound sincerity which precisely is perhaps a fault in the eyes of some. But in spite of the generally accepted opinion, these songs in which only a portion of his great and gloomy soul finds expression, is not the best in Rakh-maninoff's creative work.

The last years before the great Russian Revolution, Rakhmaninoff traversed a new stage in his creative art in a cycle of songs to words by Russian symbolist poets, a cycle dedicated to the singer Nina Koshits, in whom the composer had found the best interpreter of his gloomy and passionate lyricism. Life once more invaded Rakhmaninoff's world as a composer, and in lieu of the tragedy in sounds there appeared for a moment the ghost of a living tragedy. The composer's creative art, as it were, felt a new upward urge. At least his poem *The Bells,* for chorus and orchestra, on the gloomy and impenetrable text of the pessimist genius Edgar Allen Poe, many of the traits of whose personality are similar to those of our composer, may without contradiction be said to contain his best inspiration and is his most complex, weird, gloomy and pessimistic creation. It was, as it were, his last burst of inspiration. Then came the War, and the Revolution toward which the passive and will-less temperament of the composer could feel nothing save abhorrence. Too strongly disappointed in the world and its illusions, too securely locked up in himself and too misanthropic to be revolutionary even in the slightest degree, or to be enticed by unrealisable dreams of an earthy paradise, which pessimists have no use for in the first place, Rakhmaninoff greeted the Revolution with the austere reserve and pessimism peculiar to him. He sensed concealed hatred and notes of enmity in musicians and the musical world. His noble and disinterested impulse, which once more recalled Liszt—his performance of Skryabin's works after the death of his genius-comrade and involuntary rival and foe, a performance in its own kind stamped with genius, like everything that pertained to Rakhmaninoff's performances—even this impulse was dashed against the murky and stolid sectarian hatred of the too unreasonably zealous admirers of the new Messiah, Skryabin. His enemies decided that the performance was poor beyond words. The Revolution which came soon after with its accompanying discomforts of life, the tribulations and material ruin, utterly unsettled Rakhmaninoff. The composer left Russia for new lands, taking with him an ardent love for his former fatherland, taking with him his proud and unbending Russian soul, kindly but firm, passive but heroic.

With the year 1918, a new era opens up in the life of Rakhmaninoff. Until then, a purely local figure, not even Russian, but almost "Moscovian," Rakhmaninoff at one blow, like the Roman hero "came, saw and conquered" the musical world of the West, and particularly of America. His colossal technique, his Titanic temperament, his adamantine rhythm of execution, in general, all that which was of the very first rank in him and which had not been honoured, as is always the case of the prophet in his own country, astounded the musical world of the West with its might. Evidently his sentimentality, which lived in harmony with this might and power and had become repugnant to the esthetes of Russia and Europe, had not yet been experienced in business-like America and astonished it. Rakhmaninoff won in a foreign land the laurels which his fatherland had withheld from him and rapidly rose to the front rank of world pianists. His subsequent life became a series of uninterrupted triumphs and even his earlier creative work has been meeting with belated recognition, illumined by the light of his inspired playing.

But apparently the tragedy of being torn away from his country is still gnawing at his being. Curious is this silence of the tomb, literally sepulchral, which has overtaken the creative genius of the composer since the moment of his departure. True, he has composed his Fourth Piano Concerto. But still a period of eight years of silence is an enormous span for a composer. As if something had snapped in him at the time he parted with his native soil, his genius, rooted by mysterious ties in his fatherland, has no longer been able to issue a single sprout. Perhaps it was not only severance from his country that played the important part here but also other circumstances; grief over the fatherland on which the Revolution had left utterly new and indelible traces and changes to form an ineffaceable demarcation between Russia of the past and Russia of the future.   A stranger to politics, the composer perhaps lived through these politics on a plane of deeper feeling than had various sworn master-politicians.

Since then the musical world has changed.   Music has entered upon a new era.   If Skryabin already seemed terrible and destructive to the guardians of the old traditions of music, one of whom Rakhmaninoff undoubtedly was, what could he say and feel about the new, the newest music? He, the servant of the ancient gods, saw the new generations follow the new music, saw it please, saw it conquer.   He felt that the old music was perishing in this new understanding.   And to him, will-less, by nature uninclined to blaze new paths for himself as the vigorous innovators were blazing them, inclined rather towards a passive contemplation of events, it may have appeared that none wanted his creative work any longer, that he was doomed always to be old-fashioned.   At the same time the honesty of a sincere musician did not allow him to force himself to pretend to adapt himself to these sounds of a modernity which he did not understand, and he felt only amazement that he, a musician and unquestionably a good musician, should be so deaf and blind to all these phenomena.   Who is wrong then?   What magic power has spell-bound the musical world and made fine and great musicians deaf to beauties in music and at the same time turned into great and profound connoisseurs some former agents of electrical societies who could not distinguish one note from another and would not recognise their favourite composer if the name had not been given them?   Who would inveigh against him another composer's name ascribed to them through error or purpose? No doubt this is favourable soil for everlasting pessimism and musical despair, a soil the more favourable because

Rakhmaninoff's creative art in general had even previously been subject to such spasms and interruptions. Doubt of himself, doubt of his own powers, of his own gifts which overcame Chaykovski and himself in earlier days, doubt of the integrity of the highest musical values and only a vague notion of the world's musical rebirth which had taken place, with its destruction of old values and the coming of a new generation with tastes forever vitiated here was enough to destroy the artistic equilibrium in an organism as unstable and passive as Rakhmaninoff's, and temporarily stop up completely the well-springs of creative art.

I have already said that to our mind the inimical shouts against Rakhmaninoff and the belittling, which was very fashionable at one time, cannot diminish the importance of this important and sincere composer. Rakhmaninoff is not one of those who die and are forgotten. In the history of Russian music his is too prominent a figure. Years of seeking new paths and wandering will pass by. Spasms of musical taste will be over, if indeed we are not already on the threshhold of a new musical era and the genuine renaissance of the musical world. Rakhmaninoff will take his place in history as a great and original personality, not only as a pianist of genius, in which capacity he has already become a part of history, but also as a prominent composer with flashes of true genius which he could not put into flesh and blood at the very end, prevented, as he was, not so much by the inadequacy of his gifts as by the peculiarities of his temperament.

He stands side by side with Chaykovski, not only as disciple and follower, but also in musical personality. Rakhmaninoff is the extreme expression of turbulent Russian Bohemianism, a passive and heroic soul. He is not a culminating phenomenon but one of the very great ones. The relation between him and Chaykovski is approximately the same as that between the Frenchmen Ravel and Debussy. It is a kinship of inner worlds with the preservation of the characteristics of the "species." Speaking biologically, the genus is the same but the species is different. Rakhmaninoff is a great master and we know that mastery is eternal and determines eternity even when lacking certain attributes. Rakhmaninoff's compositions bear within them, in common with Chaykovski, an inharmoniousness of form, which in the case of Chaykovski was overcome by a genius's insight of the general structure and dynamics of feeling and emotion. Rakhmaninoff lacks this insight and hence his compositions seem more formless, frequently more verbose.

The very long interval of silence on his part permits us to scan his creative work as a whole that is finished. Perhaps it is really finished, and new compositions, should they appear, will hardly alter anything in its mature and settled mastery. But in spite of this completion because of which we no longer await anything unexpected from Rakhmaninoff, it would be a source of sorrow to think that this great composer should be silent to the last. Recent information that he has composed new works in larger forms, justifies the hope that his silence, whether enforced upon him by yearning for his native land and musical fatherland or for the "old musical world perception," has come to an end and that our self-centred and impenetrably reserved composer, in accordance with his psychology, will still fearlessly say the words which he has to say, without considering how they will be received by the ever-changing, accidental and inconstant world.

VLADIMIR RYEBIKOFF

(1866–1922)

STRANGE was the fate of this composer who went to his grave unnoticed, after a humdrum life, against the darkly ominous and turbulent background of unfolding revolutionary events. He was forgotten even in his native land, and many musicians there were who went out of their way to humiliate and belittle a composer who, in the light of historical criticism, had played a prominent rôle in the last period of Russian music.

Ryebikoff did not escape that strong coating of artistic dilettantism which, in one or another degree, is peculiar to the mightiest geniuses of Russian art, Musorgski, Borodin, even Skryabin. Perhaps he was born too early or out of place. An early impressionist, the first "decadent" in Russia, which at the time had not grown up to impressionism, one of the early pioneers of that school of "destruction of traditions" which subsequently swept over the whole world in huge waves, Ryebikoff's only fault was perhaps that his too advanced ideas about musical theory and esthetics proved unsupported by an equal intensity of the creative art itself. His talent, which can in nowise be called feeble or poor, is below his ideas as an innovator. He elicited ridicule on the part of some and ardent love on the part of others, who alas, were at that time too youthful and too weak in art themselves to create epochs and influence them with their personal opinions.

Occasionally it happens that persons endowed with creative gifts in a moderate degree, but not with the gorgeous super-abundance of genius, loom up importantly in historical perspective. Nearly all early pioneers of any movement whatever are such. Their contemporaries pass by them either with ridicule or indifference, for their creative art does not possess that dazzling quality which makes even a foe stop, while the truth which they bear within is still incomprehensible to the many or has not yet been legibly re-. vealed or disclosed.

When Ryebikoff began to do creative work, the Russian musical milieu was still primitive. The great masses of the public did not understand their own greatest geniuses. With a feeling of perplexity and frequently with hate and contempt, even the most prominent musicians still passed by the works of Musorgski. Borodin and Rimski-Korsakoff called forth puzzled feelings and frequently biting and inimical criticism; Chaykovski was just beginning to gain a strong hold on public opinion. The most prominent musicians of that time were strongly coloured in conservative hues, and greeted with hatred and unconcealed hostility anything that smacked of innovation. Wagner, Liszt, Berlioz, even Grieg and Brahms, who unexpectedly fell into disfavour in Russia, possibly owing to Chaykovski's personal tastes, were regarded as enemies and the end and ruin of musical art. But one would in vain seek a harmonious system of esthetics and taste in these conservatives. What there was was accidental, and merely the youthful snobbishness of the first Russians who had been initiated into Western European classical culture in the conservatories just then founded by the Rubinsteins, valued this new acquisition highly. Russian musicians had just come to feel the beauty of form in classical music, and after a period of dilettantism, had just succeeded in learning and gaining faith in the immanence of musical laws. Suddenly a musician came who called once more to innovation, to the destruction of form, who sowed once more the seeds of doubt in the immanence of music laws taught in the conservatories.

Inevitably, the first and older generations of musicians, pioneers in conservatory culture, took a hostile and contemptuous stand against a young, unknown composer who moreover, after Richard Wagner's example, was even preaching his musical theories. In the nineties of the last century, when Ryebikoff was beginning his work, Richard Wagner meant to the Russian musicians a black and sombre scarecrow, whom it was considered a mark of musical good taste to hate. . . .

But in reality Ryebikoff was not at all dreadful. The views which he had conceived and formulated in a series of articles are often naïve in form, and almost always display a small amount of information in the philosophy of art. His school may be called "sensualism." "Music is the language of the senses," said Ryebikoff. He believed naïvely that every feeling is adequately expressed by one or another musical melody or harmony. In his pedagogical work he educated pupils to compose music for strictly defined "feelings." The naïve philosopher-musician believed that every feeling can be expressed in words.

"Music is a language of feelings, and feelings have neither form, nor laws, nor rules," so preached Ryebikoff. Hence, his slogan of complete freedom of chords and his admission of everything "forbidden." No limitations, no restrictions for the creator. Be "filled to the brim with feeling and be able to express it adequately" in sound.

And Ryebikoff strove to destroy boundaries, and strove to be bold and impudent as far as his essentially modest and somewhat phlegmatic nature permitted him. But there was a literary quality in his impetus; insufficient force was felt in his threats addressed to the existing musical régime. Possibly this very "shallowness" of feeling, his lack of a revolutionary form in thought or the genuine might of the innovator, were responsible for the fact that he attracted much less notice than he deserved. At one time, nevertheless, he gained great popularity in the newly-born circles of Russian youth with tendencies toward innovations. He became a sort of local idol and there were people who seriously deemed him an epoch-maker, one who had something new to say in music,—a genius.

His music, if we disregard all his discussions and prefaces, which frequently hindered more than helped, is in closest kinship with the "impressionist" Grieg. Without casting any reflexions, one can say, nevertheless, that without making the proclamations and the manifestoes in which Ryebikoff anticipated the futurists, Grieg long before had in actual music practically arrived at many of those liberties which Ryebikoff only preached. Possibly the innovating tendencies of Ryebikoff were nurtured by still another composer whose personality and fate were touchingly similar to the fate and personality of Ryebikoff himself; I speak of the French "Father of impressionism," Erik Sati, also unrecognised in his time yet important in the history of French music, who somehow suddenly and tardily came into bloom. Ryebikoff is the "Sati of Russian music." Even the psychological shallowness and miniaturism of his musical thoughts are similar to Sati's. And both are drawn to the fairy-tale, to a child's world, where such Lilliputian innovators can, without harm, follow their musical taste and produce tempests in teapots and revolutions in tumblers of water.

But occasionally we chance to hear wisdom even from children. And miniaturism in art is not a negative quality, but an attribute only, and strangely, Ryebikoff really innovated with his feeble yet persistent hands and blazed certain new paths in his limited and miniature world. He was the first to "dare" conclude his miniature compositions with dissonances, a trick to which considerably later, Debussy and Skryabin resorted, and now almost all composers. He was the first to begin to cultivate chords in fifths, fourths, and the harmonies in which even an inexperienced hearer will detect a kinship to those which subsequently made Debussy famous.

This fateful injustice of unrecognised priority in the realm of creating new harmonies and establishing new liberties, constituted the tragedy of Ryebikoff's life. He could not reconcile himself to being left in the shade, while Debussy and Skryabin, his "imitators" as he proudly declared, won recognition and world-wide fame. Debussy has been acclaimed as a genius; Ryebikoff who created the new world of harmonies, is little known even in Russia. His miniature self could not grasp the fact that genius is not the creation of the means, but the accomplishment of an end by them. That after all the merit of "invention" in art is of secondary importance, for the centre of gravity lies in thought and its adequate embodiment.

As I have already mentioned, Ryebikoff began in the style of Grieg and partly of Chaykovski. From Grieg he has the tendency to miniatureness of external form, that laconic language of little preludes and poems. Anticipating that same hated Debussy, Ryebikoff gave his smaller pieces fragmentary poetic headings, such as *An Urge to the Infinite*, etc. He was the first Russian musician to set his songs to texts by the Russian symbolist poets, Balmont and Bryusoff (then called "decadents"). Once more, anticipating the French impressionists, Ravel and Debussy, he composed fragments for Kryloff's fables, for performance on the stage, endeavouring to gain admission for that didactic genius of literature into the current of music. However, in this instance, Ryebikoff was not outside the influence of the great realist Musorgski and his famous *Nursery*. In his restless impulse to widen musical form, he created psychological tableaux—*Slavery and Freedom, Impulse and Achievement*—striving to express abstract thoughts in tone. His *Melo-mimics* represent an anticipation of the craze for the mimic ballet with music, which is characteristic of the early years of the twentieth century. These *Melomimics* are musical miniatures planned for accompaniment by mimics in movements and dances. Here he undoubtedly anticipated the latest Russian and French ballets of Stravinski and Debussy. His miniaturism never leaves him for a moment, not only when he develops childish and fairy-tale themes, such as the opera *Christmas Tree*, the Suite *Mila and Nolli*, Kryloff's *Fables*, etc., but even when he enters into the realm of subjects majestic and serious, philosophical and cosmic.

As early as the beginning of the twentieth century, it became clear that Ryebikoff had been outdistanced by others in his own field. His ideas several years before had been too new and fresh, too extraordinary, and he was too early a pioneer of his modernism, correctly previsioning the future though they did. But he lacked the power of a pure musical talent. His talent was pleasing and lovely and filled with fine musical taste, but it was not puissant, as the talent of a pioneer must be. While eager to destroy norms and boundaries, to start a revolution in music, he was by nature an exceedingly modest and pacific musician, and did not by far destroy all that he wished to destroy and what should have been destroyed long before. Other more powerful and striking talents made their appearance and Ryebikoff's ideas, then already floating in the air, were accepted by them and given more striking and convincing expression. These descendants of Ryebikoff, or "his imitators," as he used to say in his obstinate pride, were able to convince the musical world and public of the truth of his ideas, for the recognition of which he himself had fought in vain. And beginning with the twentieth century, Ryebikoff felt that his name and his creative work were already fatally put into shade by other more recent and brilliant talents, who were robbing him of what he had with such care invented and nurtured in his miniature hot-houses. He was tortured with the torments of envy, the most terrible envy of all, artistic envy. He would not surrender, he strove to conquer for himself and began to invent afresh things still more novel; but his talent, having reached full growth, was completely formed and no longer supple. It would not yield to new directions and his creative work began to give the sense of mental effort and "intention," the constant presence of the tenseness of invention not of inspiration. It became strangely schematic. He endeavoured by means of it to conquer the age and his rivals, and constructed compositions on some sheerly concocted principle. For instance, the whole opera *The Abyss*, on a subject taken from Lyeonid Andreyeff, and essentially naturalistic and not musical, is built up exclusively of chords in seconds; the psychologic tableau *Alpha and Omega*, on a cosmic theme, exclusively on augmented triads. His creative spirit was drying up and the once fresh and naïvely miniature inspiration had deserted him.

And at that very time new idols, new gods had appeared on the musical horizon. Impressionism conceived by Ryebikoff, was being developed by the powerful hands of Debussy, Rimski-Korsakoff and Skryabin, all his musical innovations were snatched up, of course mostly without any evil intent, and even without knowledge of committing plagiarism on the part of these "great ones," simply because the time had come for it in music, and it rang forth victoriously from the hands of these giants. He was completely pushed into the background, and in the light of the conflagration of the maturing grandiose World War events, his miniature world seemed still more trivial and feeble than before. Deserted and forgotten, alone with his profound tragedy of non-recognition and injury, even with a feeling of having been robbed, Ryebikoff died during the Revolution, when none any longer had use for "psychologic tableaux," or "melomimics." He died in extreme straits, deserted by the musical world, forgotten even by his pupils.

But we, descendants and recorders of events, must pay due homage to this martyr of musical history; Ryebikoff was right in many things, and in many respects he was a true pioneer, the true father of modernity, the sire of mighty sons of modern music, and as such he is deservedly entitled, not only to recognition but to profound regard. Musical practice and life are pitiless, and without remorse or conscience, forget the intermediate and the initial, remembering only the fulfilment and the culmination. Who remembers the ancestors of Bach or Beethoven? How many know how much the great author of the Ninth Symphony has in common with the modest and now forgotten Clementi? But musical history is juster and more grateful. It cherishes the memory not only of those who have reached the peaks, but even of those modest toilers and workers who, though unaware of it themselves, have helped others to climb the summits and made their glory possible. To these intermediate, historically important personages belongs Ryebikoff.

NIKOLAY METNER

(Born 1879)

NIKOLAY METNER, the youngest member of the famous pleiad including Skryabin and Rakhmaninoff, presents the interesting type of half-Russian, half-Germanic composer, belonging to Russia by his musical education and to Germany by blood and artistic sympathies. But it would be an error to suppose that the "Germany" to which Metner belongs has anything whatever to do with contemporary Germany, the Germany of the twentieth century.

Descendant of Livonian Germans, almost perfectly Russified during his long residence on Russian territory, Metner retained German traits, if any, only atavistically—the German traits of old romantic Germany, of Schlegel and Schiller, Goethe and the great period of literature and music. The musical phenomenon of Metner is utterly inconceivable in other countries except Russia. In order to grasp his significance for the Russians, one must bear in mind that precisely German music, in spite of its unquestionable and enormous inner influence, was treated with a certain scornful neglect in Russia. The most characteristic manifestations of the German spirit were considered bad or amusing, deserving of ridicule and irony. The German spirit was to a considerable part of the Russian musical intelligentsia synonymous with either pedantism and crumb-picking or sentimentalism. World phenomena, such as Beethoven, were usually left out of account, but our characterisation of the Russian attitude toward the Germans would be incorrect and incomplete if we did not mention that the leaders of the musical world who gave tone to the whole Russian musical society, namely, the chiefs of the mighty *Koochka,* always spoke scornfully and disapprovingly of all great German musicians. In the imagination and catechism of Balakireff, who was the *Koochka's* law-giver in taste, Bach was a sort of composing machine and not infrequently called forth scornful jeering; Beethoven was the "composer of marches for military revues," Mendelssohn, a sentimental and salon composer, the synonym of bad taste in music. The genuis Wagner was accused of being devoid of talent and possessing poor discernment; scornful ridicule at his expense filled the whole critical activity of the composer Cui, one of the leading pillars of the *Koochka.* Nobody wanted to know anything of Brahms and could not stand him. He was considered a most ordinary "German" and even Chaykovski did not understand what, "really speaking, distinguished him from Raff." A certain feeble exception was occasionally made in favour of Schumann, but even that, so feeble. Russian culture, especially in the striking nationalistic aspect, which it manifested in the *Koochka,* separated itself decisively and categorically from German culture. To a degree, it scorned also Italian culture, in the narrow sense of "Italian Opera," and French culture. It decisively asserted the hegemony of Russia in music.

An antagonism of this sort might seem queer, particularly toward cultural phenomena which themselves had unquestionably given origin to all Russian music, but the explanatory and to a certain degree justifying circumstances here are the historic conditions of the development of Russian music. For a long time Russian music had been in the cultural bondage of "Italian Opera" which was the favourite music of aristocratic society and hence, in the eyes of Russian musical patriots, the obstacle in the way of development of genuine *Russian* music. Russian composers could not forge ahead; in their own country they met with complete disapproval. The public of aristocratic circles, which properly speaking was at that time the only "public," scornfully dubbed the compositions of the original genius Glinka "coachmen's music," and unequivocally preferred the Italians and their opera. Hardly having somewhat escaped from the captivity of Italian culture, Russian music fell into that of German, and this captivity grew the worse, thanks to the Germanophile sympathies of the founder of the Russian conservatories, Rubinstein. The activity of the Russian National School in the seventies of the last century, with Balakireff, Musorgski, Stasoff and Cui at its head, was chiefly a struggle with Germanophile influence in the Conservatory under Rubinstein and his party. Rubinstein was a "classicophile," and admirer of Beethoven and Mendelssohn. Balakireff and his party, convinced that Russia should be original and that it could become so, hated both Beethoven and Mendelssohn and all German music more strongly than wisely. Everything German was considered synonymous with haughty lack of talent and a sentimentality which took the place of genuine feeling. The whole science of music to which, not without reason, a German origin was attributed, was declared unnecessary, and musicians were invited to seek musical laws within themselves for their own creative art and not in Conservatory routine and rules. The Russian National School was ideologically very closely related to the Slavophile movement then fashionable in Russia. Developed on the soil of Russia's growing political might, it maintained that "the West had rotted through to the core and could give nothing to us, a young nation, that we had to seek within ourselves, in the innate riches of the Slavic race the foundation of our own culture, distinct from that of Western European." Political Slavophilism found an echo both in Russian literature and in music, giving origin, in the latter, to the whole movement of national art. In politics, as well, it created its own ideals, unlike the Western European ideals of democracy and parliamentarism, and always it waged fierce war against Occidentalism, personified by Rubinstein and the Conservatory in the field of music. Under this banner of musical Slavophilism Russian music developed, for the gifts of the group of Slavophiles, Musorgski, Borodin, Rimski-Korsakoff, were considerably greater than those of their adversaries, among which one could mention only the names of Rubinstein and Chaykovski. But not even these latter could escape the influence of the intensity of musical gifts of the National School, even though at variance with them ideologically. Therefore the anti-German tastes of the *Koochkists* gradually gained general acceptance in Russia, although in no pronounced degree. The protracted non-recognition of such figures of genius as Brahms and Wagner is a particularly striking testimony of the hypnosis of anti-Germanism which had developed.

This hypnosis continued until the twentieth century. Only then began a natural and of course correspondingly stormy reaction. In the first place Wagner was "discovered," and then followed Brahms, accursed of all Russian authorities. In Moscow, in 1905, there was even formed a special Brahms Society. And one cannot but conclude that the musical phenomenon of Metner was essentially nothing but a reaction against anti-Germanism, and a trend in the direction of active Germanism.

The reaction was intensified also by a series of accessory circumstances that had an indirect bearing upon it. At that time, the triumphant march of modernism was beginning. Impressionistic moods, complex harmonies, the cult of formlessness and musical arrhythmy, vague, nervous and elusive rhythms, were coming into vogue. Old musicians did not understand the new music. Others were bored by this arrhythmy, by these formlessnesses of the new creative art, by the "unmusical element" intruding into it. The phenomenon of Metner had a double meaning. On the one hand, Metner meant, as it were, the paying of our debt to the Germans and the restoration of the influence of German music. He sprang wholly and entirely from the bosom of the "most German Germans," from Brahms, Schumann and partly Wagner. And to Russian music these influences, unadorned and underscored, appeared as a novelty, although the absolutely new elements in Metner's creative work are not numerous. He was just new to Russia. His very portrait which recalls the antique engravings of old masters or organists, was typically German. In his ethical and artistic make-up, we see numerous similarities to Tañeyeff. The same uprightness, the same purity and holiness of attitude towards music which in the full sense of the word was not a "career" but a service, the absence of all compromises with his musical conscience. Metner did not understand and did not recognise new music. Even the last compositions of Skryabin provoked the feeling of aversion in him; he disliked the new Frenchmen for their formlessness and arrhythmy, his sympathies came to an abrupt end with Wagner and the last Russian romantics. From the very beginning of his creative past, Metner was himself, and his style, sharply pronounced even in his earliest compositions, subsequently underwent no essential changes.

There is no doubt in my mind that Metner was a sort of Renaissance of the Brahmsian spirit in music and the first manifestations of this spirit in Russian music. Hence he appeared many times more "original" than he appeared in the eyes of German musicians who precisely did not credit him with the qualities of originality. True, Metner's originality and Metner's independence are of peculiar finesse. It is not a decorative, coarse originality which of itself strikes the eye and ear. Metner hardly resorts to the complex chords beloved of the moderns. His originality expresses itself mainly in a vivid and specific rhythm, in which precision and definiteness combine in an original manner with a sort of mental *a priori* content. Occasionally it seems that the composer invents these rhythmic combinations like mathematical formulas and on this basis apportions his inspiration. Austere and severe in style, somewhat niggardly and dryish in melody, Metner does not appeal immediately to the customary and broad sentiment of the public. On first hearing his music may appear somewhat dry and planned. His rhythmics, like everything too specifically characteristic, possess fatiguing qualities. In this he is similar to Schumann with whom just such hypertrophies of rhythmic monotony are not infrequent. His music is not that of a man of frank and free sentiment, but the music of a profound thinker, a philosopher-musician who feels deeply in his own way and with severe reserve, that chastely leaves many things unsaid. Metner has lived his life in a select intellectual circle, mingling with the best and highest-minded representatives of Russian literature and philosophy. The influences of German idealistic philosophy and that of its Russian branch, the Russian philosophic school, have stamped his creative art and expressed themselves in his sympathy with the great German poet, Goethe, with Nietzsche, to whose texts Metner has set many of his songs, and with the Russian philosopher-poets, such as Andrey Byely and Tyutcheff, who also supplied him with texts for music.

Like every other "philosophy," Metner's music is for the few. And apparently this is more a source of joy than sadness to him. He is least of all a "composer for the crowd and for fame." Even in appearance similar to the old masters, locked up within himself and solitary, he still prays in the silence of his solitude, to his ancient beloved god, having lost no faith, as all others have, either in the perceptive faculties of human reason, or in the great effect of sentiment and love. Partly sentimental, as are all Germans by nature, and simultaneously severely reserved, he has impressed on his creative art the eternal traditions of Bach, Beethoven and Brahms, and his music really possesses much which comes in a direct line from the "three great B's" as the Germans call them.

I have already said that in Metner's make-up there is a similarity to Tañeyeff. But there is also a great difference. In reality Tañeyeff "dreamed to be what Metner became." Metner's talent is more definite, his style is more sustained, and he is far better educated, both as a man and as a musician. Tañeyeff lived, worked and developed at a time when the innate Russian dilettantism in music was beginning to die out. Searching and deeply intelligent by nature, he lacked, to his own great sorrow, a true, profound education, except in music. Metner was more fortunate. He was born in the age of developed intellectualism. He lived in a select circle of thinkers. He displayed a more clear-cut and completely formed taste and sense of musical style. His attitude towards music is perhaps still more consistent and profound than Tañeyeff's. And he is more severe towards himself as a composer. Possessing as he does a uniformly sustained technique, he is a true master of composition.

For a long time Metner was Moscow's recognised composer. In that city, the centre of Russia's intellectual forces, he was warmly acclaimed by a small but powerful group of musicians. The conjuncture of the musical world shaped itself so that Metner was obliged to become the opponent of Skryabin for whom he personally felt great respect, although only for his early compositions. Musical life had placed Metner and Rakhmaninoff at the head of the party of conservatives who fought for the old ideals of music against the innovations and excesses of the young school, headed by Skryabin. These two composers, bound to this day by the ties of deep friendship, were united by musical events as representatives "of one musical party."

In opposition to the vagueness of the impressionist rhythms, Metner put forth his own almost classical clean-cut rhythm. In opposition to the enthusiastic and half hysterical excesses of "emotional expressionism," he put forth his modesty and reserve of feeling; against the violence of the complexity of harmonies, simplicity of harmony; against music as a sort of "magic, intoxicating remedy" and application to occult magic, the idea of pure "music in itself." The Moscow group of Metner's admirers was already numerous in 1915, and the responsible word "genius" was uttered, though it is hard to say how much justification there was for applying it. But St. Petersburg, in the persons of its most prominent musicians, had not yet recognised the new genius. The Revolution came and Metner went abroad, where he is still living. And here the strange fate befell him which emphasised the fact that the appreciation of talent in a given country depends in an extraordinary degree upon the history of music in that land, and that what had appeared unquestionably striking on a Russian scale and against a Russian background, dwindled exceedingly on a scale of European and world modernity.

But of this fate—later. Meanwhile, let us return to Metner's creative work. His intimately serious talent naturally clung to "intimate forms." He composed almost exclusively for the piano (he is a first-class pianist himself), and for the voice. Metner does not seem to display any strong desire to step beyond the drawn limits of this narrow world, in which he apparently finds sufficient depth and in which his characteristic earnest gravity and dislike for external embellishment find a natural medium.

Metner is a graphic in his music. He does not like and does not genuinely feel the tonal charm of colour. His music is minus colour, his tones are not living substances which sparkle with the hues of the rainbow, but thought-out formulas. Involuntarily, a comparison with Brahms suggests itself. And indeed, just with this composer, Metner has very many traits in common, though Brahms with all his austerity is softer, more passionate and more varied than

Metner, to whom the quality of tonal eroticism so developed in Skryabin is exceedingly alien. Metner is a composer sexless in his creative work, intensity of feeling is replaced in him by intensity of "thought about feeling." Compared with him, Brahms is well-nigh an enthusiast. With Metner, the reserve of feeling is so strong that occasionally it does not reach the hearer at all, remaining as the inner quality and experience of the author.

Metner deserted the intimacy of creative art only to write two piano concertos, the second still unpublished, in which he came in partial touch with the world of the orchestra. This contact, as could easily have been foreseen, was purely formal; in Metner's eyes the orchestra is merely the generally accepted method of accompanying the pianist and not a world of its own with its own laws. And in spite of the fact that Metner, who made a late début with these orchestral compositions, had succeeded very well with them, they are not characteristic of his creative art.

His creative work is best characterised by his *Fairy-Tales*, a type of composition invented by him and partly similar to the old romantic form of the Ballad. Metner's *Fairy-Tales* unquestionably belong not only to the best in his creative work, but to the productions of romantic inspiration in general. But Metner's romanticism is peculiar. It is not the romanticism of enchantment, but rather the romanticism of the grotesque. Metner's fantastic world, which opens for us through the sounds of his *Fairy-Tales*, is not the world of elves and witchery, but the poetry of ancient heroic legends, and most of all an echo of the underworld of Nibelungs, gnomes and mountain kings. Such I feel this music to be. It has no brightness and radiance, but dusk and darkness. Occasionally it has ominousness and a certain closeness. In his *Fairy-Tales*, Metner is neither heavenly, nor ethereal, nor in the clouds, but earthly, even earthy, subterranean. Fleeing from the world which intrudes into his abode, fleeing from this tumult of modernity, seeking to be a recluse in a lonely tower, Metner willy-nilly breathes stifled air. Having no exit "to heaven" he yearns for earthly moods, goes down into the subterranean Nibelheim and there finds his fairy-tale moods. His isolated chapel where he prays to his ancient gods of music, is visited by underworld "elementals" who annoy the musician-philosopher with their appearance, and this is natural, for in our times one has to pay the penalty for hermitage, at any rate if it does not assume a religious character. And Metner's music, with all its seriousness, is "philosophical" and not religious. And the philosopher-ascetic, involuntarily conjures no rainbow-hued, fascinating pictures, no captivating world, but a world sombre and weird, a fantastic and nightmare world, and he embodies it in his creative work.

The *Fairy-Tales* are the most powerful compositions of Metner. But his creative work in the realm of sonata is no less interesting. Metner is a genuine classic in this sphere. Over his compositions hovers the spirit of Beethoven's last Sonatas. Further it is difficult to characterise these compositions. They are as a rule written in a broad form, massive in exposition, profound in content, and are always provided with a certain amount of that musical "erudition" which makes them hard to grasp and at the same time paralyses emotional impression from the numerous details of beauty. Something heavily Gothic is felt in this creative art. A mass of embellishments, rhythmic details which intertwine bizarrely and fantastically, screening the perspective of the composition's large lines. A mass of most painstaking labour, of minute designs which recall the sculptured details in great Gothic cathedrals. And all executed in so masterly and complex a fashion that first impressions are unable to appreciate it justly. A non-musician will surely be taken aback by this composition and will not even understand all the mastery that has been lavished upon it. Metner's sonatas

are creations of the same category as Bach's and Brahms',—
"one must go to meet this music, it will not come to meet
us," as Liszt said of Beethoven.

The Beethoven and Brahms traits are strong in Metner.
But this apostolic succession alone would not of course be
sufficient to indicate a supreme talent. I should say, on
the contrary, that this Beethovenism which brought Metner
to the front ranks of composers in Russia and now spells
ruin for him in the wider world, is too heavy a burden, for
thanks to it, his true countenance is invisible at first glance.
Metner is not so big as Beethoven and Brahms, there is no
doubt of that, but he possesses some things of value which
in turn distinguish him from them, his own individuality,
the traits of which while not so brilliant may however be
perceived even by the non-musician.

His songs also are interesting, in which our Russian composer definitely continues the line of "great German creative
art" begun by Schubert and brought to a close by Hugo
Wolf. Metner's songs are almost of the old German type.
The style of "Russian artistic song" is entirely different.
Emotional melody is not in Metner's spirit, nor is free,
broad tunefulness. His melody is scantish, austere, reserved,
his pathos never possesses the traits of frenzy. There is
always the thought checking the sentiment, yet simultaneously deepening it. Like the wise composer and intellectually
experienced man that he is, Metner makes exclusive use of
first-class poetical works for his texts. He sets the music
of his songs to words by such lights of Russian and world
literature as Goethe, Nietzsche, Pushkin, Tyutcheff. Strange
as it may seem to our mind, much in this music does not
appear to be in harmony with the text. The "pagan"
Goethe, and the no less pagan and epicurean Pushkin, singer
of Apollonic beauty and voluptuousness, are not at all consonant with Metner's creative art, in which there is no pagan
radiance at all, but on the contrary the colourless and

graphic complexity of the Gothic. Nietzsche and the profound yet lapidary Tyutcheff, attain a successful embodiment in Metner's musical fabric. Things grow still worse when our composer, in spite of his serious and awkward nature, suddenly conceives an impulse to express in music moods of elegance and grace; these moments are the weakest in his creative work.

Metner is a productive, persistent and assiduous composer, though it cannot be said that he composes rapidly. His work always shows marks of labour. It is not facile; it is the product of much thought and its rapidity is determined only by the composer's mastery. He achieved this mastery and this style almost at once, and they were highly esteemed by the Russian musicians of the War and pre-War periods.

We are now coming to the exposition of the "tragedy of Metner" which, in its general outlines, coincides with the "tragedy of Rakhmaninoff" and possibly posesses roots in common with it. This tragedy began with his settling abroad after leaving Russia, swept by the fire of the Revolution that completely upset the usual "rhythm of life" for the composer. Locked within himself and isolated, he came with horror to the conviction that his inner world was no longer insured against invasions from without. However he might try to separate himself from the outer world with a Chinese wall, the thunders of Revolution penetrated into his refuge and brought him to a state of madness. His creative work had no contact whatever with the Revolution. The recluse philosopher,—what feelings could he have towards people who desired to establish heaven on earth by means nowhere tried before? Rudeness and the physical discomforts of the trying revolutionary régime completely unbalanced him and the composer left Russia a short while after the departure of Rakhmaninoff, apparently for similar reasons.

On going abroad, Metner was already a prominent composer in Russia and a recognised quantity. Moreover, as I have said, he was a determined and "uncompromising hater" of everything modernistic. He disliked Strauss and Debussy, let alone subsequent musicians. Great was his horror when out of his isolation he got into a noisy European world infected with materialism, almost entirely devoid of that "holy" attitude towards music which alone had value in Metner's eyes. There was no music at all to his liking and his straightforwardness making him say so, made him uncomfortable and life a torture. His compositions met with no success; it was a sad fact which very soon became clear to him. It was not the lack of success that hurt; Metner was not of those musicians who are prostrated through lack of success. The tragedy lay in the fact that he grew more and more convinced that his musical conception of the world was becoming an anachronism, that he was alone in the world and that not the crowd alone, but musicians as well, had completely changed and begun to feel music in a different manner. Nowhere did he find people who held similar feelings and similar views. The musical world suddenly became a hostile and incomprehensible agglomerate of persons, speaking a foreign tongue. This tragedy was Rakhmaninoff's, too, but perhaps Metner lived it more deeply. The European public's failure to understand him had deep roots. First and principally in German zones, Metner's music could not produce any impression simply because in the eyes of Germans he was but a mere imitator of Brahms and other composers of the "obsolete school." They could not descry anything new, the new that was new for Russia. At the present time the German musical world is passing through an epidemic of eagerness for novelty, ancient tradition has broken down, and those who represent tradition cannot boast of possessing talent. The musicians of Germany could not help seeing in Metner but "one of many," a composer of the antique style in which nobody takes any interest at present. They had neither time nor desire to delve into the details of this music and find out what it had to offer. The American public to which Metner made his bow, was in a still greater state of innocence regarding his "historical importance." The austere and too reserved style of Metner did not strike conviction on first acquaintance. Disappointment was still greater in France, where utterly different tendencies reign, where musical modernism marches triumphantly over the shards of smashed idols, and where, instead of tradition and deep respect for art, fashion and changing tastes have always held sway. Nobody noticed Metner as a composer; at best he proved to be one of the "composing pianists," and the same condescending attitude was assumed towards his creative work as to the compositions of Josef Hofmann and others. They could not understand the austere and, in a modern sense, too serious make-up of the new musician. Metner remained unrecognised, and this must not surprise us, for even the greater and more brilliant Skryabin was scarcely noticed against the background of the contemporary European Vanity Fair of music.

He has withdrawn into his own inner world and continues to create therein, evincing both heroism and the nature of a true philosopher. If the music which he loves and worships has become silent throughout the world, if the world feels no need for it just now, it is nevertheless his, Metner's, duty to create what he, what his inner conscience believes is needed. Generations will pass, the fickle wheel of fashion will revolve many times, carrying into the stream of oblivion many names now acclaimed, and sometime in the future, in its geological researches, music will hit upon vestiges of an honest and courageous composer who has this incontestable advantage over many of his contemporaries, that he knows what he does and is convinced of the necessity of exactly this work.

Metner is not so small in magnitude that he can sink into

the abyss without a trace. On the contrary, there is great likelihood that he is just the composer for the future, the composer for the coming era of a calmer and more objective attitude towards art. But if really old music has died and will never return, then Metner's musical sunset assumes outlines of epic grandeur. The heroic death at the post of a faithful soldier of the ancient musical faith.

A. GRYECHANINOFF

(Born 1864)

In reality Gryechaninoff already belongs to the old generation of composers. He is sixty, great renown is his, and
some of his compositions such as his popular song *The
Steppe* are known the world over. Gryechaninoff was educated and developed in the surroundings of the "old musical
culture," as it existed in Russia forty years ago, when nothing
was heard of any modernism or innovation save that of the
Russian National School, and when Musorgski's daring
seemed more than unpardonable. Gryechaninoff's first essays
in composition placed him in the ranks of the adherents of the
Russian National School. His first compositions, among
them many of his songs and the opera *Dobrynya Nikitich,*
produced at one time on the stage of the Moscow Grand
Theatre, were written in the tones and the tuneful Russian
melodies, with the Russian themes and methods of harmonisation found among the chiefs of the Russian National School.
At the same time Gryechaninoff cultivated with great success two spheres in which he was destined to create a style
of his own and win for himself a really great name as a composer of church music and music for children. In the latter
field Gryechaninoff has created a number of genuine master-
pieces, proving a truly loving penetration into the original
and peculiar world of children. Gryechaninoff's "children's
music" is not Musorgski's "psychologising" directed at the
child's world. On the contrary, in these works the composer
can enter into this world himself, not as an outside observer,
but by becoming a child himself. Their enormous popularity
and the exceptional pleasure which the little musicians derive

from performing these compositions, offer the best proof
that Gryechaninoff has succeeded in solving brilliantly the
most difficult problem of "children's musical literature," without either the insincerity or the condescension of the usual
"children's composer." With infinite art and taste, Gryechaninoff introduces into this musical world of childhood
elements of Russian nationalism in the form of a folk-struc-
ture in his melodies and rhythms and in his favourite method
of using fairy-tales, adages, and proverbs as texts. Besides
their specific importance for children these compositions
show a great amount of purely musical invention, wit and
original application of musical resources as well as the genuine masterly technique of an experienced·and knowing composer. But however great the importance of this childhood world he has created, and to which he has devoted
much of his creative work, it would not be sufficient to
make Gryechaninoff what he stands for at present.

His work in the field of church music is unquestionably
more important than his "children's realm." In the creation
of artistic Russian church music, Gryechaninoff has been
continuing the line begun by Glinka, the father of Russian
music. The idea of this work is to utilise the old Russian-
Byzantine Church melodies and to work them over artistically, abreast with modern requirements and at the same
time, not to contradict, in matters of style, the melody itself
and the accepted type of Russian church service. This
problem is not as simple as it might appear at first glance.
Russian church singing is ritually locked in a choral world,
for the Russian Church does not permit the use of any
instruments in the church. To this day, it demands a well-
nigh antique style of musical exposition, at any rate, a style
which in its harmonic complexity has scarcely advanced beyond Palestrina and the music of the sixteenth century. This
singing imposes very burdensome conditions upon the composer. Under these conditions, to give music an interest and

a current significance, specific gifts are required. An ordinary composer as a rule cannot acquit himself of the problem without departing from the proper limits of style. Even the greatest of Russian composers, such as Chaykovski and Rakhmaninoff, turned to this field with a consciousness of great responsibility, and frequently the solution of their problem did not prove completely satisfactory, and produced results, musically interesting but departing too much from the style and its limitations. Being of ecclesiastical origin, Gryechaninoff from childhood had been familiar with the liturgy, and understood better than the others the inner meaning and structure of this style, which in regard to its grandioseness and impressiveness undoubtedly vies with that of Roman ecclesiasticism, and with Protestant choral music. A perfect master of choral orchestration, if one may use this expression, knowing ideally and to perfection the properties of the human voice, Gryechaninoff can extract from choral masses utterly unexpected and frequently overpowering effects. Along with the composer Kastal'ski, his senior, who confined himself almost exclusively to church music, Gryechaninoff at present stands out as the highest exponent of Russian church composition, a field which is almost unknown in Europe and has somehow always been left out in reviewing the achievements of Russian musical art.

In this field Gryechaninoff is also an innovator, if you will. His innovations must here be understood to be relative. Gryechaninoff widens the scope of the effects of music, displaying broad plans and a certain grandioseness of conception but without trespassing the limits of its style, as in the *Demyestvennaya Liturgy. Demyestvenny* (the word *domestica* in false disguise) meant in Russia in the seventeenth century, a liturgy composed in a rather free form with the addition of an element of greater solemnity, magnificance and even virtuosity. Gryechaninoff, availing himself of what the term *Demyestvenny* covers, still further widens the rôle of

music in the liturgy, bringing it more closely to the Western
European mass. In addition to the choir, universally accepted in Russia, he introduces into it as well, the organ and
symphonic orchestra, without at the same time, depriving the
music itself of its specific contours of Russian ecclesiastical
tunefulness. At its first appearance, Gryechaninoff's *Demyestvennaya* called forth numerous criticisms, principally in
ecclesiastical circles, who saw therein the collapse of the tradition of old choral singing. But the more liberal representatives of the clergy well understood that such broadening of
artistic effects was both inevitable and extremely useful. So
far, Gryechaninoff's *Demyestvennaya* has been the culminating point of his innovations, but in addition to it he has written numerous Canticles and Liturgies in the usual choral
form.

Quite apart from these two great departments in which
Gryechaninoff appears a prominent and original composer,
are his compositions in the field of worldly and instrumental
music, his symphonies, opera, chamber compositions and
songs. In instrumental music, he follows the traditions of
the Russian School and partly those of Glazunoff. His music
is of a comparatively neutral colour, being neither of too
national a hue nor too devoid of it. We do not find
originality in the direct and immediate meaning of the
word, we find the splendid composition of a master composer, and no more. His songs stand out from the mass of
his compositions because as one knowing in a masterly
fashion the field of the voice, and more at home therein,
Gryechaninoff is a vocal composer *par excellence.* Even the
songs not distinguished by originality are beautiful in the
masterly use he makes of vocal means, in their fitness for
singing, for which reason they have long enjoyed popularity
among singers and have been favourites of the public, not
only in Russia, but elsewhere.

The years 1910-1918, when enormous interest was shown

in Russia in new tendencies in music, laid their impress on the creative art of Gryechaninoff, who was generally rather unshaken by the winds of fashion. But time and fashion combined to produce their effect. In the group of songs published during this period, Gryechaninoff, as it were, pays tribute to vogue and the age. He leaves the national style, the Russian tunefulness vanishes, he begins to cull the texts for his music from the works of contemporary poets and · publishes collections of songs to words by Vyacheslav Ivanoff, Baudelaire, etc. Sharp, disssonant harmonies make their appearance in his style, vaguely recalling now Rimski-Korsakoff and then again, Debussy. This was not organic in our author's creative work; most likely it was a stray waft from the atmosphere surrounding him, a composer's involuntary and probably unconscious reaction to it. Subsequently, these accidental traits disappeared from his creative work, which unquestionably is something original and considerable in spite of the fact that Gryechaninoff was no seeker of new musical means of expression. Gryechaninoff's style in his creative work for church and children, in his bright and sincere melodiousness, in the immediate manner in which his musical conceptions impress his hearers, together with the true mastery of his art, have won him a great name not only in Russia, but abroad as well.

NIKOLAY MYASKOVSKI

(Born 1881)

NIKOLAY MYASKOVSKI came to the fore chiefly in the post-revolutionary era of Russian music, beginning with the year 1917. Prior to that time his creative work remained comparatively little known and even somewhat neglected. A pupil of Rimski-Korsakoff, a conservatory fellow-student of Prokofyeff, who was his junior in age (though not in success or fame), Myaskovski at first attracted no attention. But those were different times. Then there lived and worked such striking figures as Rakhmaninoff, Skryabin, Metner, upon whom the eyes of the whole musical world were fixed. Myaskovski was never so extreme an innovator as to attract attention by the mere extravagance of his manner, nor was he so strict and consistent a reactionary as Tañeyeff or Metner. Being neither "cold nor hot," he was too serious and too severe with himself as a musician to bring himself before the public gaze by artificial methods. And in one way or another, it required the setting of the principal luminaries who had worked in the creative sphere to permit the midnight star of Myaskovski to shine forth, and find admirers for its strange, dusky effulgence.

Myaskovski is, in the first place, a profound and interesting human individuality, and only afterwards a musician. He is a splendid musician, alert, understanding, profound and eagerly omnivorous; too interested in music, in musicians, too painstakingly studying their compositions. But all these musical traits are a secondary matter. First and foremost comes the image of a man of depth, morbidly and originally sensing the world. Myaskovski's attitude toward

149

the world has something in it of Dostoyevski, that complex, broken, sickly spirit in which neurasthenia passes into psychopathy and the realm of mental darkness. Russian music already possesses enough representatives of such psychopathological emotion, in whom diseased breaks of psychic emotion occasionally are transformed by genius into artistry. Musorgski, Chaykovski, Skryabin, these greatest geniuses among Russian musicians, were in reality abnormal in many respects, and now their number is increased by Feinberg and Myaskovski. Another queer feature makes Myaskovski akin to Dostoyevski,—the insufficient artistic re-creation of this diseased and great psyche.

In all probability, to appreciate Myaskovski's music and come to love it, one either must personally know the composer and grasp this personality, which as a personality is far more interesting than its musical expression, or one must by some transcendental method, come to feel this personality in his music which, as we have already said, expresses it but inadequately. Dostoyevski, too, was like this; his literary style and diction were gnarly and poorly polished, his prose could never be called artistic. Heavy and fatiguing to the sense of perception, he is nevertheless a genius, for so great is the psychological potency contained in his creative work, and so deep are the psychological abysses he plumbs. Of course it is too early to speak of Myaskovski's genius, although among his admirers there is a group of persons who credit him with it. But it is indubitable that, like Dostoyevski, Myaskovski is a man with a great soul, with a great experience, with morbid emotion and enormous lack of balance, and these qualities are partly expressed in his creative work; only partly, for his musical language is too often too primitive to utter his emotions. His musical style is too unfinished, uncouth, and unmodern. His musical material at first produces the impression of something too ordinary, non-original and imitative.

Music is a mysterious art. Occasionally by some transcendental means, it proves capable of telling the contents of its creator's soul, in spite of the exterior faltering form of the telling. At all events, Myaskovski can engender veneration, awe and respect. He can create around himself an atmosphere of genuine and profound friendship and musical devotion, of which no ordinary musician can boast. He is surrounded by an authoritative clique of friends who make propaganda for him sincerely and not out of fear, and who are genuinely and disinterestedly devoted to him. These musicians consider him the rising star, they deem Myaskovski the legitimate, natural and only successor of the two greatest Russian musicians, Musorgski and Chaykovski.

On the other hand, a musical analysis made without any friendly prejudice, but also without any hostile preconception, an objective analysis, shows nothing remarkable in this music. Is Myaskovski an innovator? No. Is he the creator of new musical means of expression? No. Do his compositions produce the impression of Titanic force and might, like those with which Wagner crushed the musical world? No. Myaskovski is no Titan and no giant, but a neurasthenic, and in this respect his descent from the neurasthenic Chaykovski is clear. In Myaskovski's creative work there are no traits upon which critical thought might pounce, to characterise him and say: "In this and that respect this composer is remarkable." But Myaskovski is elusive. Like an eel he slips out of the critical grip and no unusual external characteristic traits are found on him. "Features ordinary; has no special distinguishing marks." But what is it in this ordinary face that still without distinguishing marks does attract? and that brings him just now to the front ranks of young Russian music?

Perhaps Chaykovski, too, in his time, appeared to be like him. He too had no special distinguishing marks or qualities. Devoid of the instincts of the inventor, he never strove to discover anything or break down anything, and yet he possessed a physiognomy, his creative art possessed a quality whereby his compositions could at once be distinguished from any other. Myaskovski does not possess such a physiognomy in his creative work.

Having begun to compose approximately in Glazunoff's style, Myaskovski from the very first joined the ranks of the moderately inventive group, consisting of those who did not keep aloof from novelty, but combined it with demands for the organic descent from the past. Even when compared with Skryabin, Myaskovski is a reactionary, rather than a "revolutionary." But his creative work is strongly distinguished from Glazunoff by its organic restlessness. Glazunoff is formally clear and emotionally calm; Myaskovski is turbulent and emotionally broken. This brokenness lacks the Apollonic spirit of Skryabin, he does not recreate his brokenness, but enjoys its sickliness with a sadistic ecstasy at times. With his music he pulls at his own and other people's nerves. At the same time, this is not a mighty and puissant effect, but the pestering irritation of one mentally deranged, with a whimsical poverty of ideas, occasionally characteristic of such patients, sometimes with their sudden gorgeous efflorescence, at other times with malicious sadistic "bytaste." He loves dissonant, "tart" harmonies. He loves annoying, cutting harmonies. Occasionally he deliberately disregards the sense of measure in monotony and hypnotically wearies his hearers. Clarity is entirely foreign to his music; his music is a heavy, disorganised dream, or an oppressive, sickly idea. There is no doubt that a hearing of his compositions leaves an impression, but it is hard to say, just as it is hard to say in the case of Dostoyevski, whether this is the impression derived from a superabundance of content, or from the morbidness of the accompanying irritation.

Occasionally it would seem as though the composer deliberately did not want beauty of sounds, as though he forced his hearers to reside in a world of deliberate musical ugliness, of poor sonorities, of irritating harmonies, out of private artistic considerations. Occasionally it is as though he deliberately wished to strike us with extreme melancholy, with an oppressive poverty of thought, in order that we might feel the more glaringly the void caused by its absence. If he is a great artist, then it cannot be otherwise. The composer's sincerity is not subject to doubt. He is not Stravinski, who has many visages and can be everything, because in reality he is spiritually "nothing" himself. Myaskovski is too saturated with Myaskovski to become "nothing," or anything save himself. And he gives himself in his music, he strives to give the whole of himself. It seems to us that he does not give himself completely, that his talent for self-expression is inferior to his gifts as a rich and strange human individuality.

His kinship with Chaykovski had been observed long ago and by many. What makes him principally of a kind with Chaykovski is their common pessimistic and dismal spirit, their insistence on universal vanity and uselessness, their religion of annihilation and hoplessness. This is not the eschatological, terrible and rapturous pessimism of that ecstatic and religious mystic Skryabin; it is not the pessimism of Wagner, gloomy as the Scandinavian gods whose forms he assumed, and infinitely beautiful in its terrible gloominess. It is the pessimism of a sick spirit, a spirit without a wide sweep; a pessimism without prospect, hopeless, dejected and imprisoned. It seems to us that Myaskovski not only denies life in favour of another existence, but denies the other existence as well. Hence the feeling that there is no escape, hence the despair which has no desire even to justify itself. Hence the deadening twilight of beauty in this music. Hence Myaskovski, the heir and successor of Chaykovski the lyric, turns out to be a poor lyricist himself, for in his music there is no love at all, no pathos of enthusiasm, no lyric ecstasy, no oblivion of reality even in a dream. He is completely in the power of longing and torment, and whenever his music gives anything like a glimpse of enlightenment, one does not believe in it,—it seems as though the composer had written these lines "just so," in order to give his hearers a respite, in a fit of rare sympathy for them, or simply from "formal" considerations.

Compared with Myaskovski, Chaykovski seems to be a composer of infinitely wider scope. He knew both the enthusiasm of lyric sentiment and oblivion in beauty. The gloomy and self-centred Myaskovski, "a pessimist raised to the cube degree," is a specialist in one category of moods, which the composer of the *Pathetic Symphony* had once touched. It is not for nothing that Myaskovski almost began his work with a symphonic poem on the theme of the terrible and incomprehensible *Silence* of the morbid Poe. We cannot conceal from our readers the fact that we consider Myaskovski's embodiment of this terrible page of Poe in any degree its match in genius. Both the latter and the former were mentally unbalanced, both of them had various psychopathological visions, but this similarity is not sufficient. One must be a genius even greater than the great Poe in order to embody silence in sound.

There is still another composer who has points of contact with Myaskovski, and that is Musorgski. Principally, of course, not the Musorgski of the *Nursery* or the *Classicist*, in general not the realistic and positive Musorgski or the early militant period, but the later mystical, strange, half-ill and half-insane singer of the *Songs and Dances of Death*. In the creative work of Myaskovski, who is not purely Russian but rather German by blood, we occasionally meet episodes of a Russian national character. On the occasions when his melody makes its appearance, it assumes the form of Russian tunefulness, and therein approaches Musorgski, who had fathomed the secrets of this tunefulness more deeply than any

other composer. But whereas the Russian spirit was rooted
firmly and solidly in the creative art and very spirit of
Musorgski, it crops up in Myaskovski as if by chance, as
if coming to visit him, and occasionally the composer man-
ages without it altogether, composing Pan-European music.
But the gloomy idea of death, which is native also with
Musorgski, predominates in Myaskovski. Not counting
Silence, which is so closely related to death, Myaskovski
frequently cultivates in his compositions the ominous chorale
Dies Iræ, as a leit-motif of death. It appears in his Second
Sonata for the piano, and it appears in his Sixth Symphony.
This shows that, as a rule, in Myaskovski's creative work
there is a certain concealed programme, which for some
reasons the composer has no desire completely to disclose to
the hearer. But the idea of death nevertheless rises before
the hearer, being evoked not only by the hopeless gloom and
the fatal melancholy of this created wilderness, but also by
this constant return to the symbolism of death, either in
the form of a mediæval "chorale of death," or in the form
of the ancient verse of the "old-believers" which found a
place in the same Sixth Symphony, and whose text speaks
of death with the same annoying persistence and conviction.

Death holds sway over this creative art, just as it held
sway over Chaykovski and over the final period of Musorgski's life. These three composers are composers of death
par excellence and in this is their kinship. But let us not
speak of the sizes of their gifts, for neither time nor conditions have come for detailed appraisals. Let us recall that
in the eyes of Chaykovski, Musorgski was nothing but a
barbarian and dilettante, while in ‘Musorgski's eyes, Chaykovski was a "German" and a "conservative." And now,
both of them are ranked as geniuses, so recognised by the
world and not Russia alone.

Myaskovski tries his gifts in various fields. Like nearly all
composers of the new school, he has a negative attitude only

to the operatic dramatic form. He is a symphonist by both conviction and calling. His compositions possess breadth of structure which frequently endows even his larger chamber pieces with a symphonic character. But this is not the symphonism of Beethoven, but rather Chaykovski's symphonism, and in this point they have their closest contact. Myaskovski's symphonism is, like Chaykovski's, intimely psychological, not epic and heroic, like Wagner's and Beethoven's. His leaning towards symphonism separates Myaskovski from Musorgski. Whatever one may say about his qualities, his musical fabric is unquestionably dynamic. It is created by a single impulse, and he is fond of this large form of musical thought. Though Myaskovski has written rather numerous vocal songs and several piano pieces on a smaller scale, these do not show his characteristic qualities. His physiognomy outlines itself clearly in his sonatas for the piano, in this "intimely symphonic" world (in this respect his sonatas are like Beethoven's without any comparison of the calibres of their talent) and in his symphonies for the orchestra.

Symphonism in no degree connotes "orchestrism," if one may use this expression. One may be an amazing master of the orchestra and its world of colours and yet be no symphonist. Examples are numerous. The whole Russian School, beginning with Musorgski, Rimski-Korsakoff, Balakireff, save perhaps Borodin alone, was an utter denial of symphonism side by side with a masterly manipulation of the resources of the orchestra. Such also are the French composers, Debussy and Ravel and nearly all contemporary modern composers. Their creative work is an emphatic denial of symphonism, in spite of their masterly work with the orchestra. Symphonism denotes first of all a dynamic unfolding of thought, and the ignoring of the "picturesque qualities" of musical matters in favour of the psychologic and emotional ones. Usually symphonism proves antagonistic to musical picturesqueness and colourfulness. Only the grandiose genius of Wagner, and the talent of Strauss descended from him, could somehow combine the symphonic breadth with strivings for picturesqueness and colour. As a rule, we find that a composer purely symphonic in his gift, does not place the centre of gravity in the qualities of orchestration, and that for him the orchestra is merely a certain symbol of the macrocosm, the personification of the cosmos or of the complexity of the inner world of the soul, and not a bright palette of sonorities. Such were Beethoven and Brahms and Schumann and the Russians, Chaykovski and Skryabin. The grandeur of musical thought and the dynanism of its embodiment, abundantly compensated for the defects of orchestral fabric which were present in the works of all these composers. Here is where Myaskovski approximately belongs. This is the type of musicians "most profound and serious" in creative problems. External colourfulness, tonal ding-dongs, hold no lure for them, nor are they fascinated by the problem of the picturesque, once a very fashionable problem, turning music into a sort of interlinear translation of other sensations. They see in music more serious problems. In this respect, Myaskovski is no exception, and accordingly we shall not reproach him for shortcomings we have just admitted are characteristic of the symphonist.

This characteristic is the ignoring of colour, the colourlessness of inspiration. To such composers music turns its psychologic side and not the tonal. This slight interest in tonal colourfulness is usually accompanied by "contrary, mutual dislike." The colourful world of the orchestra does not disclose its secrets and mysteries to the composer who dislikes it. Neither Brahms nor Chaykovski nor Skryabin in particular could boast special abilities as colourists. Similarly, and in a still smaller degree, can Myaskovski. With him "non-interest" in orchestral sonority occasionally turns into plain contempt for it, into formal orchestral writing according to a system recalling the great "musical feuilletonist," Anton Rubinstein, who wrote operas and symphonies as a newspaper reporter writes reviews in straight copy, without rough draft. Myaskovski's orchestra is a definite psychologic quantity and its physical embodiment frequently leaves much to be desired. His sonority is thin, of dull colour, and hard. Occasionally one may think even that the author cannot handle it, that he does not know the fundamental laws of sonorousness. Myaskovski's difficulties with the orchestra, for which he nevertheless reserves his best inspirations and the compositions which mature within him the longest and most intimely, began as far back as his student days. This idiosyncrasy recalls another great musician and composer of genius, Schumann, who likewise was devoid of any gift of orchestration, or of any notion of sonority. As we have said, in reality this is not an absolute drawback, only an extreme manifestation of a common peculiarity of convinced and pure symphonists. It is no surprise to us that Myaskovski, who psychologically represents the extreme expression of subjective pessimism in music and a like extreme expression of symphonism, proves just as extreme in the faults connected with this manifestation.

Yet in spite of it all, this composer proves to be the most productive of all Russian composers in the field of pure symphony. He has written eight symphonies, as many as Glazunoff, but he will probably write as many more, which can no longer be said of Glazunoff. Myaskovski's musical ideas somehow mould themselves most naturally into symphonic forms. Not all his symphonies have been published, nor have all of them been performed by an orchestra. We have never heard his first two symphonies, they have not had a single performance. His Third Symphony was played long ago, before the World War. His latest symphonies have all been performed. An author of eight symphonies can in nowise be considered a composer of insignificance.

But skeptics occasionally point significantly to exactly this quantity, as a sort of symphonic graphomania. Are his ideas worthy of this form consecrated by the greatest composers beginning with the classics? As I have pointed out, it is hard to make an estimate of Myaskovski's vague and strange talent, and in this book I resolutely forego attempting it. Some consider him a new genius, a "Musorgski of the symphony"; others, no less authoritative, maintain that he is an inflated quantity, a mere epigone of Glazunoff, a composer without a countenance. What is remarkable is that apparent proofs are more numerous on the side of the enemies, for theirs is the "formal" method. They can "prove" that there is nothing new in this creative art. But then, there was nothing "formally new" in Chaykovski either. But the power to sway many, and Myaskovski's indubitable and evergrowing success with the Russian public, are facts which must be taken into account.

Myaskovski's eight symphonies are strongly individualised even in the monotony of his prevailing moods. We shall not speak of the first two, still unpublished, and of the last one, still in the composer's portfolio. The Third Symphony is most like Chaykovski, and in many respects it is the freshest and most powerful. The Fourth Symphony, of rather small dimensions, was written in the War years and, musically speaking, is a combination of the influences of the Russian National School, Chaykovski, and in part, of Glazunoff. The Fifth Symphony surprisingly is the clearest in moods and the most formal, and comes closest to Glazunoff. The Sixth Symphony is full of the greatest gloom and tragedy. An interesting point in it is that its Finale requires a chorus, like Beethoven's Ninth Symphony (or rather like Liszt's *Faust-Symphony*), a chorus which sings the old-believers' Russian verse about death, while at the same time in the orchestra, are interwoven a number of revolutionary themes, *Carmagnole, Ca ira* and others. To these is added the gloomy motif of the Chorale *Dies Iræ*. This implies a concealed programme in composition. What inter-relation there is between the gloomy death motifs, couched in two languages, the lapidary tongue of the ancient chorale and the soft contemplative folk-tones of the song of Russian *raskolniks* (sectarians), and the stormy militant tunes of the revolutionary songs, it is difficult to say. But there is no doubt that this juxtaposition has been brought about by the events of Russian revolutionary reality, the epoch of the years 1918-1920, during which the symphony was created. And the motifs of death assume a new meaning in this light, in the plan of the symphony. Instead of being purely psychological, it becomes epic, as with Beethoven.

The Seventh Symphony, on no large scale, begins with an episode which deceives the hearer by a contemplative character unusual with Myaskovski. But the composer soon plunges his hearer again into his habitual world of despair and neurasthenia. Of all the symphonies, this is the most nervous, the most despairing in mood, the most hopeless, and this hopelessness is not palliated by one episode of "pantheistic" character, which instead of serving as a contrast, in reality only emphasises the gloom of its fundamental background.

The world of sonatas is another and more intimate department of Myaskovski's symphonism. Here the author is in reality very similar to his symphonic world, as he has embodied himself in his symphonies, save that his language is more intimate. But tonal charm is alien to Myaskovski here also. Not only orchestral colouring, but even the comparatively modest mysteries of piano sonority remain a "book sealed with seven seals" to him. There is no doubt that this too "pure" symphonism, this psychologising which has no desire to employ tonal matter or heed the present-day demand for it, may affect the popularity and spread of Myaskovski's compositions. Of his sonatas, the best is the

Third, in one movement, nervously lyric and passionately dramatic, recalling Chaykovski in its first theme and in spots not without boldness in harmonic language. The Second Sonata, more ordinary as music, recalling Glazunoff in places, is woven in a masterly musical fabric. It is the most popular with the pianists of Russia. The Fourth Sonata, recently written in three movements, pays tribute to some recent musical fads, the cult of complex and "atonal" harmonies and to certain "retrospective fads," but taken as a whole it is less individual.

Myaskovski is productive and persistent in his work. He is severe with himself and extremely modest. In this man there is no advertising, nor any desire "to push ahead." As an ethical figure, his loftiness recalls Tañeyeff but without the academical old fashion of the latter. There is no doubt that precisely "human" qualities have won great popularity and respect for the author of the eight symphonies and placed him in the position of a "respected teacher" at a comparatively young age. At the present time Myaskovski is Professor of Composition at the Moscow Conservatory, and among his pupils there are a great number of young composers of the latest generation, who will also be treated in this book.

Strange and enigmatic he passes before our gaze, and if in us personally his creative art does not strike an echo, it cannot be denied that it moves many others. The inner meaning of a musician is frequently perceived from his musical sympathies and antipathies. Myaskovski does not like Wagner, nor particularly Liszt. He does not like Beethoven and has an aversion for Chopin and Bach. His idols are Chaykovski and certain Russian contemporary composers, among them his comrade Prokofyeff, whom he considers a genius. It is difficult to draw a conclusion from this collection of likings, excepting that we apparently must deal here with a man who perceives the musical world and the musical elements very queerly. The strong and the potent in music is as foreign and incomprehensible to him as the tender and the intimate. They rouse neither sympathy nor rapture in him. This cruel autosadist has lovingly selected the field of wicked melancholy, of neurasthenic and hysterical emotion, of hopeless moods which do not even possess the fascination of force for his world. This art, basically unhealthy, anti-social in its tendency towards isolated individualism, might nevertheless prove artistically valuable and possibly even a genuine treasure if, on the scales of the historical "test of time," it turned out that the potentialities of musical talent underlying it are sufficient to overcome the terrible psychologic material with which the author operates, and which will yield artistically only to the talent of a genius.

SAMUIL FEINBERG

(Born 1889)

SAMUIL FEINBERG made his début in the epoch of enthusiasm for Skryabin. His strange characteristic and sincere talent, so unlike the talent of any one of his contemporaries, took form and strengthened at that time. He is now a mature composer, perfect in his mastery. Nevertheless few people can be found who would definitely and properly perceive the essence of this profound and diseased talent.

Certain external traits of Skryabinism in Feinberg may strike the superficial hearer and obscure Feinberg's very quintessence, which only in one respect, namely, its extreme exaltation, touches the character of Skryabin's gift. His other traits are well-nigh antipodal to the creator of the *Poème d'Extase*. Feinberg is a romantic to the marrow of his bones, like Skryabin, but he is a romantic in an incomparably higher and more acute, I might even say a more "aggravated," form than Skryabin. In this romanticism, in the concealed philosophic character of his creative art of which Feinberg does not speak so openly as Skryabin but clothes it in chastely enigmatic garb, lies the anachronism of this composer. His dissonance with our century of positivism and deliberately atavistic reversion, of deliberate simplification, which perhaps betrays the weariness of the civilised world after the great upheavals of recent years, and, perhaps, betrays even the degeneration of thought and feeling, especially noticeable in the new generation.

Feinberg therefore may share Skryabin's fate and probably will. This restless fantast, possessed by nightmares, must

163

seem queer and foreign to the modern listener who comes to hear interesting, piquant, witty music, but not that which agitates and turns the nerves inside out. Feinberg sets for himself exactly this goal, or more correctly his personality being what it is, his music does turn the nerves exactly inside out. Skryabin was full of joyous ecstasy, of some sort of triumph and victoriousness, and if his highly wrought up state was not perhaps at bottom joyous, for after all, like all eschatologists he was a pessimist, it at least pretended to appear as such. But in Feinberg's ecstasy and convulsively gloomy elation the exaltation is not the joyousness of Skryabin, but a nightmare frenzy, a whirlwind of weird hallucinations forged into images of sound. It is something akin to Schumann, that first romantic seer in music, and through Feinberg's compositions flashes the Schumann of *Kreisleriana,* and *Nachtstuecke,* the Schumann who in the depths of his spirit and creative art was psychopathic. This psychopathism is not something that vitiates, but perhaps a species of new vision; this obsession may not perhaps be below, but above, normal. However, it is apparent that the unceasing action of spiritual life is undermining the physical, and we have to do with an artistic psychopathism that gave the world perhaps its greatest achievements in Schumann, Poe and Dostoyevski.

Feinberg, too, belongs to this species of half-mad artists, "touched" by some sort of hyper-vision, which destroys certain norms and foundations. In this morbidity and diseased self-consciousness he is much more severely and deeply ill than Skryabin, who was obsessed by only one idea, but otherwise was generally speaking healthier than many others. On the other hand, Feinberg is more the artist than Skryabin, less dilettant, less inclined to go beyond the boundaries of art or consider music merely a means to something extraneous to it.

He is more modest than Skryabin. He is wiser, for he

knows better his limitations and does not venture beyond them. Having ascertained his place, deep and narrow and dark as a bottomless pit, he makes no attempt to get out of it. He is a splendid, and just as fantastically morbid, spasmodically nervous pianist as, composer, and lovingly cherishes this piano-world, this microcosmic instrument of the human soul, which served the genius of just as self-centred an individualist, Chopin. Piano compositions and occasional songs are his sphere, which he has drawn around his creative work like a magic circle and from which the spirits possessing him, the creative "elementals," have themselves no power to escape.

As I have already said, Feinberg began to write when Skryabin was still alive, and began, as is not difficult to understand, almost in the spirit of Schumann; this is symptomatic and important for the subsequent characterisation of his creative art. His first sonatas are permeated with the spirit not the imitation of Schumann. The similarity to Skryabin upon closer examination proves perhaps to be no more than the little "something" which Skryabin himself drew from Schumann. At all events, one may rest assured that the modest and chaste Feinberg will under no circumstances attempt to make one believe that his sonatas contain anything "cosmic," or that the world will shiver and tremble from the tones of his piano. Not for a moment does he assume the "Titanic pose" so characteristic of Skryabin, which occasionally overwhelms even the impressions of genius which his music produces.

But on the other hand, we see here also the narrowness of Feinberg's talent. First, Feinberg is chiefly a composer of harmonies and rhythms. He is almost no melodist at all. His melody is rudimentary and frequently intangible. His musical fabric is bizarrely wavering and turbulent. These compositions are some sort of tonal tempests and whirlwinds, not music. In a terrible tumult mad sounds are pursuing one another and rushing with a speed which is the utmost possible in musical tones. We witness the birth of ghostly ideas that swarm and vanish at the will of a fantastic sorcerer; elemental spirits personifying perhaps whole symphonies of feelings and ideas. Feinberg in general is a composer who recognises virtually no slow tempo. He is no contemplative visionary; his visions are dynamic and madly precipitous, recalling the hallucinations of a sick man. The torn and spasmodic rhythm becomes still more spasmodic in the composer's own performances. The destruction of the rhythmic web and substance occasionally frightens the auditor with its abnormality. In this Feinberg is the psychopathist, and in this destruction of the unity of rhythmic musical sensation resides the psychic defect which somehow harmonises with the composer's appearance as a creative artist and performer.

It is easy to wave aside an enormous talent with the word abnormality or psychopathism. But it is far more difficult to understand this constant mingling of the planes of genius and psychopathism in the phenomena of artistic life. To the psychologist and "geniologist" studying, in Lombroso's manner, the mysterious relationship between genius and mental disease, Feinberg affords one of the most interesting problems beside Skryabin, Schumann, Poe and Dostoyevski. He is not a simple psychologic problem. In his mental make-up may be discerned indications of uncommon depth of feeling that is frequently philosophical and not merely philosophically decorated. Occasionally one imagines that Feinberg's entire creative work is only some sort of a result of this psychic life, incomprehensible or little known to others. He has strange ideas which deserve to be stated here, the more so as the author of these lines has had numerous opportunities to arrive at similar ones himself. For instance, Feinberg is the creator of the original theory of unintoned sounds, or sounds imagined, which the performer merely "thinks of in addition" to what he plays, colouring whatever is to be heard into entirely different tones. With him the perception of music is not the simple process habitual to average persons, who come, listen, enjoy and depart. No, it is a sort of slow entrance into a special world which is not revealed to every one at once. There is some peculiar depth of finesse of perception in this assertion of non-existing sounds. The musical fabric is not merely the usual, the realised, the known. From first to last it becomes some tonal and psychological sphinx. On the degree of clairvoyance in the performer hangs his power to divine and feel the "unsounded" which is hidden in this art; and upon the clairvoyance and "sensitiveness" of the auditor hangs his power to divine the unsounded fulfilment of the performance. In this theory of "unsounded tones" or unintoned sound perception, there is a deal of romanticism and much in common with Schumann and Hofmann, and with the romantic "mysticism of music," in general, that regards music as an art mystic and inconceivable in its essence and filled at every step with new mysteries and occult revelation. It has something in common also with Skryabin's theories, but it must be observed that in Skryabin, all this was far more schematic and geometrically clear. A mystic in his religious creed, he was, however, a positivist and a clear thinker. His musical world held no "secrets," but only "qualities." His musical material was some sort of powerful "potion" for producing mystical states. Feinberg does not set out to produce definite states, they happen with him "by themselves," and in his make-up there are incomparably sharper traits of obsession, psychopathism and entangling of sensations than in Skryabin, who could remain Apollonically clear and transparent even in chaos. Feinberg's whirling snowstorms in sound are perhaps more kindred to the Russian poet, Blok, who died during the Revolution, than to any other. This Russian poet, from the psychological and literary points of view one of the most enigmatic figures in Russian art, in whose verse there is left almost no room for "thought" and its clarity, but only for the "divination" of something from beyond, is frequently reflected in Feinberg's work. He writes cycles of songs, set to his texts. And these strange songs, in which there is almost nothing recalling melody, are musically nearer to Blok's creative work than are any other Russian composer's set to the same texts. Feinberg loves the intimate vocal world in which he can embody his favourite "uncanny" moods. In his partiality to it he is again similar to Schumann.

Feinberg's Schumannism manifests itself also in a number of other slight traits besides his general partiality for the piano-vocal field, and the general "thickly romantic" colour of his art. Metaphysics is present in both, and philosophical ideas penetrate into the music and colour of their fabric. Over his Sixth Sonata for the piano Feinberg placed an epigraph from Spengler's widely discussed book, *The Decline of the West*. This epigraph is just as mysterious and as enigmatic, and its connection with the music just as untold, as in Schumann's numerous epigraphs and subtitles. Also his partiality for the "rhythmic element" of music makes him kindred to Schumann, except that his rhythms are far more fantastic and, coming a century later, more complex and ingenious.

A strange figure is this belated romantic on Russian soil, who has come into the world either too early or too late, either as the harbinger of a new spring of romanticism, or as the funeral singer of the past. Russia, which has always paid less tribute to purely formalistic and esthete tendencies in art, does not, in general, part with romanticism as quickly and easily as Western Europe. It is not yet entirely clear to us how far the anti-romantic current in the world of music is organic and enduring. Perhaps, and it is quite likely, it is only the fashion of a decade. A fashion, perhaps, which has not been called into being so much by the actual tendency of the world's creative forces in the realm of music as by the esthetic discussions of critics, who invariably desire to characterise epochs in most pointed and decorative terms. Traces of orthodox romanticism are observable in the work of the most acutely modern composers, such as Stravinski, Schoenberg and Prokofyeff. Formalism and esthetism, which desire to create the fashionable taste of the epoch, are in reality observed chiefly in certain German and French composers, and there only. As regards Russia, it is beyond doubt that the eradication of romanticism in music is well-nigh impossible. At all events, we are convinced that the future rise of romanticism in Russia will occur ere its last vestiges die out under the pressure of fashion. If we look at the work of the most prominent composers of Russia, we can see the truth of this. Myaskovski and Feinberg, and the deceased Skryabin, and almost all the youthful talents, have not broken with romanticism by far. The belated nationalism of the Jewish school, in the persons of Gnyesin and Alyeksandr Krein, is also indicative of the living force of the typically romantic current. Perhaps Feinberg will not be sufficiently comprehensible in the West, owing to his too tempestuous expression of romanticism, and his psychopathism which is too obviously expressed in tones incompatible with the contemporary "business" poise there, but in Russia his appearance does not interrupt any current, for here it is natural and logical. We might suppose that Russian music is lagging and but repeating what Western music has already done with, and there is a banal logic in this view. But we know too well the law of ebb and flow in the realm of artistic movements, we know too well that every phenomenon, if it is important, may with equal right be considered either the belated echo of the past or the call to a reawakening. In the realm of art, whatever "survives" is right.

Feinberg is a great master of his art. He does not undertake large contours, he labours in a limited sphere, but in that sphere he is a master. A splendid and interesting piano style reveals him a true pianist, loving and knowing his instrument and setting new tasks for it. His creative line is gradually growing more complex, but it presents no abrupt advances and no breaks. Like Schumann, he began almost at once in his own spirit, almost escaping the period of manifest imitation, but thereafter he did not seek new paths, and was preoccupied only with self-expression within limits early established. His creative work is almost unknown in wide circles. It is too difficult and complex; so far there has been almost no pianist who dared attempt his sonatas with their terrific difficulty. By this time his portfolio contains seven sonatas, almost unknown to any save the narrow circle of close friends among the musicians of Moscow and of Leningrad. Even in this age of haste it seems odd and absurd that an important phenomenon should remain so unknown, and it causes a European to believe that the "content" of this creative art may very likely have been exaggerated. But one must know the psychology of a Russian musician, particularly a composer, in order to understand that such reasoning is inapplicable to him. To this day a Russian composer is an idealist. He is as modest as an old master, loathing self-advertising and fearing it, and profoundly convinced that every value will "in time to come" receive its proper appreciation. In this age of haste to attain fame in one's lifetime, when the very name of a composer seems to many but a step towards renown, Russian composers almost without exception, save among the very youngest generation, which has been infected with the positivism of the times, work for eternity and do nothing to spread their own fame, but leave it to posterity to render judgment on their labours. To them, and particularly to such of them as Feinberg, the procedure of self-advertisement appears even degrading to their art. The mercantile spirit which has already infected wide circles of musicians, and in Europe turned them into a special genus of musical businessmen, is utterly foreign to the Russian composer. In this respect a Russian author is a totally incorrigible romantic and idealist, and here, of course, more than elsewhere, it is possible to speak of Russian "backwardness." In this never ceasing race for fame, notoriety, honour, and money, instead of spiritual values, Russia lags behind the world. It is still an outlying province, untouched by the plague of the ever-hastening tempo of civilisation, where people pray to an ancient god.

In our opinion, this severe, profound, highly gifted artist, though morbid in his talent and unbalanced in his psyche, is one of the "great possessed," an integral and original type, who stands out like a peak in contemporary Russian music. Whether he is writing for the present, and whether the contemporary world will appreciate him, is of course a great question. We think that it will not. Just now we do not see, in the musical sentiments of the world, anything consonant with Feinberg. At any rate, his is music for the very few but, for that reason, more valued hearers. Feinberg's aristocracy of creative spirit makes him akin to Debussy and Skryabin. They, too, did not write for the wide world but for the select few to whom they alone could, with full conviction, apply the high title of "humanity." And in our age of democracy and the equality of everybody's ears, when the very idea of the revaluation of values becomes a value, Feinberg is an anachronism, not in the style of his music, not in its technical expression, but in the very point of departure of his musical and artistic self-perception, in which there is the fullest absence of any elements of democracy.

MIKHAYIL GNYESIN

(Born 1881)

Mikhayil Gnyesin was a pupil of Rimski-Korsakoff and, moreover, one of his most beloved pupils. As in his creative work, so in his instruction, the famous maestro possessed a certain elusive tinge of pedantry, a certain dryness combined with a broad artistic nature and an extraordinary amount of taste. Perhaps Rimski-Korsakoff's Swedish-Teutonic ancestors were responsible for his punctuality and exactness, so rare among the Russians. But undoubtedly Rimski-Korsakoff passed certain of his qualities on to his pupils, together with the artistic formulas, methods and stencils which every strong artist inevitably communicates to his pupils, and which only later the strong individuals among them transform into something of their own.

Mikhayil Gnyesin began his career as a composer when the fame of the leaders of the mighty "coterie" began to dim perceptibly, and the former innovators began definitely to feel themselves the preceding generation, and no longer innovators but defenders of the past. Rimski-Korsakoff himself was at bottom rather a conservative and a guardian of tradition, and felt particularly keenly and deeply his severance from contemporary life. But in fairness to the great composer, it must be admitted that to his very death he battled for himself, to his very last composition he did not surrender his banner of champion of the "new." On the one hand, he showed in his last compositions an extraordinary susceptibility to the very latest currents of thought, and on the other, a no less keen sense in divining great talents among his pupils, whose tastes obviously diverged from those of the old generation.

There was then rising the star of Skryabin, of whom
Rimski-Korsakoff himself said: "A star of the first magnitude has risen, the broken and somewhat self-opinionated
Skryabin." The old composer felt this "first magnitude,"
felt it even through the traits of opinionation and "brokenness." At the same time people who were themselves geneti-
cally connected with the activity of the Russian National
School, were carried away by the neo-impressionism of the
French, seeking new harmonies, new truths and new freedom. And at that time Mikhayil Gnyesin, too, began to
write with a certain impressionism, in whose features were
simultaneously felt the strong influence of the new harmonic
revelations of Skryabin and Debussy, and the no less powerful and even overwhelming influence of Rimski-Korsakoff's
manner and methods.

It may be said that Gnyesin began brilliantly for a young
composer. The rather famous conductor and pianist Silotti
noticed him, and so his Cello Sonata was performed with a
brilliant ensemble, Silotti and Casals, and though it was a
flat failure, its very failure was success. The traits of the
young author's individuality had manifested themselves. An
austere, gloomy, and even colourless musical inspiration,
which possessed both hardness and a certain odd "looseness
of parts," such as is occasionally found in young, strong
animals. At any rate, through all these qualities was felt
a strong and original talent, though lacking clearness and
ease.

Soon Gnyesin began work on a broader scale. He wrote
Lieder, symphonic compositions, the Cantata Worm the Conqueror, and chamber pieces. All this was a self-enclosed and
severe world. The composer himself was not particularly inclined to spread his compositions. Self-reserved and taciturn,
he worked stubbornly, overcoming the really ill-yielding element of his talent. The greatest success and fame fell to
the music he set to Alyeksandr Blok's drama The Rose and

the Cross. Certain passages of this music, particularly the heroic and powerful *Song of Gaetan,* became popular, thanks especially to the fact that one of Russia's most interesting artists of the time, the famous tenor Ivan Alchefski, a man easily carried away by enthusiasms, grew enthusiastic over Gnyesin. He sang Gnyesin's songs in a number of his concerts with enormous success, due less to the compositions themselves, which were hardly understood by the public, than to the name of the popular singer and the charm of his inspired interpretation.

But, strangely, in spite of the fact that he composed a great deal, Gnyesin's work possessed characteristic signs of groping. He produced experiments and essays more than complete compositions. It seemed as if he did not clearly know his own path. The contact in his texts and themes with the world of Russian symbolist poets, was not the organic contact of the musician's creative art with the world of the poet, but determined by his personal intimacy with these literary circles, the external accident of mere neighbourliness. In truth, both the visionary mysticism of Blok, and, even more so, the poetry of the haughty and brilliant Bal'mont, were entirely out of keeping with the spirit of Gnyesin himself. His "spirit" was not that; it was the spirit of a bookman, of a scholar, of a great and industrious worker, of a brainy and deeply-feeling man of whom it is difficult to say with what he composes more, with the mind or the heart and inspiration. Least of all was he the type of the inspired artist to whom musical visions come of themselves without effort. And apparently, endowed with a keen critical sense, he was himself dissatisfied with a great deal, and persistently sought the sphere in which he might and must manifest himself. This sphere he found considerably later in national Jewish music. Thus fate involuntarily united him with the artistic work of Alyeksandr Krein, with the pleiad of all those creators of the Jewish national musical style on Russian soil. Apparently ideas of the sort must have been floating in the air at the time. It is difficult otherwise to explain why just then nationalism was resurrected in Jewish music, at the time when it had already lived through and died in the creative art of almost all other nations. The wave of nationalism in music travelled through various nations and lands. Having victoriously traversed in its time first Germany in the persons of Weber and Wagner, then Poland in the person of Chopin, then Hungary in the person of Liszt, and Norway belatedly in the person of Grieg, it finally reached Russia and gave rise to the Russian National School. Then, ultimately, when the very idea of nationalism seemed obsolete, it came to life anew in one of the most musical nations of the world, the Jews. Apparently independent of Krein but in close connection with the work on the essence of Jewish folk and religious melodies by numerous Jewish "scholar musicians," Gnyesin set himself the task of creating a national artistic style on a level with the modern development of musical art. Not in a style intentionally primitive "after the folk manner," but national in the spirit of Chopin and Rimski-Korsakoff. There is no doubt that the influence of his teacher Rimski-Korsakoff manifested itself in this choice of his creative path. "The Jews are awaiting their Glinka," Rimski-Korsakoff once remarked in a talk with his pupils. And soon after the lyre of Glinka's successor in the realm of Russian music and its national style had grown silent, several competitors appeared simultaneously for the title of "The Jewish Glinka," the creator of an artistic Jewish style.

It is very difficult to establish priority here. Ideas of this kind float in the air and come into the minds of various persons simultaneously. The simultaneous appearance in Russia of several talented Jewish musicians doubtless played the principal rôle here. The idea of a national creative art possesses enormous attraction for a composer in general. It becomes especially active and actual in the cases where this national creative work implies pioneering, in the field, where he must plough up virgin soil and indicate the first paths. In such circumstances it is easy to be organically new and interesting, almost invariably the stale wine of civilisation is replaced by the new of unfermented folk inspirations.

With his somewhat "scholarly" bent, this was the easier for Gnyesin who had been a great student of national Jewish music even before. He plunged into the study of the ancient melodies of one of the most ancient nations in the world, he even undertook a special journey to Palestine, perhaps in order to gain a more accurate and profound communion with the spirit of this culture. Since then his creative art has become national and his name one of the most prominent among those of the creators of Jewish musical style. But with it, another phenomenon is observed,—his music grew simpler. The erstwhile rabid modernist, the seeker of new harmonies and new "means" of musical expression became more unaffected and lapidarily austere. He had leaned in this direction before. Even in his early compositions, in the music of *The Rose and the Cross,* might be discerned the indisputable presence of traits of "Judaism," despite their incongruity in the subject. Clearly, the Jewish element had been organically rooted in Gnyesin, and his course as a composer meant but its disclosure.

But frankly speaking, we cannot say that Gnyesin's creative art gained freshness from this communion with folk sources and the ancient melodies of the synagogue. On the contrary, the impression of a certain "heaviness" of the scholar is increasingly prevalent. Even the simplification of his music, indubitably striking the ear though it may, does not seem to us a simplification coming from the simplicity of immediate perception, but a simplification of selection, a constructed simplification. His music does not make an immediate impression, but only gradually, after one has gotten into and studied it. At all events since then Gnyesin has departed from his former modernism for good.

His figure stands apart not only among other Russian composers, but even among the composers of the Russian "Jewish group." He is incomparably more a bookman than Alyeksandr Krein, his colleague and competitor in the creation of a national art. His music lacks the passionate emotion so peculiar to Krein, and the earthly feelings and the orgiastic view of the world. The semi-pagan character of Krein's music, its saturation "with flesh and blood," its ecstasy, passionateness and sensuality, have not entered Gnyesin's world at all. They have divided between them two polar manifestations of the Jewish spirit. Krein has taken the fiery and passionate protestation of ancient Israel, ever insurgent and ever succumbing to temptation with the same transport of joy with which it subsequently repents. Gnyesin has taken the cabalistic element, contemplative and characteristically heavy in its wisdom and unyielding in its profundity. Perhaps the true beauty of musical contemplation and feeling is equally alien to both, for perhaps it is not in the style of their national spirit. But with Krein there is at least left the charm of passion, comprehensible to the masses, and that tenseness of utterance which creates an impression aside from, and above, the music. But in the case of Gnyesin, his lore and his aspiring austerity are not created for a wide public. The "bookish composer" in general risked misunderstanding by that public at large, and bored even the masses of his own people for whom his art was being created.

Nevertheless, one cannot say that specific pathos is not inherent in Gnyesin. On the contrary, he possesses it in more majestic form than Krein. But the absence of the sensuous element, and the asceticism and asexuality of his music compelled him to content himself with the sacred ecstasies of the ascetic; and the essence of the oriental eroticism of the *Song of Songs,* for which he wrote music, remains a bookish and not a personal experience in his score.

His biblical opera, *The Youth of Abraham,* set to music to his own text, must be classed as the most important work of this period. In addition to the common widespread Wagnerism of our times, the music of this opera shows many other influences of the great master of Bayreuth. This music is written in the lapidary style, partly recalling Rimski-Korsakoff's last compositions. The externals of this opera are extremely modest and austere, containing only two characters, Abraham and his father. This limitation reflects the whole of Gnyesin with his archaic, truly biblical view of his own art. The whole meaning of the opera lies in disclosing one rapturous emotion, the glorification of the Sun by Abraham, who has not seen it before. The episode has been portrayed by the composer with restrained austere force. The absence of any erotic or love element in the opera is no less characteristic. Gnyesin's talent has few points of contact with the sphere of tonal colour. We have called his musical perception "colourless." Hence the orchestration of his instrumental pieces is abstract and does not possess any physiognomy of its own. Like Brahms or Schumann, Gnyesin dwells somewhere outside the orchestral element. Accordingly we think that his opera hardly gains in a stage performance with its poverty of plot and minimum of movement, in comparison with which even the Wagnerian Tetralogy seems overfilled with action, and its absence of orchestral colours which might have enhanced its effect. In reality the oratorio style is more akin to Gnyesin, and his Opera, both in idea and execution is a "concealed oratorio" to a considerable degree.

Gnyesin is not productive as a composer. He writes slowly and cumbersomely, and his compositions appear at long intervals. He has been standing apart among the Russian composers, enjoying no considerable popularity. He is held in respect; his endeavours to found a Jewish national style meet with a welcome, but his creative work is somehow overlooked. The years of the Russian Revolution and the trying circumstances of life connected with that time retarded even the usual slow tempo of his work. However, Gnyesin was one of the few Russian composers to respond actively to the revolutionary spirit and choice of subjects in his creative work. As I shall point out in the chapter "The Musical Creative Art of the Russian Revolution," the commands of society for monumental and majestic music which would express the revolutionary break in Russian history, and celebrate various revolutionary occasions, festivities and other manifestations of the new social order, has so far been filled by the incapable artisan hands of second-rate composers. The Russian composers, in the great majority of cases, were and are utterly apolitical individuals, who previously had felt at a loss in political problems or had been uninterested in them, and were now overtaken by the Revolution unawares. If we are to except N. Roslavyets, who of his own accord endeavoured to accomplish something to correspond with the new demand for "music for the masses," Gnyesin alone made a heroic attempt to create important revolutionary work. The history of music is full of proofs that filling specific requisitions from society has only in the rarest cases resulted in productions of art that were important in the artistic sense. The complete assonance or contact of the composer with his subject matter, the complete sympathy with his theme, is necessary in order to create an artistically lasting production. Apparently, as it turned out, Gnyesin possessed more revolutionary feeling than other Russian authors. The *Sketch of a Symphonic Monument* is a sort of symphony cantata, the text being a poem of the late Sergey Yesyenin, who acquired passing notoriety by his marriage with Isadora Duncan. Essentially the text does not at all reflect the communistic spirit of Soviet Russia, nor the Marxian doctrine, nor the urge to build which, above all, possesses new Russia. It is rather an echo of those unbridled moods which swept throughout the Russian land during the first years of the Revolution. And so Gnyesin, a revolutionary when judged by his choice of text, appears to us rather the anarchist singer of unbridled liberty. Curious it is that the musical web of this piece proved to possess many traits in common with the style of the Russian National School. Gnyesin, as it were, returned from his Jewish Palestine to the fold of his teacher Rimski-Korsakoff, and even the basic theme of the Cantata, a tempestuous song, is strongly reminiscent of one of the operatic themes of Rimski-Korsakoff.

Whether this composition is something organic in Gnyesin's creative work, or a chance turn of a formerly rigid and cautious author from his once chosen path of life, the future will show. But one thing is beyond any shadow of a doubt. Gnyesin has worked on it with great zeal and put much of himself into it. Under no circumstances was this the filling of commercial "social command." It was the artist's own requisition upon himself. A Jewish composer in the rôle of singer of Russia's freedom is, of course, a queer play of nature, and reflection on this point makes us think that a certain blindness befell the composer, who failed to perceive the disparity of this style and himself. For this style is organically derived from his "modernistic" period as a seeker of new paths, not from his persistent "Zionist" labours in the cause of Jewish national music.

ALYEKSANDR KREIN

(Born 1883)

ALYEKSANDR KREIN is one of the most gifted composers of contemporary Russia. His vitality and actuality are based on his live contact with folk elements. It is an old truth that art always gains vitality from contact with the earth of folk music. The element fructifying the art of Alyeksandr Krein, giving it life, freshness and "full-blooded-ness," is the element of the Jewish folk melody.

However, Krein did not immediately come upon this path and this folk-soil. Jewish composers made their appearance in Russia principally on the eve of the twentieth century. By that time certain national wants had matured and people grew conscious of certain national needs. It is curious that the majority of our Russian Jewish composers, who with Krein formed a sufficiently solid and individualised Jewish National School, are almost all of the same age regardless of the fact that they were born and studied in different places. The Jewish national idea awoke simultaneously in Krein from Novgorod, in Gnyesin from St. Petersburg, in Akhron and in Saminsky as well as in Engel from Moscow. Approximately on the threshold of the twentieth century, all of them remembered their nationality and resolved to embody it in music. But the paths thereto were different with each. Krein in particular began as an orthodox modernist, as a partisan of the traditions bequeathed by Ryebikoff of liberating music from the vise of "science" and the vise of "theory" and from dead laws. This revolutionism expressed itself practically in the fact that the young composer began with tones which partly recalled Grieg, partly

181

the early Skryabin, and were not without a strong trace of Debussy and Ravel.

In spite of the fact that even then this creative work attracted attention by the freshness of its musical inspiration, a definite harmoniousness and an "inborn feeling of muscianship," and in spite of the technical erudition of the composer, who vigorously and defiantly "denied" all norms and rules, Krein's true countenance did not disclose itself in these compositions. It disclosed only his "epigonic essence," present in every composer, especially in the embryonic period of his development.

The break in Krein's creative work began with his nationalism, at the moment when he felt himself musically a Jew and decided simultaneously with, and apparently independently of, a number of others to repeat the experiment which had once been performed by Chopin, Liszt, Glinka, Grieg, and produced splendid musical results each time. This experiment was the fructification of personal creative art with the folk element.

But Alyeksandr Krein does not seek tunefulness in the contemporary music of the Jews. His gaze penetrates further back into the epoch when, in his opinion, the race was purer and the melody mirrored more exactly the psychic essence of this race. He makes a profound study of the ancient synagogue melodies, investigates their odd, now severe, now bizarrely ornamented, melodic structure, and begins to feel within himself the blossoming of his creative art from these seeds.

Krein does not follow the road which the Jews have taken in music until now, he does not plant himself on the ethnographic soil, he does not arrange the ancient tunes in "European fashion." He creates new ones in their image. Such was the path of Glinka, Grieg, Chopin. He pays attention principally to the tense character of this expression of the synagogue, to its declamatory recitation, but not to the gorgeous ornamentation of the melody, which blurs its severe basic lines.

Psychically Krein is really called to embody musically the image of ancient Jewry arising to new life. The foreground in his music is held by emotion, hot, passionate and even coarse in its insatiable, earthy sensuousness. Krein is no mystic and is not inclined to transcendentalism. He is all of the earth, life, and its joys and activities. His eroticism is not Skryabin's mystical eroticism refined to all but total disembodiment; it is the earthy, healthy, blood eroticism of the *Song of Songs* and oriental hymning, and his music has assumed the nature of these ancient prototypes of Semitic music. His melody becomes heady and erotic, and is insistently dynamically half recitation permeated with passion and fire. He is not a Talmudic Jew nor the studious bookman which I imagine his fellow-worker Gnyesin to be. He is the incarnation of that ancient Jewry which in its time had painfully struggled between religious passion and the orgiastic of heathenism. The image of Jewdom has perhaps been imprinted most vividly on his *Kaddish* a kind of grand symphonic cantata in which the solo tenor personifies the struggling and protesting "earthly personality," while the chorus symbolises the religious and passionless law. But if Krein's melodies are drawn from synagogue melodies and their ornamentation, his harmony is of mixed origin. Herein are influences of Skryabin, Ravel, and even of the Russian composers of the National School, chiefly Rimski-Korsakoff.

The tone of Krein's moods is sufficiently uniform for him to be reproached with a certain monotony. He is always emotional to the saturation point. He recognises almost no quiet lyricism, nothing visionary, no static picturesqueness. In this respect his music approaches Chaykovski and departs furthest from the impressionists who gave him origin and first aroused his musical imagination. This is naturally as was to be expected. The earthly image of the passionate and seeking, ever-wandering Jew reconciles itself uneasily with static esthetic colouring. It reconciles itself with difficulty with the cult of harmony, typical of impressionists, to the disadvantage of melody. Krein is essentially a melodist. He cannot get along without melody. In spite of his long practice as a composer, he is not a master in the full sense of the word; he is in the position of one ever-seeking and restless. His compositions, like Chaykovski's, are rather unified by dynamics than by real form. As with Chaykovski, his colour and exposition always recede to the background before sentiment, which expresses itself in melody and dominates over and determines all.

Krein is a definitely formed and clear-cut figure of Russian contemporary life. Of course it would be rash at this moment to place him in the "left wing." Krein was never especially an innovator, and if at one time he was somewhat conscious of musical solidarity with Ravel and Debussy, these authors have long been recognised as "academy." But even then he was moderate in his mimicry of the innovations of the time. Like Chaykovski, Krein is original not in his originality or in the breaking down of current norms, but by another "different originality," which has laid the stamp of a definite style on all his compositions, especially the most recent, although one can hardly put finger on it.

He is a productive and industrious author. Having begun in the modest field of the piano and songs, he soon began to try his powers first in chamber music and later in the orchestra. His first symphonic composition which already partly reflected his new enthusiasm for Hebraism, the symphonic poem, *Salome,* proved unsustained in form and exposition. Soon his great Piano Sonata appeared, one of his best compositions, and then his First Symphony, related to it in its themes. In this latter his style became strongly monumentalised and partly even more simplified. Along with these was created the aforementioned *Kaddish* and numerous groups of songs, many of which have been set to Hebrew texts, while others, as for instance his *Gazelles,* one of his finest inspirations, were set to words by Jewish poets. Krein has also laboured much in the field of Jewish music for the theatre, and here he has created a great deal that is curious and occasionally of genuine interest, as for instance the music to Perets's drama *The Night at the Old Market-Place.* And curiously he almost never stoops to the borrowing of folk tunes, always preferring his own melody, created in the image of the popular or religious melody. But the lines or the "profile" of his melodies, with their characteristic fioritures and ornamentations, declamations, conjugations, and imprecations, all saturated with emotion, have somehow an inordinate "inner closeness" to the true spirit of Judaism, that subconscious essence, that racial psychology which but partly reflects itself in folk melodies, and may as brightly shine in the creative art of a cultured musician who is imbued with this spirit and this psychology. Krein, who sprang from the impressionists and Skryabin, is now the complete antithesis to both the former and the latter. Impressionism occurs in him now only accidentally and reminiscently, as for instance at the beginning of the Second Movement of his Symphony. But even then he is always tuned to definite oriental hues, not to the semi-tone and the indefiniteness characteristic of impressionism. True, Krein's harmonic language is often "formally" similar to that of Ravel, but its substance is utterly different. In Ravel the same chords ring like a refined dream, a vision, an almost intangible hallucination; in Krein they ring with reality, they are a "living piece of emotion." Krein illustrates clearly how the same material may serve utterly different artistic purposes, how the psychology of the creator completely changes the significance and meaning of his material.

At the present Krein is in the full bloom of his creative

powers and energy. But though we acknowledge him to be the central figure of the Russian-Jewish group, or at any rate the most brilliant and dynamic figure in it, it must be admitted that so far no vestige of his influence on other composers has been observed. And perhaps there never will be, for reasons similar to those that prevented the manifestation of such influences after Skryabin. The style is too specific, the characteristics are too striking, and every imitation immediately "convicts" the imitator more than he finds comfortable or desirable. Only in the young champion of the Jewish school, Vyeprik, may one trace Krein's influence, though in a form weak and "innocuous."

Recent years have brought Krein something even in the way of world-wide recognition. His compositions have begun to penetrate abroad, and, unlike many other Russian compositions of recent years, win a firm place. At all events, if any contemporary Russian composer is to be awarded the palm of pre-eminence in the expression of the national spirit of Judaism, Krein is most likely to be the one selected. His music is more national in emotion, more typical in structure, less permeated with the influences of antecedent Russian music, and the very spirit of the Judaism it manifests is more characteristic than, let us say, that which is revealed by Gnyesin, who next to Krein, makes the strongest bid to being regarded as the founder of Jewish National music in Russia.

GRIGORIY KREIN

(Born 1880)

GRIGORIY KREIN is somehow always over-shadowed by
the brilliant and popularly written works of his brother
Alyeksandr. Grigoriy Krein is a far more abstract and less
real musician. First, in spite of his closeness to Jewish musical
moods and ideals, he has remained mostly aloof and has not
grown too enthusiastic over "obviously expressed nationalism." Nationalism manifests itself in him, if at all, in the
form of a native expression. It appears of itself, forced
to the surface by the mighty impulse of the race. He began
his career as composer somewhat earlier than his brother.
In distinction to the latter, he was not self-taught, and
in spite of his former radicalism, he has gone through a
serious and formal school of work and training as a composer. Unquestionably he was one of the first and most
active innovators at the time when Skryabin was just rising
on the horizon. His sympathies have always gone out
towards the French neo-impressionists and Skryabin. Grigoriy
Krein was perhaps one of the first before Skryabin to cultivate complex chords and polyphonic combinations. Though
lacking the primitive lyricism of his brother, and rather
contemplative in sentiment, he is endowed with strong emotionalism and profound expressiveness. Genuine power may
often be felt in his music, and his melody is always noble
and full of dynamic power. He is more profound than
Alyeksandr Krein, though he is inferior to him in passion
and in lyricism, as well as in the capacity of affecting great
masses. His is the typical "music for the few." A strange
fate has persecuted this thoughtful composer, bringing to

mind the bitterest pages from the annals of "martyrs of
music." Non-recognition, ridicule and early oblivion fell
to his lot, while in reality everything in Grigoriy Krein's
music is still in the future, and very few have so far justly
appraised this sincere and noble artist. It is enough to say
that Grigoriy Krein's inventive powers perhaps exceeds Skryabin's, and that he has "invented" much more. Moreover,
his creative work is considerably more varied than that of
Alyeksandr Krein, who writes his compositions in one
colour, while the palette of Grigoriy possesses several. Nor
can he be accused of writing too little; Grigoriy Krein has
to his credit several piano sonatas on a grand scale, major
chamber pieces, violin sonatas, poems for the violin, and
many songs.

The sphere of the orchestra is the only one in which he has
not tried his powers, but his austere and self-enclosed talent
somehow has no predilection for orchestral colour and magnificence. Ridiculed in his time by light-minded critics, he
has nevertheless continued his line of creative work, making
no concessions to public opinion, and even now, in the epoch
of general "revaluation of musical values," he continues to
worship his ancient impressionistic musical gods. His is the
type of an artist severe and inexorable towards himself, who
does not expect recognition although he would not refuse
it. While he is generally classed with his brother under the
group of the Jewish National School, the classification as I
have said above, is hardly justified. Grigoriy Krein has much
more kinship with Ravel than with his Russian compatriots,
but he does not possess Ravel's "fascination of sonority."
He is more austere and reserved, and less "colourful." The
workmanship of his compositions is never lapidary nor decorative, on the contrary it is elaborate and all its details
carefully written out. One might say that many traits
which have become characteristic of Alyeksandr Krein, first
appeared in his brother Grigoriy, but the latter could not

endow them with the brilliance or popularity within reach of the former. And thus this great artist lives unrecognised by the world, not even properly observed by his musical intimates, keeping up his creative work in spite of all discouragement. Creative work of this kind is usually rewarded with fame after death, or with a belated if firm recognition. One hopes that the time is not distant when it will become known on a scale which it justly merits.

Among his compositions must be noticed a Violin Sonata and a splendid Violin Poem, full of restrained passion and deep pathos. Splendid also is his last Piano Sonata written in monumental style. Grigoriy Krein has no particular leaning towards miniature forms of self-expression; even in his minor pieces he prefers the more expansive forms, and the ideas he expresses in music are usually indeed so considerable as to require larger forms. Hence comes his partiality for the sonata as the most substantial musical form. The enormous technical difficulties in which his compositions abound are among the causes which stand in the way of their becoming familiar even among musicians. In general, they are among the most complex and difficult compositions that have ever been written in the field of chamber music. Of course, all this is relative, and what some years ago frightened pianists and violinists, and deterred them from performing Krein's compositions, now seems a bugbear no longer.

ALYEKSEY STANCHINSKI

(1889–1913)

I CANNOT leave unmentioned this short-lived meteor of talent which flashed into view with a dazzling flame, only to be extinguished prematurely and without having had time to leave the proper impression on the world. There is no doubt that in the death of A. Stanchinski, the world lost a greater composer than the one it only knew in his person during his brief lifetime. He began his creative work at the age of sixteen, only to meet an untimely death at twenty-four. Unfortunately, fate had not prepared for him the fame of a Pergolese, and among his compositions, quite numerous for his age and span of activity, there was not a single one which could gain popularity with a wide public. He was a man of self-enclosed and exquisite mentality, a refined and strange soul which but few knew, and still fewer sensed, and which, being the most tender part of him, was doomed to fall ill earliest of all.

At first a pupil of the Moscow pedagogue and theorist, Zhilyayeff, and later of the famous S. I. Tañeyeff, Stanchinski entered upon the path of creative art at the time when Skryabin had just begun to rise in Russia, and the first rumours of Debussy's fame arrived. The youthful Stanchinski, a passionate admirer of the two new geniuses and aflame with new musical ideas, naturally succumbed to the influence of their powerful individualities. His first compositions, which aroused the displeasure and even the harsh protest of the conservative Tañeyeff, were executed in the form of musical miniatures, which in form and content closely approached the compositions of Grieg and Skryabin. The fresh and juicy harmony, the strange semi-tone moods of this music, in which was felt some suppressed and fantastic tragedy like the horror of a fairy-tale, attracted the attention of musicians. The youthful Alyosha Stanchinski became the fashionable rising star in the musical circles of Moscow; his compositions in manuscript copies circulated in the capital, far ahead of their publication, rousing perplexity on the part of some and rapture in others. The beginning of his musical career was really extraordinarily brilliant, and early success and even the beginning of fame were his during his lifetime. Even the word genius was, perhaps prematurely, used in connection with him. However, we think that potentially even that word was right, but time did not allow the composer's talent to unfold to the proper degree.

Soon, however, tragedy broke into the life of the youthful musician. His spirit, abnormally delicate, could not withstand the too hard and harsh contacts with life, though possibly the real cause, about which we are left in the dark, was heredity. However, before reaching his twentieth year the young composer, like Hugo Wolf, began to exhibit the symptoms of mental disease. At first his delirious ideas involved only the musical realm, but soon they spread into other spheres as well. He could not withstand the pressure of his own creative forces. He was placed in a psychiatric clinic suffering from "dementia præcox," in circular form. Attacks alternated with moments of comparative lucidity, during which the unfortunate composer attempted to continue creating his musical images in the midst of a mass of suppressed delirious ideas, which filled his incurably diseased consciousness. The compositions of this diseased period are distinguished by much greater mastery and maturity of form. It is curious that in these he departed from the line of impressionism and romanticism in which he had begun. New, purely formal problems loomed before him. This is the more interesting because we all know now that formalism has at present vanquished romanticism and is, as it were, the more modern and newer tendency. In his being carried away by formalism, during the years when impressionism and emotionalism were celebrating victory along the entire front, Stanchinski manifested a sort of artistic prevision of the future, which alas, he was not fated to meet.

His first compositions, preludes and poems in the manner of Skryabin and Grieg, no longer satisfied him, in spite of their great merits. Besides the fantastic moods and fairy-tale gloominess peculiar to him, moods of jest and sarcasm appear in his music. In this he anticipates Prokofyeff, but his jest is of a sickly semi-psychopathic hue, and not the jest of the healthy, perhaps over-healthy Prokofyeff, the youthful "Scythian." It is the psychopathic patient's laugh behind which is felt a swarm of hallucinatory images. Such are his *Sketches* for the piano, the only ones published so far. In other compositions—*Canon, Fugue, Sonata*—Stanchinski is a formalist who carefully combines the constructive world of polyphonic forms with the new world of harmonies, and who mates Bach's old technique with harmonies in the style of Schoenberg. Stanchinski's world of sound-combinations becomes ever more hard, in this definitely anticipating a number of the most modern composers, Schoenberg, Stravinski and the contemporary polytonalists. Definite, polytonal structures occur in his compositions and at the same time, under the influence of disease, a certain dryness and constructive planning appear in his writing of music.

In a fit of new madness accompanied by hallucinations, Stanchinski destroyed his early compositions and they would have been lost to posterity, had they not been reconstructed from memory by devoted friends. The periods of lucid states grew rarer and rarer, though Stanchinski did not cease composing. Friends who were intimate with him, assert that he was full of musical ideas and still more of interesting and strange "ideas about music," part of which apparently must have belonged more properly to the sphere of psychopathogy. The subtle construction and schematism of his music, taken in connection with the hallucinatory and fairy-tale tone of its moods, make this talented sick man kindred to another such unfortunate, the diseased painter, Churlyanis. He, too, created hallucinatory dream pictures, and these, as the disease made its triumphant progress, grew more and more schematic; geometry invaded fancy; in Stanchinski's case geometry defeated musical intuition. These parallels will perhaps be of interest to the psychiatrist, under whose department Stanchinski came more and more.

Curiously the great musicians who were his contemporaries did not recognise his talent. Some, like Metner, failed because of inborn conservatism; others, like Prokofyeff, owing to the vague protest of a healthy nature against a diseased one; others, like Skryabin, because of the isolation which distinguished the author of the *Extase* from all other authors. His new style of creative art roused particular criticism, precisely because it was original and anticipated the music that was to come.

His strange and short life broke off just as strangely as it had run, his death being as much of a mystery as his life had been. He was found dead on the bank of a river, near the village where he went to a rendezvous with his secret wife. Whether he was drowned or died from heart failure, whether it was a case of suicide on the part of the unfortunate sick man or he fell victim to a crime, has remained unknown. Various versions of suicide and drowning were popular.

His compositions saw the light of fame only after his death, and even then, for but a brief period. It was wartime; other more real and cruel interests cast their shadow over the world. People could not be concerned about hapless composers. The publication of his work was difficult and complicated, expensive and beyond the means of his friends, while war conditions were not favourable for the performance of his compositions. A veil of oblivion began to drop over Stanchinski's name. The musical world was shaken by two greater losses, completely obscuring the memory of the unfortunate, insane talent. Skryabin and Tañeyeff died, one shortly after the other. Then came the privations of the pre-revolutionary period, the tumult and storm of the Revolution, the October upheaval of Bolshevism. Stanchinski was buried under the ruins of tottering historical values. There was nobody even to recall him.

Now that the world atmosphere again seems like the first reappearance of the sun after storm, a sun timid and yet scattering the clouds, the time has come to recall the prematurely dead composer who in intensity of talent was unquestionably comparable to Skryabin and Prokofyeff and Stravinski, and considerably beyond many now active composers. There was nobody to intercede for him when he died amidst world cataclysms, and the flower of his fame was still so tender and frail that it shriveled at the touch of the fiery breath of the Revolution. But already under the Bolsheviks, the musical sector of the Government Publishing Department undertook to engrave his compositions. And possibly now fate's historical injustice to this extraordinarily gifted musician will be rectified.

FYODOR AKIMYENKO

(Born 1876)

IT is not granted to all to be powerful and proud, but in
art even the miniaturist and creator of a certain limited
world, if it be his own, has a right to exist. To these possessors of "small worlds," belongs the composer Akimyenko,
whose compositions are known both in Russia and abroad,
especially in France.

It cannot be denied that Akimyenko possesses a world of
his own, a convincingly stable world. It is not a chance
whim of fancy, nor a chance practical choice, but it is
precisely his own native world. Akimyenko, least of all,
"a man of this world," has estranged and shut himself off
from people. Isolated, somehow even unfamiliar with the
earth and its inhabitants, unpractical and infinitely naïve as
saints and children can be naïve, he seeks neither fame nor
money and in his attitude towards art there is a holy touch
and some antique devotion and purity which seems almost
insane to us moderns. The world which he endeavours to
embody in sounds is the world of heaven. In a strange
naïve design, worlds of seraphim and cherubim interweave
in this heaven with worlds of the Saturnian rings and scientific nebulæ of Newton and Flammarion, intertwined with
the world of mystic legends. But it is a genuine "heaven"
which he has spiritually experienced. Friend and comrade of
the renowned Flammarion, he received from that great
preacher of scientific celestial glories both his love for the
nebular world and his indifference and indolent contempt
for the earthly one. With a weird artistic fancy he has
peopled the world of stars and nebulæ with seraphs and

cherubs, and fused the dreams of the Middle Ages with those of scientific beauty. This conception of the world possesses something of the naïveté of an ancient monk who accepts Aristotle along with the Holy Scripture. It might be thought that these themes,—grandiose among the grandiose, the most colossal ideas of mankind, the idea of a mystic heaven peopled with terrible and mysterious beings combined and unified with mighty æons standing before the Lord, and the no less grandiose idea of cosmic infinite space peopled with grandiose nebulæ, whole star-worlds of which each is a sun-world,—that these ideas in the refraction of the composer's creative art would produce grandiose annihilating music. Nothing of the kind. Quietly and tranquilly, as if in a child's head, these grandiose ideas have gotten along side by side, and produced a quiet and holy radiance in which it is possible to observe charm and beauty and even a sort of salon politeness, in a word everything save grandioseness and might. One might begin to think of insincerity and the affectation to circulate in the midst of grand images. But no. Akimyenko is a man of unquestionable sincerity, a man organically devoid of snobbery. In his brain grandiose ideas simply reflected themselves as evenly and peacefully and tinily as the skies reflect themselves in a crystal ball in a garden. Tiny and cosy, with the cosiness of a child's soul that knows neither malice nor doubt.

Akimyenko is a miniaturist of grandeur. The paradoxical nature of his being causes the oddity of his music. All of it is incorporeal, bloodless, "astral," as if it were not woven of passionate tonal matter, having nothing of that sanguineous and burning matter of which Wagner had built his Titanic worlds. Akimyenko's musical matter is of extraordinary chastity, music of the monastery. And there is in it also an element of femininity. One might easily believe that some young nun in her revery would evoke just such sounds, so bloodless and passionless, chaste with unruffled chastity, full of holiness and childishness, dreaming of the grandiose and the sublime, but in some sort of a miniature microscopic world.

The femininity of Akimyenko's music, the simultaneous presence of the salon and sublimely grandiose themes, make him kindred to Skryabin. And not without reason were the two composers great friends in their lifetime, and the author of the *Poème d'Extase,* who as a rule assumed a skeptical and grudging attitude towards contemporary composers, did divine a friend and a man of congenial ideas in the quiet and naïve Akimyenko. His difference from Skryabin as well as his similarity to him, strike both the eye and the ear. The difference lies in his anæmic sinlessness, in his musical "sexlessness," if not his femininity. As much as Skryabin is passionate and even erotic, just so chaste is Akimyenko. Yet some common element created them, and the miniature and simplified inner world of Akimyenko, with its salonishness beside its tendency toward the grandiose, is but the diminutive of the truly grandiose created by the puissant talent of the author of *Prometheus.*

Both his chaste reserve and the inner consciousness of his own worth made Akimyenko kindred to Skryabin. Like Skryabin, he has a predilection for the intimate world of the piano, but he lacks even the impulse to write for the macrocosm of the orchestra. He feels free and at ease in the two piano lines in which he holds with perfect comfort the rings of Saturn and the myriads of nebulæ and the choirs of quiet and by no means terrible cherubim and seraphim. It is a quiet and domestic starry religion, whose altar is the piano and in which the whole world becomes a sweet and pretty fairy-tale. This music may appear watery, but after a time one begins to feel that the author is right, that there is some specific beauty in this world, that in this wateriness there is the incorporeal beauty of some astral vision, that this salonishness does not come from the lack of depth in his nature, but from its purity, from the fact that the composer's unmalicious and starry soul really has nothing whatever to do with evil.

Starry dreams, beautiful scientific fantasies about planetary worlds, the sublime infinity of space, dances of nebulæ watched through some sort of a telescope and turning into a graceful ballet, round dances of fantastic beings, elves, seraphim, cherubim, who in some way combine with the world of nebulæ,—this is Akimyenko's world. At first this seems boring and too sugary, then somehow it carries one away with its purity, and then it begins to grow sugary again. Either we, who are not holy, feel crowded and bored in the atmosphere of such moral rarity, as if we were indeed in "inter-planetary" space, or there is too little flesh, too little blood, too little passion here, and this creative art is too ethereal, too chaste. At any rate, we cannot survive for long in this atmosphere of Akimyenko's cherubim, and the very ideas served up in such microscopic expositions begin to require some sort of magnification. After all, a modern auditor is a being of flesh and blood, not a schoolgirl prematurely immured in a convent.

It is hard to criticise Akimyenko's music. The imperturbability of this nature is so great, that all critical thrusts glance off his bodiless vision, which, while it is music, perhaps does not desire to be. In this again lies his similarity to Skryabin, who considered it a disgrace "to be only a musician." Akimyenko creates his seraphic songs because such is his inner necessity, and he does not need "the justification of his music" at all. One might imagine that his inner world does not express itself sufficiently in his music, that he is richer than it, more grandiose. No, this is not true either. On the contrary, I suppose that his inner world adequately expresses itself in his visionary music, that he is just as visionary, just as fleshless as the spirits at spiritualist seances. In the midst of other musical compositions, woven of flesh and blood, of nerves and passions, Akimyenko's music struts like a pallid ghost and passes through hard bodies without difficulty, easily entering the psyche and perception of the hearer, and then with equal ease and without hindrance, passing out of it, leaving neither too deep nor too clear an impression, truly like a musical ghost.

But on the other hand, is not this some great and profound originality? One cannot deny the external similarity of Akimyenko and his music to the child literature of the Loeschhorns and similar authors, but the difference lies in the fact that the latter adapt themselves to a child's mind, while Akimyenko thinks and feels so himself. And at the same time, without astonishment, the hearer discerns in his creations a certain specific gracefulness, and occasionally a subtle, almost indistinguishable originality, no longer an originality of contents and ideas, but the originality of the embodiment itself. It is difficult to separate Akimyenko from his seraph-astral-planetary world, and it is hard to say that his music, deprived of titles, deprived of this verbal explanation of "what it ought to mean," would make any impression whatever. But is not the author's music the synthesis of his thought and his form? Cannot the same reproaches be levelled at Skryabin and Debussy, and have they not been flung at Richard Wagner himself in his time? Akimyenko has created a strange and small world, but it is his own world, and in spite of the vagueness and ghostliness of its exterior it possesses an originality which permits one to single Akimyenko out of the host of pallid epigones and award him a certain substantial significance.

Akimyenko has written much, all of it in the same intimate spirit. His muse cannot boast of variety. His seraphic songs always discuss the same thing. He is just as much a man of a single love in his creative work as Skryabin. His best works are just these small semi-salon, semi-mystical piano compositions, semi-astronomic in their theme and graceful in their form. The composer himself plays these with a tender charm and with a certain ineffable originality. His works rarely appear on the concert stage, but they have not been created for it. The salon, the medium-sized drawing room, offer the largest area and space for these tender creations, whose very meaning flickers out in surroundings which even slightly exceed the limits of intimacy.

NIKOLAY ROSLAVYETS

(Born 1880)

N. Roslavyets stands alone in the group of contemporary Russian composers living and working amid post-revolutionary conditions. But the beginning of his activity belongs to the pre-revolutionary period. At the time when Skryabin lived and worked, when the modernistic group was making its victorious march upon the stronghold of Russian music, in the period of the casting down of old canons, the first compositions of Roslavyets appeared. They were coloured in ultra-modernistic hues, with bold complex harmonies in which musicians could at first hearing discover nothing but wild cacophony. At that time his work met with no sympathy, and somehow he became part of no composers' group of the musical world of the time.

But his rise at that time was nevertheless interesting. That pre-War era bearing the motto "Fight against the old musical foundations," and possessing a strong revolutionary colouring in a musical sense, differed exceedingly from the inventive impulses of the former romanticism of the Russian National School of Borodin, Musorgski, Balakireff, Rimski-Korsakoff. The former innovations were naïve and arbitrary, asserted in the name of the freedom of creative art, and overthrowing the old canons and rules merely in order to establish the complete power and arbitrary will of creative genius, in their stead. In the epoch of which we speak, we observe something else. The innovations both of Skryabin and those grouped around him (among whom Roslavyets doubtless occupies a formal place) were quite different. Old canons were overthrown only in order to set up, in their stead, new rules, new theoretical foundations, just as strong and categorical if not still more rigid. Skryabin's harmonic tonal system of which we have spoken bears within it all the external and internal earmarks of a sustained specifically "severe style." Skryabin did not establish freedom of creative art. On the contrary he placed his own limits on himself, bringing his own creative work within the limits of the law.. He wrote according to certain rules, new it is true, but rules nevertheless, and within these he wrote with such punctuality and strictness that in comparison a Schumann or a Chopin, let alone a Wagner, seemed a sheer anarchist. Formalism of musical thought, hatred of anarchy in creative art (which was precisely a commandment in the romantic era), love for theorising and anticipating the musically creative process by some sort of reasoning and plan, were characteristic of the pre-War epoch in which the experienced eye of the historian discovers, with some effort, a similarity with "Byzantinism" and other typical forms of art which were already on the decline though still powerful.

It is not without reason that the musical formation of Skryabin and his associate composers exhibits such closeness to the literary current of symbolism in Russian literature of the day. The search for external means, new means, new excitations, and the partiality for formal problems of art, is common to both. In this we do not touch upon the emotional side of Skryabin's art. Skryabin himself was fiery and passionate, his music illuminated from within by a certain light which could and did paralyse the formalism that came to Skryabin as the spirit of the time and the epoch. This was not the case with his followers.

The others who were nurtured by the same time and the same epoch, under the same esthetic standards, did not possess this fieriness. But formalism was triumphant nevertheless. It was still more triumphant because it was not paralysed and hidden by emotion. Skryabin did not notice his own realism and he was not acute in observing it in general, but in the case of Roslavyets, who must be classed officially as the closest to Skryabin, we find not only attentiveness to his own formalism, but an esthetic deification of it, and the placing of it in the very centre of creation.

If in the pleiad of Russian musicians who reflected in sounds the spirit of literary symbolism, Skryabin is analogous to Balmont to a certain degree, Roslavyets is rather analogous to Bryusoff, that cold well-balanced master, admirer of mastery and stylist to the marrow of his bones, in whom the very creative process occasionally seems reduced to a series of scientifically reasoned calculations, which nevertheless produce the impression of inspiration.

Roslavyets began where Skryabin ended, proclaiming a new musical catechism of a purely formal character, and constructing a new theory of harmonies which was to replace the old. With Skryabin theory was a sort of "super-structure" on mystical philosophic edifices, just as all his music in general was to his mind but a "reflection" of some legitimate considerations not of a musical but of a cosmic order. Roslavyets has no ties with mysticism and with philosophy. His world breaks off right here behind the sounds; behind the sounds there is no "stir of chaos," as Tyutcheff would say. Everything is simple and clear. He is a positivist in esthetics; and accordingly he begins with his theory which he applies in an orderly and consistent way. With him music is the organisation of tonal matter, neither more nor less. Emotion does not interest him; he is interested only in the methods of organisation. Hence Roslavyets is in his essence an esthetic formalist, an inventor of bizarre tonal designs behind which he does not wish any other substance to be seen, priding himself on his anti-emotionalism and formalism. Thus his external similarity with and closeness to Skryabin become his contrast to him as well, ending in the ranks of the composers whom the mystic Skryabin had always disavowed precisely for their being out of touch with the "mystic wellsprings of music and art."

It is interesting to note that just as an "idea" becomes a religion with certain inventors, so this theory with Roslavyets became a dogma to which he sought to attribute universal obligation. His theory was a super-structure on the old theory of music, a "second-story" added to the original edifice. The old theory enters into his new as a "particular case." Roslavyets, the evolutionist who thinks that everything must necessarily develop and grow more complex, considers his theory the only musical truth, absolute as the laws of nature. He teaches it to his pupils as a truth verified and exact, and if he could he would make his new "musical dogma" compulsory. Like all dogmatists Roslavyets is intolerant and cruel towards representatives of any other creed in music. He treats the classics with scorn, he denies the yesterday of art for the sake of his tomorrow as it pictures itself to him. With him the foreground belongs to his theory, and mastery within the limits of this theory.

These qualities bring him near to the type of academist. He is a strange yet natural type of "academist innovator." To him everything is clear in the world of music and he has but to apply his technique to "produce things musical." It is a combination of "mastery" and artisanship, a mixture of art with something that in no way differs from the work of a watchmaker or jeweller. These are exactly the views of Roslavyets, a convinced master and a convinced "specialist in musical business," as he calls himself.

I shall not enter into a detailed examination of his theory, for that is comprehensible and essential only to the musical specialist. I shall say only that the principles of tonal "organisation" by which Roslavyets creates, lead him to the creation of very complex, very bizarre harmonies. Formally his music is quite perfect, it possesses an external dynamism and invariably a beautiful design. The complex world of

his harmonies makes him forget the difference between dissonances (sharp harmonies) and consonances (pleasing harmonies) which are entirely swallowed up by the former. His
compositions resemble one another just as the standardised
productions of any specialist resemble his others. It is obvious that these "musical things" come from one workman in
one firm. If one seeks emotional saturation, "the utterance"
of something trans-musical reflected and recorded in tones
by a mysterious force, one finds in Roslavyets only dry ornament, ingeniously and bizarrely complex, devoid of any
antique simplicity. His mastery astonishes but never moves;
that is not part of his task.

Roslavyets, positivist and Marxist in his convictions, laughs
at emotions and the "soul of music." According to his theory, which has no trace of mysticism, though it possesses
dogmatism, music can and must express thought, not feeling. It must express its own organisation. This is something
intermediate between ornament and an ingenious chess problem. To compose an organism of this kind affords the composer joy similar to the "scientific joy" of a mathematician
solving a difficult problem. He does not even love sound in
itself overmuch and one of the tenets of his theory maintains
that soon music will not be heard in performance but merely
"read through" with the inner ear in the same manner as
verse is now inwardly read. There is a great deal of "musical
aristocracy" in his theorising, and he composes for the circle
of the "connoisseurs of formal perfection," and not at all
for the emotional crowd. He counts upon the most highly
qualified hearer, or rather "reader," of his music.

The style of his art has remained almost unchanged even
after the great upheavals which have occurred in the world
and Russia since 1914. It is difficult to differentiate even
the style of his early Violin Sonata written in 1911 in the
era of Skryabin's predominance. Already he employed a far
more complicated language of harmony than Skryabin and

possibly Schoenberg, but just as elaborately "differentiated" and without any traces of "decorativeness." Roslavyets is a miniaturist in his tonal matter; like both Skryabin and Schoenberg, he lovingly writes out the minutest details. The only thing wherein his later compositions differ from his earlier ones is a greater perfection of elaboration, an ever-growing academic formalism and a striving for precision, harmoniousness and "abstract perfection."

The change which revolutionary events brought to his art consisted curiously in the fact that in some way or another he managed to combine his esthetic theories with the general ideas of Marxism, and deduced it from his premises. His theory of music as "organised tonal matter" fits in with the general system of social order organised by the creative will of communism in such a manner that the greatest economy of forces and energy may be observed. Here, too, Roslavyets's dogmatism and theorising have manifested themselves in the highest degree, once again recalling Skryabin, who also fitted his musical system into a harmonious relationship with the cosmos and its creative process.

Roslavyets's Marxism and his association with communistic theories and practice could not fail to affect his compositions. He considered it his duty to come out as composer of revolutionary music. Beginning with 1918, revolutionary music in Russia was created in bulk and poorly, and in accordance with specifications and requests from the respective organisations. Roslavyets was the first "convinced" composer of music for the proletariat. He set himself the task of eradicating the dilettantism from composition of this kind and their invariably poor style and taste, usually derived from the repertory of the operetta and "light" music. Even for the proletariat Roslavyets endeavoured to write masterly and complex music. But in spite of his theoretic premises that the most complex music is within the grasp of the working-man, if it but "organises tonal matter" well, Roslavyets finally had to make a number of concessions, and his revolutionary compositions, written for workmen's clubs, differ strongly in style from his "serious" compositions. Everything is simpler, more primitive and his usual complex musical language (the modernistic language) gives way to a plainer one. As an intermediate essay, Roslavyets wrote several songs to revolutionary texts by present-day Russian poets and some of bygone years, preserving his style intact. Such are *Songs of the Labouring Professions,* and *The Songs of the Revolution,* two volumes which cannot be denied their structural musical merits.

Roslavyets has worked almost exclusively in the field of chamber music and only during recent years has he attempted to pass from the chamber into the orchestral auditorium, with a Symphony and Violin Concerto. He is very productive, as a real master is, and his creative art process occasionally appears mechanical in its facility. He has written a mass of sonatas for the piano, violin, 'cello; trios, quartettes, and various minor pieces for the piano and violin. All these pieces are of nearly equal merit; Roslavyets's manufacture is so standardised that the pieces he puts forth are technically indistinguishable one from the other. His fame began only after the Revolution; previous to that his compositions never found even a comparatively decent performer owing to their difficulty and unusual language.

BOLYESLAV YAVORSKI (Born 1880)
AND HIS PUPILS

THERE is almost cause to leave B. Yavorski out of the list
of Russian composers, for he composes so little and is so
capricious and bizarre, hardly ever publishing his works.
The contrasting traits of a mediæval alchemist like Agrippa
of black magic fame and a meister-singer are interwoven in
him with those of a modern scientific investigator and theoretician. But one thing is indubitable, among modern Russian musicians B. Yavorski is one of the most curious and
interesting personalities not only as a composer but as a
great influence upon the musical world, as an original, whimsical thinker, occasionally flashing genius and enormous
subtlety of ideas, occasionally revealing half-insane symptoms,
queer madness and almost fanatic dogmatism bizarrely combining to form a musical Cagliostro of contemporary Russia.

Yavorski is a theorist in the field of music. As I have
said, his compositions are not numerous but they show the
refinement typical of his Polish nationality, and the clever
and brightly recreated characteristics of Chopin, Debussy
Liszt and Skryabin. They are mostly vocal miniatures, songs
set to texts always carefully chosen from the greatest names
in Russian and foreign literature, and composed with an accuracy of melodic design which recalls Musorgski. Yavorski
was one of the first in Russia to undertake the important
cultural work of re-establishing Liszt as a composer. Liszt
had been forgotten in Russia. He was considered as merely
a virtuoso composer, the author of graceful and noisy trifles
for the purpose of astonishing with brilliance of technique.
The Liszt who had composed the *Faust Symphony,* sonatas,
masses and a great number of symphonic poems was entirely

obscured and altogether unknown. Yavorski was one of the fore-runners of the Liszt revival in Russia, and reflected partly in Skryabin himself. But Yavorski's principal importance does not lie in that, but in his creation of a musical theory. A fine and forceful pedagogue, he could hold the young generation in a sort of hypnotic subjection and he brought up whole generations of young composers in the spirit of his theory.

Yavorski's theory is original and vague at the same time. In it a genuine insight of genius into the nature of the musical fabric is tangled up with a species of half-mysticism which is not presented as a result of research but rather as "a teacher's divine revelation" subject neither to discussion nor proof. Profound knowledge and occasionally unparalleled subtle understanding of music mixed with dilettantism and ignorance and even Cagliostro in the worst light,—these are the features of the theory which the extraordinary hypnotic power of the teacher himself over musical minds found few to withstand. Nearly all composers of the younger generation have in one way or another, indirectly or directly gone through his hands, nearly all of them have tasted of this knowledge which, according to Yavorski's audacious confidence, was to crowd out all the old withered theories and take their place.

I shall not undertake a discussion and exposition of this theory, since its very vagueness makes an exposition of it exceedingly difficult. Being original in whatever he undertook, Yavorski did not publish his theory but handed it down merely by word of mouth as a "sacred tradition," excepting only for a few articles of aphoristic character in which the propositions of his theory were given as the fruits of a higher perception requiring no proofs. As he put it, the nature of musical "speech" is based on the fact of the gravitation of some sounds towards others. In Yavorski's opinion, purely *a priori* and not devoid of mystical features, this

gravitation is "the same" mundane gravitation which Newton discovered. But the lore and mysticism of the new
musical occultist and magician is not important. What is
important is that from this gravitation Yavorski derives a
series of consequences, and in particular his theory of musical
ladӱ (Russian for modes, tonalities). The *ladӱ* are various
systems in which the gravitation expresses and moulds itself.
It is curious that a number of phenomena of new music as
well as a number of formerly insufficiently explained phenomena of old music are magnificently explained by this
theory of gravitation and *ladӱ*. Herein is the positive side
of his ideas and theory, which both appealed to the mind
of youth and attracted those who delighted in musical analysis and awaited new theoretical standards to replace the
withered old ones.

But like all dogma Yavorski's theory contained a new
despotism of musical thought over creative art. The immediate experiments even proved that the new basis which this
original theorist had prepared for music offered less than
the old one, for the latter had at least the advantage that all
forceful composers had long forgotten to pay any attention
to it. And the disciples of Yavorski's School soon became
in their turn "meister-singers" of a peculiar order who had
mastered the new tablature and professed faith in it with
the sincerity and zeal of neophytes. Whether for good or
for evil, all musical Russia at present is divided into "Yavorians" and "Old-Believers," with the former inclining towards
aggressive action along the whole musical front. Though
still insufficiently verified, the new theory is being introduced into institutions of musical learning, its half-mystical,
half-cabalistic propositions taking the place of the simple
recipes of old naïve theory which possessed the advantage
of not requiring obedience.

The number of Yavorski's pupils is enormous. This musical Cagliostro has managed to capture the minds of promi-

nent musicians. In this he was helped by his sharp novel speech, ever seeking original forms of expression, and his invariably subtle musical taste. Some of his disciples have become disloyal and have fallen into "anti-Yavorianism," heresies which at times approach the old creeds and occasionally even sheer theoretical anarchism. His most pronounced, convinced and firm followers are the young composers Alyeksandr Myelkikh (born 1889) and Sergey Protopopoff (born 1890).

A. Myelkikh is a composer of small scope but fine schooling. A certain formalism which is peculiar to all Yavorians fetters his fine but not profound talent. Imperceptibly but in inevitable keeping with his theory, Yavorski gave his pupils so great a mass of musical formulas that their manner of composition received a certain general stamp which obliterated their own individuality. Characteristically Russian is this anarchism on principle that soon turns into a formalism and dogmatism which are its own negation.

Yavorski's "theory of ladӱ" has laid a heavy imprint on the creative work of Myelkikh, filling it with formulas that occasionally overshadow creative freedom. The scope of his talent is not great, and perhaps these formulas do aid the average talent. But woe unto the forceful genius who comes under the training of this new Loyola. His talent may be crushed in the vise of this new theory, more severe, more narrow and more uncomfortable than the soft and weakening clutch of the old and inexacting one.

Myelkikh has composed several important symphonic pieces, among them the beautiful music for *Aladdin and Palamida*. His *Revolt Sonata* for the piano shows Skryabin influences (parenthetically, the most compatible with Yavorski), and a fine style of piano writing.

His colleague, S. Protopopoff, is a more convinced and severe Yavorian; ladӱ discipline hangs heavily over all his music. Structural theory occasionally hides creative freedom.

This goes so far that in certain places the composer inserts in the text of his composition the names of the various *ladÿ* in which the given passage has been composed. But apart from this, which is essentially external, Protopopoff's music likewise smacks strongly of Skryabin. Skryabin survives easily and with perhaps the best results in the fold of Yavorski, himself such a strong admirer.

It is difficult to foretell what will be the final form of this movement which can no longer be called new, for it is over fifteen years old. And in the course of these years much has happened in music. The obvious tragedy of Yavorski and his group lies in the fact that their excessive theorising and excessive confidence in their theories have made them overlook the fact that music during these years took a turn to other forms, and that Skryabin together with his theories has not emerged at the head of the procession. As we have said, he is a musical "blind alley," interesting in itself, important and significant, but without continuation. Just at present music shows a strong tendency towards simplification of harmony, and in a number of other features towards a return to former standards. The line of super-refinement breaks down and in its place comes a new line of coarsening and decoration. In place of Yavorski's theory of *ladÿ*, practice presents us with the phenomena of "polytonalism" and "atonalism." Like all sectarians, the Yavorians declare all these tendencies to be a departure from righteousness, a heresy, not music, and we arrive at the rebirth of old musical hatred in a new form. Whenever a theory is placed in the foreground against the practice of art this is the result. Inevitably there are found compositions which do not fit in with the theory, and inevitably they are declared *false*.

But is this just precedure? Ought not musical theory be similar to any "natural science" theory? Ought it not derive from facts instead of prescribing them? Having discovered a new, unusual type of animal, no zoölogist will ever take it into his head to declare it "false." Yet the musical theorists, a people who in our scientific, experimental age have preserved a mediæval manner of thinking, fall into this very absurdity.

THE MOSCOW GROUP OF CONSERVATIVES

PERHAPS from the point of view of a strictly scientific classification the above grouping may not withstand criticism; I introduce it merely for the purposes of advantageous exposition. The composers whom I have brought together under this group of "Moscow Conservative Musicians" have as few common features as composers, as have those I have grouped together under the Leningrad group. What is common is geographical and that elusive general hue found in the works of composers who do not possess a striking individuality in their art and have not aimed at "blazing new paths." Furthermore, their "generation," too, is a common factor, all the musicians enumerated being practically of the same age and of the same training in the same Conservatory under the same musical "mentors." Subsequently each selected his own path in fields suited to his peculiar endowment.

The oldest of this group and the one most associated with the "old musical view of the world" is Georgiy Konyus (born 1862), a musician with a strange career and a curious fate. Having been graduated from the Moscow Conservatory as a pupil of Chaykovski and Tañeyeff, together with Rakhmaninoff and Skryabin, he distinguished himself at once with a number of other musicians who rightly or wrongly roused expectations, and came into the category of candidates to succeed the great generation of Chaykovski and Rubinstein. His first compositions created a sensation. And truly the youthful composer, a Frenchman by blood and a Russian in culture, oddly combined the refinement and elegance of the typical Gallic musician with the lyricism and melodiousness of Chaykovski's school. A musician of fine native taste, he immediately set himself apart as a subtle

instrumentator whose orchestra sounds delicate and transparent, in the melodic contours of whose creative art, Russian
tunefulness and an exquisiteness oddly intertwine, of which
it would perhaps be idle to seek prototypes in Russian music.
I especially emphasise the fine taste of Konyus as a composer.
In this trait there is much which anticipated Skryabin, and
in the graceful and minutely refined piano style of Konyus'
compositions we can now without effort discern certain traits
in common with that which subsequently distinguished the
author of the *Poème d'Extase*. "Tasteful" underscorings of
dissonances, extraordinary purity of part-writing, along with
a tendency towards the pungent in harmony,—all were
characteristic of Konyus, anticipating Skryabin, and unfortunately remaining but striking promises without subsequent performance.

His *Suite from Childlife* in whose graceful style we feel a
certain musical anticipation of the "childlife" inspirations of
Ravel and Debussy, gained immediate renown for him. At
Chaykovski's solicitation, Tsar Nicholas II granted the
young author a life pension of twelve hundred roubles which
he received until the collapse of the monarchy in Russia. But
as often happens, the encouragement was not properly directed. Konyus composed slowly and with effort, elaborating
details with painstaking accuracy. His urge to compose
waned rapidly; other musical activities attracted him,—the
activities of research work in musical theory. Whether
rightly or wrongly Konyus exchanged his small but elegant
world of composition for the still uncultivated field of
musical scientific investigation, and here his "painstaking"
and extraordinary pedantic accuracy have probably found
better application. Since 1900 he has practically been out
of the ranks of active composers, studying as he does the
field of musical theory and the laws of symmetry in musical
works. The old comparison of music with architecture,
put forth by Anton Rubinstein and Hanslick, finds a most

zealous follower in Konyus. He has given himself up to it
with a zeal approaching lunacy, and really arrived at some
interesting generalisations which constitute the essence of the
enormous labour occupying him for twenty-five years of his
life. An accurate and conscientious scholar, he subjected
thousands of musical productions to "measurements" and
analysis, to arrive at the laws of musical symmetry which he
considers his most valuable contribution to musical art, a
sort of "discovery of Copernicus" in the world of musical
forms. What the true significance of Konyus' "discovery"
may be, it is still too early to say. Despite the great importance of some of his assumptions, one cannot but perceive that the general outline of his theory is somewhat
strained with that tendency to "dictate law" unto art, which
is characteristic of all theorists. Experience shows that such
dictation leads in practice but to swifter revolution. But
be that as it may, Konyus has stepped out of the ranks of
Russian composers to swell the thin ranks of Russian
theorists.

Beside Konyus it is natural to place Georgiy Katuar (1861-
1926), a great musician who, in his lifetime, was distinguished
by the single but nowadays unpardonable fault of undue
modesty and inability to advertise himself. Like Konyus,
Katuar is a Frenchman by blood, a descendant of old immi-
grants who became almost completely Russianised during
their long residence in Russia. His French blood tells in the
refinement and taste which permeate his compositions, in his
tendency towards exquisiteness and harmony, and in the
masterly elaboration of details. Katuar began to write long
ago, but his modest and tender nature which shrank from
light and the world was incapable of booming his own works.
One of the first Moscow musicians to "recognise" Wagner
and bow before his genius, Katuar in his creative work combines the mastery and fundamentality of German music with
the elegance of the French and the profound lyricism of the

Russian. In this respect he recalls that genius Caesar Franck, the "French Brahms." But the French elements are completely transformed in him by the German and Russian ones, leaving but their elusive flare of refinement. This creative work, full of seriousness, profundity and exquisite feeling is not for the masses. To them it may and must occasionally appear tiresome, the more so since with all his positive qualities Katuar lacked an individuality of his own in his work. The models whom he imitated were no doubt musicians of genius; his art sprang from Richard Wagner and passed over paths of redemption through Chopin and Chaykovski. But of himself, there is only the strange combination of these influences and a careful fundamental technique of composition.

Katuar has not written much but he has written solidly. From his pen have come a piano concerto and a number of chamber pieces, many of which have successfully become stock numbers in the regular repertory of Russian chamber ensembles. His violin *Poem*, one of the most beautiful inspirations in Russian violin music, his songs and choruses attract attention by their exquisiteness, and the taste with which they have been written. Katuar, possessor of a fine but too delicate and timid soul, could not distinguish himself strongly beside the powerful and too brilliant talents creating at the same time and obscuring with their effulgence his talent of ordinary candle radiance. Only in the chamber world, where traditions are more carefully preserved, has his work an excellent chance of survival.

The creative art of Alyeksandr Gedike (born 1877), who, in common with the preceding composers, has a half-French origin, comes closest to the line of Russian musical art which sprang from Chaykovski and Tañeyeff and leads to "Germanophile" tendencies, for the two latter also belong to German culture. This Germanism leads to the resemblance to Brahms which we observe in Gedike's work, and this, in turn, makes. him akin to Metner, a composer closer to him both in sympathy and general talent. But Gedike's creative art is softer than Metner's, devoid of its severity, and that colourlessness which distinguishes Metner. On the other hand Gedike, while without these deficiencies of Metner, lacks as well anything that might give a character of his own to his music. As with Katuar we do not encounter any individuality but merely well-made, beautiful music, up to the best traditions of the Russian and German art. We find modesty and austere reserve which reflect the inner spirit of the authors themselves, and a holy sincerity. At a time when the presence of "originality" was considered indispensable to the point of morbidity, when even a paltry individuality so long as it was one's own, was welcome, the creative art of composers like Gedike and Katuar was driven into the shade.

Gedike is a conservative, his sympathies entirely on the side of the old "great" music of Beethoven, Wagner, Brahms, Chopin, Schumann, Chaykovski and Bach. But Gedike's soul is perhaps not so locked within itself as Metner's and much in contemporary music is clearer and more acceptable to him. Modest and quiet as a man, organically incapable of advertising his own compositions, he was long unknown as a composer. Yet he is the author of three symphonies written in Brahms' monumental manner, and of a number of chamber and piano pieces. Curiously Gedike, French by origin, German in culture, exhibits an enormous interest for Russian melody in his work. He has made splendid arrangements of a number of Russian songs for chorus, solo and chamber music accompaniment.

Like Konyus, Sergey Vasilyenko (born 1872), began brilliantly but his star soon set. His graduation cantata, *The Tale of the City of Kityezh*, was a triumph and a brilliant future was predicted for him. At the time he belonged to the left wing of Russian music but in reality the left wing was exceedingly moderate and its radicalism was based on Russian unfamiliarity with the more modern currents of musical thought. Wagner was regarded as of the extreme left. Skryabin who was abroad at the time was still little known and had not appeared in Russia, so that Vasilyenko and Rakhmaninoff were forced to play the rôle of radicals. Radicalism then consisted chiefly in not following in Chaykovski's footsteps or writing in the spirit of the Russian National School which had gained general recognition in Russia and partly even in musically backward Moscow. Vasilyenko's compositions *The Garden of Death* and *The Witch's Flight*, which had followed *The Tale of the City of Kityezh*, held throughout to the tone of Musorgski and Rimski-Korsakoff's program music. The appearance of Skryabin on the Russian horizon and the sudden strong "general swing towards the left" in all music threw Vasilyenko out of key as a composer. Unexpectedly he found himself in the "extreme right wing," and his creative work was placed under a disadvantage although he has not ceased to compose. The Russian nationalism which he had shown in his earlier compositions, *The Witch's Flight* in the style of Musorgski, and *Kityezh* in Borodin's style, has disappeared and international impressionism taken its place. In this spirit he composed his Symphony and his Suite *To the Sun*. One of his most recent compositions written in Russia under Soviet régime is the music for the ballet *Joseph the Handsome*, which was produced on the stage by the famous Russian ballet director, Goleyzovski.

Reinhold Glière (born 1874), of Belgian origin, belongs to the type of those fine masters who find it exceedingly easy to handle tonal matter, principally because they never set themselves the task of seeking out new paths or forcing originality. He possesses exceptional "lack of originality" but absorbs the most varied and usually fine influences in a masterly manner. His vocal songs composed in the style of

Chaykovski and Rakhmaninoff enjoyed enormous popularity in pre-War Russia. A splendid orchestrator, possessing in his palette all the colour effects in the very latest French manner, Glière has written for the orchestra many beautiful things, a number of which have enjoyed great success. His symphonies have been written in various styles: the first two approach Rakhmaninoff, the third, *Ilya Muromyets,* is rather an imitation of Skryabin's Third Symphony, *The Divine Poem.* Like many Russian composers who are not endowed with a striking individuality, this author has lately been working hard to create a special repertory of "revolutionary music" for Soviet Russia.

The oldest composer of this group, M. M. Ippolitoff-Ivanoff (born 1859), really belongs to the preceding generation of Tañeyeff and Glazunoff, but to a certain degree his fate is similar to that of the above enumerated composers. Ippolitoff-Ivanoff, too, began as an innovator, or at least for what then passed as an innovator, in Moscow. Possessor of a very simple and in the highest degree a naïve talent, clear and childishly pure, Ippolitoff-Ivanoff began in the tones of the Russian National School, which in itself was considered an "innovation." His *Caucasian Sketches* won enormous popularity not only in Russia but also abroad. But Ippolitoff-Ivanoff's inventive spirit was too feeble, his audiences too backward, and we soon see him back in the ranks of determined conservatives. Ippolitoff-Ivanoff has written several operas, among them, *Ruth,* on a biblical theme, and *Treachery,* on a subject taken from the Caucasus. He remains ever faithful to his inexacting but melodious style which is within the grasp of wide circles of the public. His Symphony, composed too naïvely for so responsible a musical form, and his chamber compositions, are less characteristic of him. For a time Ippolitoff-Ivanoff exerted a strong influence on the musical world of Moscow, occupying the post of Director of the Conservatory for more than fifteen years. But as a matter of fact his soft and languid character did not contribute to its flourishing or to its turning into a musical centre. The conservative party of composers whom I have enumerated embraces many excellent musicians, but all of them, from Konyus down to Ippolitoff-Ivanoff, confirm the historical axiom that only "conservative composers" endowed with enormous talent of genius to counterbalance their confirmed conservatism survive during active epochs of musical life, such as ours unquestionably is. Brahms survives, but not the ordinary "bandmaster." Hardly any one of those above enumerated can be classed among pre-eminent conservatives who have a chance of surviving, to which class, in all probability, belong but Tañeyeff, Rakhmaninoff and Metner.

THE LENINGRAD GROUP

THE Moscow group of conservative composers sprang up naturally as a sort of "selection" of less active, less original talents and, as one might easily expect, has its analogue in Russia's other capital and cultural centre, Leningrad. But the conservatism of Moscow and the conservatism of Leningrad are somewhat different, and this difference has been determined by the conditions of musical life in each.

As I have already pointed out, Moscow was more backward than Leningrad in the sense of keeping informed of the latest European musical thought. The traditions of the conservative musicians Rubinstein, Chaykovski and Tañeyeff held on tenaciously in Moscow, for here these men had been teachers and leaders. These traditions helped to isolate and make even the comparatively young generation (Rakhmaninoff, Gedike, Metner, Katuar) hostile to everything that smacked of innovation or was merely novel. St. Petersburg was different. There Anton Rubinstein's conservatism and the "German party" had long before been routed by the militant innovations of the mighty *Koochka* of Rimski-Korsakoff, Balakireff, Borodin, Musorgski and Cui. St. Petersburg came to believe in the innovations of the Russian National School much earlier than Moscow, but on the other hand this early recognition was a sort of vaccination against the contagion of subsequent innovation. Moscow of the twentieth century is perhaps more advanced than Leningrad that keeps on worshiping the idols set up in the seventies and the eighties. The authoritative teachers in Moscow were too conservative and hence youth came to a decided break with them. In St. Petersburg the guides were Glazunoff and Rimski-Korsakoff who in their time had been associated with innovation, and hence the break there was not so decisive and the activity of youth more timid. The authority of teachers of the older generation was much stronger and their very mastery appealed to youth. Hence an atmosphere most favourable for epigonism was here created. As is well known, the circle of the publisher Byelyayeff, which embraced the flower of the musical world of St. Petersburg and had the figures of Rimski-Korsakoff and Glazunoff as its "centre of ideas," gradually crowded out the old circle of active workers of the Russian National School. Finally the mighty *Koochka* dissolved, and its remnants in the persons of the aged Balakireff and Cui no longer enjoyed any authority among musicians, especially of the young generation. The atmosphere of the Byelyayeff circle with the published Maecenas as its "economic centre" and the overpowering authority of Glazunoff and Rimski-Korsakoff as "ideational centre," was exceedingly favourable to the creation of a whole swarm of disciples. These composed music according to the recipes of Rimski-Korsakoff and Glazunoff, and received their approval and the right to be published by Byelyayeff's firm. It is even difficult to enumerate the whole mass of minor composers who settled on that firm, composed music "decently-talentless" and overburdened the publisher's catalogue with their names. Many of them were forgotten in their lifetime and this is not the place to resuscitate their corpses. What I have called the "Leningrad group" of living composers is really but the most gifted part of this epigonic army, the essence of whose creative art consists in repeating cleverly and with technical perfection the musical truths which had been discovered by the genius of Rimski-Korsakoff and the great near-genius talent of Glazunoff.

Nikolay Cheryepnin (born 1873), belongs to the most striking figures of this world, and is as much more brilliant than his counterpart in Moscow as Rimski-Korsakoff and

Glazunoff were more brilliant than Tañeyeff and Ippolitoff-Ivanoff. Cheryepnin possesses a magnificent technique as a composer and the ability to extract exquisite sonorities from the orchestra. He is not hostile to the most recent achievements in musical colour. In his Poem *The Enchanted Kingdom*, he makes use of a palette which recalls not only his teacher, Rimski-Korsakoff, but also Ravel and Debussy and the other new magicians of the orchestra. His beautiful and elegant, though not profound, talent may perhaps be characterised as "external" and somewhat salonesque. This it has been all his lifetime and one may only record a certain weakening of his colourfulness and his external inventiveness.

Maximilian Steinberg (born 1881), is Glazunoff's true heir in his creative work. His manner of writing is fundamental, massive. A magnificent orchestrator, Steinberg nevertheless does not make an object of orchestral colour, and in this respect he once more recalls Glazunoff. He is somewhat ahead of Glazunoff harmonically. The influences of Richard Strauss are reflected in his creative work just as traces of Wagner's influence were reflected in the work of Steinberg's teacher. The same co-relation exists between him and Glazunoff as between Rakhmaninoff and Chaykovski. But Glazunoff's style itself does not hold the same relation, for it does not imprint traits of epigonism on the creative work of his successor. And it is hard to discover nuances of originality in Steinberg despite the fact that he avails himself of both new combinations of sound and new orchestral colours.

Yulia Weisberg (born 1882), is, after Steinberg, the composer closest to Glazunoff. She is the example, rare in general and particularly in Russia, of a woman composer who has managed to go through the process of difficult technical training which is usually far out of the reach of her sex. Yulia Weisberg is a master in the full sense of the word, and in this respect she stands above all other women composers.

However, she shares with them their common failing, the inability to reveal a strong and original idea. A certain dryness is peculiar to this creative art, a certain "rationality" is felt back of these fine and confident strokes of her pen. She has tried her powers also in the symphonic field and there revealed that she completely follows the traditions of the Glazunoff school. One of her most successful compositions is the music (written in the revolutionary years, 1923) to Blok's poem *Twelve*. It is one of the finest musical works illustrating this weird and incomprehensible, yet powerful work of the great latter day Russian poet.

N. Zolotaryoff (born 1873), is the last of the more prominent composers of the Leningrad school. He is a typical composer of the style of Glazunoff. He possesses a masterly technique which shows its greatest art in following existing models. He possesses beautiful melody and harmony which however never overstep the boundaries of the accepted, and never evince originality. Zolotaryoff was one of the most prominent representatives of the Byelyayeff circle of composers that replaced the "circle of the Russian National School," and, in Rimski-Korsakoff's felicitous phrase, differed from the former by its numbers and its abundance of "mediocrity," in contrast to the handful comprising the *Koochka*, and the genius of almost all its members. Zolotaryoff displayed his greatest productivity in chamber style, in which he has written many compositions nearly all equally masterly and equally cold. The revolutionary years have brought Zolotaryoff, as they have so many others, the title of "Revolutionary Composer"; he has written an opera *Decembrists* which enjoyed a certain amount of success at the Moscow Grand Theatre during the year 1925-1926, though it has scarcely added any to his musical laurels.

THE AMERICAN GROUP OF RUSSIAN COMPOSERS

In his tendencies as a composer, Saminski (born 1881), who is now living permanently in America, belongs to the National Jewish School of which the Moscow composers, Gnyesin, Alyexandr Krein and Grigoriy Krein are brilliant representatives. But Saminski's "Hebraism" is different in its expression from that of the Kreins or Gnyesin. Since 1910 a composer of the modernistic school, Saminski has evolved a strongly emotional impressionistic style. In his manner of composition, his splendid schooling and technique, the inheritance of masterly training under Glazunoff and Rimski-Korsakoff, are manifest. His Symphonic Poem *Vigiliae* belongs among the fine examples of Russian impressionistic creative art. Saminski entered the path of national Jewish music considerably later, and here his creative work is coloured in more direct naïve tones. He really creates a cultural Jewish song, not *Lieder* such as Gnyesin and the Kreins write. The Jewish element in his melody is less embellished and more evident, and his Hebraism itself he regards more realistically than his colleagues in the creation of the Jewish School regard theirs.

Saminski frequently sets his music to Jewish texts but his Jewish language is not the classical and academic old Hebrew of the synogøgue, "dead and solemnly sacred," but the very "jargon" spoken by millions of Jews all over the world. Like every conscious striving for nationalism this new tendency of Saminski's has expressed itself in a considerable simplification of his music, a simplification the more pronounced, because music in general has made great strides forward in complexity. Saminski, the composer, is somewhat overshadowed by Saminski the energetic musical social worker and propagandist of the Jewish national idea. At present he is at the head of the Composers League of America, the united body of all the most extreme left currents of contemporary musical thought.

The work of our other Americanised fellow-countryman, Joseph Akhron (born 1881), bears the imprint of a certain amount of academism. He is a master of style and a master of expression. His inspiration is somewhat dry and his methods seem occasionally strangely academic, but he cannot be denied a unity of musical character. He, too, is a champion of national Jewish music, although his work in this field seems more that of an artistic "arranger" than a true "creator." Akhron is a magnificent violinist and has enriched contemporary violin literature, generally poor in compositions of a substantial content, with a number of splendid pieces. Although they cannot be regarded as having originality or opening up new eras in art, they are nevertheless interesting music, full of talent and genuine inspiration and in their style approaching the "moderate modernism" which reigned almost absolutely in Russia at the turn of the twentieth century and the beginning of our era.

These two composers, so different and yet so close, play a double rôle. They are, first of all, the harbingers of the "Jewish" musical idea in America, a land of enormous musical possibilities where musical art has just begun to issue the living sprouts. The Russian Jew has been fructifying the musical soil of America, raising an art which subsequently will be classed in history not as Russian or even Jewish, but American. On the other hand, both composers are disseminators of Russian musical culture and tradition, for no matter how strong the racial trait and the national idea may be in their creative work, they are nevertheless organically connected with the Russian succession of musical thought. The Jewish nationalism was unquestionably born on Russian soil, and its type is clearly reflected in their entire appearance as composers, which shows as well the unmistakable traits of inheritance from the Russian National School in general and from Glazunoff and Rimski-Korsakoff in particular.

THE YOUNG COMPOSERS OF RUSSIA

THE youthful Russian composers naturally do not form a single organisation in the sense of tendency or style. The principal group is centred in Moscow, which has become both the political and economic centre of Russia during recent years. Leningrad which once supplied the great majority of composers has comparatively little to contribute: Shcherbachoff, son of an obscure composer of the Byelyayeff Circle, is productive and has a unique, although not yet a strikingly pronounced individuality; and Shostakovich (born 1906), who at one time aroused even exaggerated hopes. Characteristic of the youth of Leningrad and partly of Moscow as well is their moderation. Extreme radicalism with its cult of sharp dissonances, its overthrow of former laws and modes of harmony and musical theory, so characteristic of the young composers of Western Europe and America, is here almost entirely absent. As a rule they do not go further than Skryabin and Prokofyeff, and occasionally express still more reactionary sympathies, definitely returning to the style of Glazunoff and even Chaykovski. In Shostakovich's early compositions this influence of his teacher Glazunoff is strongly observable along with the imprint of the general St. Petersburg training which also marks all the work of Shcherbachoff.

Of the Moscow composers, Yevseyeff for whom the Conservatory group once entertained strong hopes, is an utter reactionary in whose manner of writing the influences of Chaykovski and Aryenski mingle with early Skryabin. His Symphony for a grand orchestra is permeated with extreme and naïve Skryabinism.

A similar imprint of Skryabin also marks the creative work

229

of the unquestionably gifted though not original Kryukoff, to his disadvantage, because the Skryabin manner is so readily recognised. Kryukoff is an assiduous composer who copies more or less successfully Skryabin's pathetic and emotional style in his symphonic productions, in his operas (he has written operas to Blok's *Unknown Woman* and *King in the Public Square*), and in his small piano pieces. But Skryabin's emotionalism has degenerated here along with an exaggeration of his salon traits, which even in him occasionally forced themselves unpleasantly into the foreground. Kryukoff's youth and his unquestionable good taste are nevertheless a promise for the future, because his ideal, Skryabin himself, began as an imitator of Chopin.

In Lyeonid Polovinkin (born 1900), whose compositions have lately been published in Vienna (Universal Edition), we notice the strongest influence of another idol of Russian contemporary life,—Prokofyeff. Polovinkin's style, somewhat external, brilliant if you prefer, is interesting from the point of view of its "piano quality," for the author so far has devoted a great part of his inspiration to that instrument. The mood of jocular gaiety and irony, of smile and satire, which is characteristic of Prokofyeff is repeated here, though indeed in more pallid forms and with less of the infectious and primitive barbarity which in Prokofyeff, thanks to its naturalness, is so attractive.

Lyof Knipper (born 1900), inclines in his sympathies rather in the direction of the idol of the West, Stravinski. This composer, himself a half-European by education, having received his musical training abroad, is full of colour ecstasy. To him music means a series of sonorities, a succession of tonal colours, witty rhythms and inflammatory accents. At the very time when Stravinski himself departed from his former colourfulness and rushed into academism, his followers in Russia were beginning to repeat the earlier stages of his journey. Of the Russian youth, Knipper is perhaps the most extreme left, the one least averse to hazardous "breaks" with the academic tradition so strong in Russia, but in his bold seekings of new paths and in his breaking with the old, it has been difficult so far to discern genuine originality. The rationalism of an author who invents more than he creates and reasons more than he is carried away, is too frequently obvious. But the painstaking and industrious young composer has occasionally arrived at interesting achievements. To these, among others, belong his *Fairy-Tales of the Gypsum Buddha* for orchestra, a series of witty, colourful grotesques in which the cold and typically esthetic psychology of the author is strikingly marked.

Vasiliy Shirinskiy (born 1904), is also a composer of the calm type, rather impressionistic. It is not without reason that in his creative work rest loving recollections of Debussy and Ravel, these most brilliant exponents of impressionism. Shirinskiy who has but lately made his début as a composer is a musician of great taste, of a fine and neat technique. He is the author of two splendid quartettes for string ensemble, of a violin sonata and a number of smaller pieces in which a certain coldness and rationalism are compensated for by mastery and beauty of exposition.

Shebalin (born 1902), a pupil of Myaskovski, bears in his work strongly marked influences of his teacher but withal gives great hopes and expectations that he will evolve a style of his own which is already outlining itself. It is a combination of Russian tunefulness with impressionistic harmony. The stamp of Russian style on his creative work joins him rather to the mighty *Koochka*, Rimski-Korsakoff, Borodin, Musorgski, than to Skryabin. But Russian tunefulness is clad in garments more appropriate to the author's modern musical taste.

The young and energetic Vyeprik (born 1892), belongs to the Jewish group of composers and a certain influence of Alyexandr Krein and Gnyesin can be traced in him. But the Jewish melos in him is obscured by general European influences among which may be mentioned those of Prokofyeff and Skryabin. He undoubtedly possesses traces of a personality of his own as a composer, which, owing to his youth, have not yet developed. In his Piano Sonata and his *Songs of the Dead*, Vyeprik comes most closely to the traditions and style of the Jewish National School in the form which it takes in Alyexandr and Grigoriy Krein.

Shishoff, Shenshin and Triodin, who cannot conceivably be numbered among champions of modernism in music, belong to the more mature generation. These composers consciously abide by the old standards. Of these, Shishoff (born 1886), possesses at least some elementary seeds of adventure in the field of Russian song melody. Oppressed by the colossal development of harmony in contemporary music, Shishoff is dreaming of turning back the musical wheel of time and restoring music to "monody" (single voice singing). This bold idea remains a mere dream which dashes against Shishoff's own practice as a composer; his natural style is the epigonic style of the Russian National School, a broad Russian melody against a background of "Borodin harmonies." It is curious that in his experiments with monody Shishoff has come across the idea of the "ultra-chromatic," or the enrichment of the tonal scale now in use in music with new tones. In this manner, he hoped to save his idea of monody and compensate for its lack of a harmonic background. While the idea deserves attention it has come on numerous occasions into the minds of other musicians, and always shattered itself against the traditions of the technical resources of music, and the necessity of creating new instruments; so far no one has created them.

Shenshin (born 1887), like Shishoff, is the innovator even to a less degree. He is an interesting miniaturist, the author of graceful vocal songs, many of which may win wide popularity, thanks to their fitness for the voice and the elegant

sentimentality of their music.   Shenshin does not attempt
to sail into the great sea of monumental creative work, being
conscious of the limits of his talent, a quality which must
also be set down as an asset.

Triodin, a dilettant composer, must be mentioned merely
because he is one of the few who are striving to resurrect the
style of the national "naïve opera" of the last century.   This
attempt must on principle be set down as hopeless; at any
rate it requires genius which Triodin, a musician of feeble
technique for all his great energy, does not possess.   His
operas were produced on the stage in Moscow and enjoyed
rather clamorous success.   *The Silver Prince* and *Styepan
Razin* are typically epigonic music in which the achievements of Chaykovski, Rimski-Korsakoff and Borodin are
repeated in weaker form and often with too great exactness.

Anatoliy Alyeksandroff (born 1889), must be recognised
as the most prominent of this group of youth "past first
youth."   This composer's beautiful but somewhat dry creative art has developed under the influence of Rakhmaninoff
and Metner.   Alyeksandroff is a typical and exclusive lyricist
most of all attracted to the intimate realm of the *Lied* in
which he has created his most beautiful things, the *Alexan-
drian Songs,* a whole cycle on texts by Kooz'min.   However
he has also worked much in the field of chamber music and
piano sonata.   (He has written five sonatas.)   Alyeksandroff
possesses the typical traits of the academy and the salon at
the same time.   He is an unquestionable master of style and
wields the technique of composition perfectly.   No particular
innovations are within the dreams of this creative art severely
locked in a world of old traditions among which certain
concessions to modern times ring like timid phrases.   Soloists
are fond of Alyeksandroff because of the gracefulness of
his compositions.   Being classed somewhere in the middle,
neither among innovators nor among extreme conservatives,
he enjoys comparative popularity on both sides.   A certain

anæmia, the absence of ardent pathos, the rationality of his work which is neither cold nor hot but lukewarm, distinguish his lyricism from Rakhmaninoff's. Closer to Metner, he is separated from him by a decidedly more "Russian placement," as opposed to Metner's "German orientation." But Metner is profounder and more severe, incomparably more substantial than the somewhat sweetish Alyeksandroff. Yet Alyeksandroff must be recognised as one of the most powerful composers of our time, and a peer of Myaskovski, who has just as little impulse to invent and is just as devoted to the unwritten laws of "former music."

Alyeksandroff is a figure already settled in style and tendencies. We have no reason to expect anything unusual or anything new from him. According to the standards of Western Europe he is a reactionary academist, but on the Russian horizon where radicalism, as I have pointed out several times, is not so widespread, his creative work holds the ear and makes a certain contribution to music. Enjoyable and never rousing too strong emotions, always permeated with taste and wise moderation in all its manifestations, neither new nor old, cleverly and securely made with that calm mastery which distinguishes the true musician, Alyeksandroff's music will in all probability occupy a firm position in the programmes of all concerts, even in case musical history will refuse Alyeksandroff a claim to a prominent niche in the Pantheon of Fame.

THE RUSSIAN-PARISIAN SCHOOL

THE great dispersion which, in the years of the Revolution from 1918 to 1922, scattered a considerable part of the Russian intelligentsia abroad, affected the composers also. Many, including composers as prominent as Prokofyeff, sought to find their musical fortunes outside their native land and succeeded. Naturally the "type" of these fugitives was utterly accidental, for they fled not as exponents of certain definite "musical" convictions, but to escape the discomforts of life and out of fear of the social explosion. Small wonder hence that the group of Russian emigrant composers who settled in France did not possess any "tendency" as a unit. Consequently this "Parisian Group" is not a musical band of persons holding similar views, but merely a geographical one. Bringing them under a single heading is again justified by the technical conveniences of exposition rather than by any inner unity among these composers. Nevertheless, there is some inner connection among them to justify our grouping them together in this way. Finding itself in France, this group came fatally and unavoidably under the heavy and despotic hand of the musical god of our time, Igor Stravinski. His authority was so all-embracing, his sway over musical minds so absolute, that even those became Stravinists who had previously perhaps no desire to do so. And as another master of contemporary Russian music, Prokofyeff, also happened to be in Paris, the Russian musical emigrants, who count in their ranks many cultured, gifted and brainy men, organised under the ægis of these two mighty musical individualities. But it is still difficult to say how strong the group is in genuine powerful talents.

235

Of this rather numerous group we shall select only a few, although in omitting the youngest we are perhaps excluding those destined to prove most "talented."

Alyeksandr Cheryepnin (born 1900), has already gained considerable fame and his career as a composer must be set down as truly brilliant. The son of Nikolay Cheryepnin, the St. Petersburg composer of the Rimski-Korsakoff School, he has already left his father far behind. The influences in the young composer's creative work are of course two, Stravinski and Prokofyeff. Cheryepnin does not inherit from the past of "romantic" Russia; he is a classical esthete of the purest water, "classical" in his perception, in his love for keen musical pastimes and hatred of great musical experiences, and he is perfectly in place in the age with his easy, flexible and unusually rapid creative gifts. In this composer we find a minimum of national characteristics, as though he were not a Russian. Neither Stravinski nor even less Prokofyeff can boast such independence in the internationalism forced on them by circumstances. He has something in common with the eighteenth century, something naïve or perhaps "seemingly naïve", most skilfully masked peers out of his creative work. He is all miniatures, tiny musical trifles. He loves this style, and profundity of content, grandeur of ideas are timidly avoided in a creative art which does not even want to be expressive. His approach to his musical material possesses the boldness of innocence, and in its indifference to the new dogma it has a certain youthful simplicity.

True his musical element is utterly different; he has been thoroughly poisoned by the new order of sound perception and an old rigourist like Tañeyeff or Metner would turn away from this art with weariness and exasperation. Indeed it expresses itself in a language which to the ears of former-day musicians is utterly "false" having lost what was the most fundamental conception of musical good and evil as personified by the worlds of consonance and dissonance respectively.

Cheryepnin's work possesses the playfulness of a man who loves sound and tone, but loves them without a thought and without a doubt, and accordingly does not know where good lies and where evil. Everything is good, all sounds are equal and all harmonies are good. On the other hand, this artistic indifference indicates the sophistication and satiety of the esthete, the true son of our skeptic age which has lost faith, believes in nothing, either in the possible and necessary grandeur of thought or the truth of musical experience or good and evil in general, let alone musical reflections in consonances and dissonances. There is also formalism in Cheryepnin's creative work. Behind his absence of expressed thought, behind his turning away from emotion in its too striking manifestations, there is felt the presence of a great reasoning mind in the actual creative process which on principle excludes all light reflected from other realms than music alone.

Cheryepnin has sprung from the same elements which produced Erik Sati in France and Ryebikoff in Russia, and still later the current of French music denoted by the nickname "the Six." The taboo on emotionalism, the rationalism and the moral indifference of this creative art are indubitably connected with the essence of the French musical spirit, ever esthete, ever rational, ever holding taste and passing fashion in the foreground. The esthetic views of "the Six" was the antithesis of the decorative and romantic esthetics of the group of neo-impressionists, Debussy and Ravel. Music without thought came from them, and was supported by Stravinski who, during his long residence in France, took a firm stand in denying romanticism and affirming "keenness of sensation" and the authority of "taste," but in Stravinski there is a decorative grandeur of conception, there is a fieriness of temperament, only physical though it may be, but temperament after all. In Prokofyeff there is a depth which he laboriously conceals from himself, and a romanticism bashfully hiding beneath raiments of jest. In Cheryepnin there is really nothing but tonal play pleasing to the author and therefore pleasing to the hearers as well, as the success of his compositions has proved. A creator of "tasty" and "pungent" pieces, in which all the attributes of the human soul are presented but as spicy condiments, and not as something "ontologic," is this composer, Russian by origin who has in Paris become more Parisian than the French themselves.

Artur Lurye (born 1889), considerably his senior, possesses an entirely different history and artistic appearance. He was once an active member of the bohemian literary and artistic association, prominent and non-prominent Russian poets, painters and musicians who, as all from St. Petersburg well remember, gathered around the "Stray Dog," the Montmartre of the northern capital. A decadent and neo-impressionist, a seeker of new sonorities, one of the pioneers of "ultra-chromatic" music with quarter tones, Lurye was really a clever, educated and deeply skeptical man. Like all skeptics, a typical esthete in his convictions, he was a lover of subtle paradoxes and a friend of the poet, Blok. His mental and artistic baggage far exceeded the usual equipment of the musician of the time. Next we see Lurye in the thick of the Bolshevik Revolution, in the rôle of a queer adventurer,—Musical Commissar. It must be stated in all fairness that he managed, during those times so trying to the art of music, to save many musical values and to defend with diplomatic adroitness the interests of "left wing art," so dear to him personally. In this turbulent period, he wrote many compositions in which his paradoxical and subtle and skeptical mind rather than his musical gifts found expression. Too brainy for his talent he rationalised his creative work. An extreme modernist at that time, he held a position at the extreme left wing of Russian composers. Perhaps the culminating point of this skeptical radicalism is his *Forms in the Air,* a composition which can with difficulty be classed in any definite field of art. It possesses more points of contact with typographical art and engravings than with music. Sundry lines of notes interweave in this composition to form a complex graphical design in which perhaps is contained the artistic task that the author set himself. This extreme Byzantinism was interrupted by Lurye's trip abroad whence he never returned to Russia.

Stravinski's powerful genius has perhaps exerted the strongest influence on this composer also coming to a peak in his Toccata for the Piano. About this time, having like all skeptics overfed on the caresses of too pungent and exquisite sonorities, Lurye turned his eyes, not without intangible prompting from Stravinski, towards the Russian song primitives of the early nineteenth century, in the style of the musical "grandfathers," Varlamoff and Gurileff. Taste and fashion are bizarre and fickle things. Once our musical snobs considered this style the acme of tastelessness and dilettantism. But time goes by and what was tasteless to Musorgski's contemporaries now whets the jaded Parisian appetite as the latest acme of taste.

A few words may be said about the strange composer Obukhoff who is somewhat outside the boundaries of artistic appraisal. Perhaps we should not have ventured to mention him were it not for the authority of Ravel, who discovered talent in him, and the benediction of Kusevitski, whose performances of Obukhoff's compositions at his concerts in Paris achieved a great deal of noise if not success. If we take Skryabin's pathological mysticism of *Last Achievement,* and *The End of the World* through his own creations, if we take the kernel of unhealthy mysticism which the composer of the *Poème d'Extase* undoubtedly possessed and at the same time leave out Skryabin's dazzling musical splendour, his enormous inborn musical grasp, his formal perfection, his innate health and lucidity despite this one obsession, we get Obukhoff as a result. The latter's art should be of greater interest to a psychiatrist, so far is the musical element obscured by the pathological. But this is not its sole fault, for the combination of madness with genius is not rare, and genius frequently illumines sick souls; the trouble is that Obukhoff's musical gifts themselves are possibly too small. Like Skrayabin and all the madmen, Obukhoff is not only a mystic but a most awful schematist as well. He invented a new musical "code of law," his musical notation differs from that of all other composers. He writes only in harmonies which include all the twelve notes of the chromatic scale. Hence his music, if this tonal fabric can be called such, acquires a colouring of extreme monotony, by the side of which even the comparative monotony of Skryabin's schematic world seems a gorgeous unattainable ideal.

The centre of Obukhoff's creative art is *The Book of Life*, a mystic composition in which the author sets himself not only a musical task (least of all musical, and herein again lies his similarity to Skryabin, making him, as it were, a caricature of him), but a mystical political one as well. He desires the rebirth of old Russia and the restoration of the deceased Tsar Nicholas II, for he is "mystically" convinced that the Tsar is alive. This mystical emperor, whom Obukhoff calls "Redeemer," is endowed with traits of Parsifal and Christ. One cannot deny a certain romantic attractiveness in the subject matter, but unfortunately, in the first place, Obukhoff has no desire to have a "subject." He considers that he is not the author of *The Book of Life*, but that it has been "revealed to him," by powers from beyond, a typical delusion of maniacs. In the second place, the very embodiment of this subject matter shows an infinite lack of fancy in developing it along with total absence of talent in musically handling the theme.

In the technique of his composition, Obukhoff does not rely solely on harmonies of the twelve notes, but resorts to sounds previously unemployed in musical art,—whistling, sneezing, hissing, weeping, and the extraction of tones from the piano by the fist. According to his conception, the characters must cross themselves during the performance and make the sign of the cross over the public. In addition to the text, which throughout consists exclusively of hysterical ejaculations, whistling, hissing and sobs, Obukhoff for some unknown reason introduces into his work one of the early feeble poems of the poet Bal'mont. The whole shows a deranged mind, a cracked brain, and the performance of such a composition with hysterical exclamations and the public crossing itself, while whistling for the first time in the world expresses "mystic emotions," must produce a genuine "clinical impression."

Obukhoff's appearance as a composer, his recognition by a musician like Ravel, the performance of his work (with apologies and not altogether willingly) by a conductor like Kusevitski, and the sympathetic or at least "serious" criticism of snobbish connoisseurs who most of all in the world are afraid to seem backward,—all this is interesting as a picture of that shaking of musical foundations which is typical of our time, as a picture of the complete disappearance of the points of departure and criteria of musical truth. This disappearance is due to the fact that an ever greater and greater influence has been gained by the opinion of people who can themselves ill find their bearings in music, who frequently do not possess the merest ear for music, while more and more frequently people are engaged in the composer's trade who should have selected entirely different occupations; who by their nature are not musicians at all but have been attracted to this work only by an acute thirst for notoriety, even though it be that of Herostratus.

THE MUSICAL CREATIVE ART OF THE RUSSIAN
REVOLUTION

THE Russian musical art, which was born under the immediate influence of the Russian Revolution, constitutes a world entirely apart. On the one hand, it shows the traces inherent in every "official" creative work, while on the other hand it discloses certain possibilities which apparently have a chance to become fructifying elements in Russian music.

Revolutionary creative art came as an answer to life's natural demands. The empire's old régime had collapsed, dragged into the whirlwind of the Revolution, people considerably changed in their psychology, their requirements and their mode of existence. Revolutionary life called forth a demand for a certain new music for the people. Many causes intercrossed in this complex phenomenon. On the one hand, the revolutionary ideology endeavoured to compromise all former Russian music in the eyes of the great masses as music of the masters, the intelligentsia, the bourgeoisie, and this agitation enjoyed considerable success. On the other hand, revolutionary life demanded new songs, songs set to new revolutionary texts, songs for the working people, for the Red Army, for peasants, for the daily needs of workmen's clubs that had sprung up in enormous numbers.

In this field, as well as in other fields of the post-revolutionary reconstruction, it was necessary to resort to "specialists" picked from the ranks of the former bourgeoisie. For only the bourgeois musician could, as a rule, write "grammatical" music. And here a phenomenon occurred, instructive in its historical significance. The most advanced and gifted musicians of Russia stubbornly abided in "neutrality," stubbornly refused to give their artistic work for the needs of the Revolution. The pathos which had been expected and which was to be analogous to the pathos of religious creative art when music was at the "services of the church," or the pathos of the romantic creative art when music was at the services of the bourgeoisie, did not materialise. The Russian musician of former days was rather a fantastic and mystic, romantic in his essence, occasionally an esthete but never a political revolutionist, and certainly not a convinced socialist and Marxist. Usually he was utterly apolitical, and found his way with difficulty in political questions.

Obviously the music manufactured in this manner, even though it satisfied the minimum of artistic demands, could under no circumstances fulfil the colossal sociological problem set for it, to become the beginning of a new era in art, to reveal to the world the unknown creative art of the proletariat. These composers wrote tiny choruses and ditties, usually of sufficiently stencilled type, partly following in the trippings of salon and park music, partly in imitation of the primitive song style. Some of them resolved to fructify the sphere of national melos and composed in the style of the Russian National School, like Musorgski, from whom they borrowed irony and satire to direct against the bourgeoisie and the former régime, against the priests, against the Tsar and his henchmen.

In this style, partly imitative of the Russian song, partly of the factory song (*Chastushka*), partly following the footsteps of Russia's greatest genius, Musorgski, and partly just borrowing whatever came to hand, the majority of the composers of the revolutionary type, the sworn purveyors of music for the proletariat, have written and still write.

Among these the following may be mentioned as the most individualised and cultured, perhaps also as the most gifted. The aged Kastalski still preserved sufficient technique and taste not to compose musically ungrammatical balderdash, even though the formerly firm ground of church hymns had slipped from under his feet. He composed *An Agricultural Symphony*, intended to do effective campaign service in collecting produce from the peasants, and also many minor arrangements of revolutionary songs. Vasilyeff-Buglay, a dilettant, though not without a certain talent, is developing a style partly like Musorgski's, though of course far less brilliant and far more amateurish. Lobachoff, a composer of taste endowed with an essentially pleasing epigonic talent, has written numerous hymns and songs, of which many breathe genuine warmth, true humour and occasionally biting irony. It is hardly worth while enumerating the others, whose compositions do not rise above the level of commonplace and do not at all fulfil their tasks.

It is curious that in spite of this heightened demand on the part of the theorists of the new Russian state, a demand aiming at the creation of the greatest possible number of such productions, the labouring masses themselves remained sufficiently indifferent towards this newly created art. If we are to except the old revolutionary songs which were and have remained in current use—the *International,* the *Funeral March,* the *Labour Marseillaise,* etc.—one must affirm an unusually laborious and slow penetration of the new compositions into the proletarian consciousness. There is no doubt at all that in addition to the general traditional attitude towards the song (among the workingmen it has not as yet given place to an "artistic appreciation" which causes everything new to be greeted with distrust while everything old is welcomed through force of habit), the low average talent shown in the new wares has also been an important drawback. Either the gift of genius or age-old tradition is necessary to win popularity for a song. Here, neither the former nor the latter was present. And thus we witness the peculiar growth of aversion for the new song on the part of the labour audiences. The labouring masses frankly preferred their old *Chastushka,* which was a song from life and not revolutionary at all, to the songs newly composed to revolutionary texts. In other strata of society there was a marked leaning towards most bourgeois music of the usual salon, "gypsy" and general varieties.

Placed perhaps for the first time in his life face to face with the unfamiliar art of sound, the working man, it turned out, went through the same evolution in the development of taste as every other human being. In the lower stages he was attracted by primitive dance forms, music with a rough rhythm, obvious melodic contour; at the higher stages he preferred, after all, Chaykovski and Aryenski, in spite of the manifest incongruity of their text and mood with the new ideology. Thus while the success of proletarian "special music" proved extremely doubtful, yet unquestionably new ranks, and those precisely from the labouring class, were drawn into musical participation. But these new audiences could be seen chiefly at the serious concerts of the First Symphonic Ensemble (the conductorless orchestra), and at the Bach concerts given at the Conservatories, etc.

Most recently have likewise appeared composers of the most serious style and type, not very numerous, it is true, but who hearkened to the call of the Revolution. I am not speaking of currents of revolutionary moods which peep out of a number of works of present-day composers as, for example, in Myaskovski's Sixth Symphony. This is not the attitude which interests us. "An attitude towards the Revolution" does not at all mean sympathy with it. But the sympathisers, or persons to whom the pathos of the revolutionary constructiveness has become customary and acceptable, are composers of greater aims who have developed an interest in the fate of "creative work in the aspect of revolution," and decided to add the mite which was within their means.

Some of them belong to the type we have already discussed, the type of epigones who had to occupy themselves with revolutionary affairs because in any other style they would have been unable to attract attention. Such is Triodin, whom I have already mentioned, the author of the revolutionary opera *Styepan Razin*, depicting the life of the famous Russian legendary hero of the Seventeenth Century. Such is Zolotaryoff (born 1873), formerly a composer of the famous Byelyayeff Circle, and pupil of Rimski-Korsakoff, Balakireff and Glazunoff, who made his début with the opera *The Decembrists*. They have not added and they cannot add anything new to art. Of greater interest are really the composers who have sprung from the labouring midst, as, for instance, the composer Dyeshevoff, who is striving to create a primitive and lapidary style thoroughly permeated with revolutionary pathos, definitely turning away from bourgeois refinement and ornamentation. Diametrically opposed to him is Roslavyets, of whom I have written separately, a Marxist composer consciously working in the field of revolutionary music. Roslavyets to be sure is a genuine composer and cannot be reproached with lack of mastery. But it is curious that, having gone over to revolutionary art, in his *Epistles to the Decembrists* and his *March of Soviet Militia*, which was made the official march, this exquisite and in his own way refined author begins to talk a language entirely foreign to him, obviously adapting himself to some unknown and presumably "uneducated" audience. The following composers laboured towards the creation of a special music, saturated with the· new revolutionary thought: Glière, who had won a reputation as an experienced and skilful but utterly unoriginal composer, and Korchmaryoff, who has composed a number of songs of pronounced salon character set to revolutionary texts. As the most valuable attempts in this spirit, one must after all set down the works of Roslavyets, *Songs of the Working Professions* and *Songs of*

the Revolution, and Gnyesin, who has recently and suddenly
enough entered on this path. Gnyesin has written a *Sketch
of a Symphonic Monument,* which was dedicated to the
memory of the Revolution of 1905, and was accompanied
with a Cantata on a text by the deceased poet Yesyenin.
As a matter of fact this was not of course the "pure revolutionary" and "Marxist" art which the powers that be had
expected from our authors, for in these compositions the
Revolution was conceived "romantically" in its stormy and
partly outlaw aspect. But the very fact is indicative.
Gradually composers in some way begin to take an interest
in the Revolution, in its idea, in the idea itself of music for
the broad masses, in democratic grandiosity, and one begins
to believe that they will gradually come out of the solitude
of their secluded "workrooms," where they have long given
themselves up to musical speculations, ignoring the life beyond their doors and begin the "exodus into the street."
How successful the exodus will be is of course a question
entirely apart.

The failure of the official music is now perfectly obvious
and it no longer enjoys actual support even on the part of
the authorities. It has become apparent that one cannot become a good composer by force, and that sincerity and the
sincere pathos of creative art are the indispensable and minimum prerequisites of genuine creative work. We should
err if we said that there are no hopes at all for the awakening
of such pathos. We have definitely observed in recent
years the seeping through into the ranks of composers of a
sympathetic mood. There now exists the formerly utterly
impossible idea of writing music on revolutionary subjects;
there has finally come a still greater doubt of the justice of
former exclusiveness and the methods of secluded studio
music composed for the few. The oligarchic attitude of the
Russian musician who liked to feel himself a "priest," "one
of the initiated few," begins to give way to the democratic

idea of music for the widest possible masses, "music of the
street" in the good sense of this word.

The causes of this are clear. The former life of seclusion
is broken up. The solitude of the private study as a rule
does no longer really exist in Russia. The musical fabric
which has become too elaborate and too fatal a cleavage
separates it from the people, to whom this music is no music
at all, but unpleasant noise. During the recent years music
as a whole has run into a blind alley, torn itself completely
away from the masses, not only from the "working" masses
but from all wide groups, and locked itself up in an isolated
circle of snobs, esthetes and connoisseurs of musical oysters.
Torn away from the soil of the people and democracy, it is
on the decline spiritually and formally, degenerating, becoming anæmic, rickety, languid, without fire. This is observed
everywhere and not in Russia alone. In Russia it has become
the more noticeable only because that class of snobs, esthetes
for whom this subtle and refined music was written, has
collapsed and vanished. The consumer has disappeared and
the terrified composer is facing the tragic question of the
meaning and need of his art.

By other equally logical paths the composer has arrived at
the new democratic art just as the Marxist theoretician arrived
at revolution. He saw with his own eyes the absence of
audiences, he saw the uncanny prospect of being doomed
to stew in his own musical juices in company of a few
musicians, friends and acquaintances. If he scanned the
history of music impartially, he could not but gain the conviction that some degree of democracy is necessary in music,
that as soon as it is locked up in an exquisite world for the
initiated the degeneration of the tonal fabric follows, bringing the rickets of creative art. These feeble, languid creations, without blood and without nerves, decadent in their
exquisiteness, unnecessary in their overelaborations, had
already begun to call forth aversion from musicians them-

selves. In Russia, music after Skryabin made great strides in the direction of anæmia. Skryabin at least had at his disposal the dazzling and insane fantasy of his mystical idea, but this idea at bottom was democratic, for by his music he wished to unite millions of mankind. On the other hand his descendants no longer wished to unite anybody in artistic rapture; they wished to enjoy their exquisite tonal dishes in seclusion. This egotism of the present-day musician became nauseating to himself. And hence has sprung the dream so striking in Russia, if less so in Europe,—the dream of a monumental national art in which the enlightened musician and the plain son of his people might join hands. The trend towards monumentality is exceedingly strong in present Russian music. It is partly the cause of the collapse of Skryabin's school; it likewise is the cause of the beginning of a return to old forms, the cause of conservatism in Russian music, and the cause of the surrender of a position formerly irreconcilable with the Revolution. This surrender may really bring many musicians into actual creative work in accordance with the revolutionary idea.

On this path the weary Russian musician, tired of refinement, hopes perhaps to find the living juices he lacks and to add to his music the grandeur, solidity and breadth which since the times of Chaykovski and the mighty *Koochka* have been neglected in Russian music.

APPENDIX

THE RUSSIAN NATIONAL SCHOOL

The Russian National School, called the "mighty *Koochka*," came into existence in the fifties of the last century. It consisted of the five prominent composers: Balakireff, Musorgski, Cui, Rimski-Korsakoff and Borodin, of whom three, Borodin, Musorgski and Rimski-Korsakoff have gained places in history as creative geniuses. This group of composers made its motto the development of the national traditions bequeathed by the fathers of Russian music, Glinka and Dargomyzhski, and inscribed on its banner the principles: "Freedom, the Picturesque, Nationalism." In its time the group stood out as one of extreme innovation, ignoring the traditional foundations of musical art and boldly sacrificing the old canons of musical rules to colourfulness and the picturesque. All the composers of this group were self-taught dilettanti.

The creative work of this group, who must be considered the typical romantics of Russian music, originated under the influence of the Russian national idea on the one hand, and on the other, under that of contemporary musicians of Western Europe, namely, Berlioz, Schumann and Liszt, with whose creative art they had many points in common. The new which they have contributed to music is principally the artistic fructification of the national Russian and Oriental musical element.

In the eighties the creative solidarity of the *Koochka* began to waver. After Musorgski's death (1881), this began to be particularly noticeable. A number of composers of the group grew convinced of the insufficiency of their amateurish musical education and like Rimski-Korsakoff, for example, at a mature age, went through a complete and rigorous schooling in musical science, which had a great influence both on the tendencies and the nature of their subsequent work.

THE RUSSIAN SYMBOLISTS

The Russian symbolists in poetry and literature who were at first called "decadents" originated on the one hand as a reaction against art too saturated with "society" and social motives (to which Russian literature had devoted too many of its forces) and on the other hand, as a return to the pure poetical mastery and restoration of romanticism in Russian surroundings. The greatest influence on the symbolists was exerted by the romantic Novalis, the whole idealistic German philosophy and the contemporary poets and writers of the West, like Nietzsche, Maeterlinck, and Baudelaire. Russian symbolism has produced a number of prominent literary figures, among them Bal'mont, Bryusoff, Vyacheslav Ivanoff, Andryey Byely, Blok, Myerezhkovski and Sologub. The most characteristic feature of their creative work was the constant contact of poetry with abstract thought and with mystic philosophy in particular.

THE BYELYAYEFF CIRCLE

The Byelyayeff Circle arose on the ruins of the Russian National School which had broken up towards the end of the nineteenth century. It came into existence at the initiative of a wealthy Maecenas, the lumber merchant Byelyayeff, who became at the same time the founder of a musical publishing house for Russian composers. A group of the active workers of the Russian National School (under Rimski-Korsakoff and Borodin) also took part in the Byelyayeff Circle which came to exert a strong influence on the destinies of Russian music. However, the central figure in this circle was not Rimski-Korsakoff but Glazunoff who had just made his first appearance. This circle was, generally speaking, less militant and less nationalistic in character than the *Koochka;* even rather academic. Unfortunately, besides Skryabin and Tañeyeff, the Byelyayeff Circle did not produce any other prominent composers, and the numerous minor composers surrounding Byelyayeff were rather a detriment than an advantage in the development of Russian music.

THE END